"The *Travelers' Tales* series is altogether remarkable."
—Jan Morris, author of *Journeys, Locations,* and *Hong Kong*

"For the thoughtful traveler, these books are an invaluable resource.
There's nothing like them on the market."
—Pico Iyer, author of *Video Night in Kathmandu*

"This is the stuff memories can be duplicated from."
—Karen Krebsbach, *Foreign Service Journal*

"I can't think of a better way to get comfortable with a destination
than by delving into *Travelers' Tales*...before reading a guidebook, before
seeing a travel agent. The series helps visitors refine their interests and
readies them to communicate with the peoples they come in contact
with...."
—Paul Glassman, Society of American Travel Writers

"*Travelers' Tales* is a valuable addition to any predeparture reading list."
—Tony Wheeler, publisher, Lonely Planet Publications

"*Travelers' Tales* delivers something most guidebooks only promise: a real
sense of what a country is all about...."
—Steve Silk, *Hartford Courant*

"The *Travelers' Tales* series should become required reading for anyone
visiting a foreign country who wants to truly step off the tourist track
and experience another culture, another place, firsthand."
—Nancy Paradis, *St. Petersburg Times*

"Like having been there, done it, seen it. If there's one thing traditional
guidebooks lack, it's the really juicy travel information, the personal
stories about back alleys and brief encounters. The *Travelers' Tales* series
fills this gap with an approach that's all anecdotes, no directions."
—Jim Gullo, *Diversion*

TRAVELERS' TALES

AMERICAN SOUTHWEST

ARIZONA, NEW MEXICO, NEVADA, AND UTAH

TRUE STORIES

TRAVELERS' TALES

AMERICAN SOUTHWEST

ARIZONA, NEW MEXICO, NEVADA, AND UTAH

TRUE STORIES

Edited by

SEAN O'REILLY AND JAMES O'REILLY

Series Editors

JAMES O'REILLY AND LARRY HABEGGER

TRAVELERS' TALES

SAN FRANCISCO

Cover design: Michele Wetherbee
Interior design: Kathryn Heflin and Susan Bailey
Cover photograph: © David Muench
Illustrations: Courtesy of San Francisco Public Library archives
Map: Keith Granger
Page layout: Patty Holden, using the fonts Bembo and Boulevard

Distributed by Publishers Group West, 1700 Fourth Street, Berkeley, California 94710.

Library of Congress Cataloging-in-Publication Data

Travelers' Tales, American Southwest: Arizona, New Mexico, Nevada, and Utah: true stories / edited by Sean O'Reilly, James O'Reilly.
     p. cm.
   ISBN 1-885211-58-9
   1. Southwest, New—Description and travel—Anecdotes. 2. Southwest, New—Social life and customs—Anecdotes. 3. Travelers—Southwest, New—Biography—Anecdotes. 4. Southwest, New—Biography—Anecdotes. 5. Travelers' writings, American. I. Title: American Southwest. II. O'Reilly, Sean III. O'Reilly, James.

F787.T73   2001
917.9—dc 21   00-053683

First Edition
Printed in the United States of America
10 9 8 7 6 5 4 3 2 1

The desert does not satisfy, nor does love.
Dust into dust—but spirit into spirit as well.
It is madness to deprive oneself of what
the red wastes are offering.

—JOSEPH FOSTER

Table of Contents

Part Three
GOING YOUR OWN WAY

Part Four
In the Shadows

Part Five
The Last Word

The American Southwest: An Introduction

Utility workers found a mammoth bone a few years ago, a quarter of a mile from my home in Peoria, Arizona. They thought it was a log and left it by the side of the road. Just to the east of this serendipitous discovery, Indian petroglyphs continue to be found in the eroded hills that grace the horizon. No more than six miles from this same location, my young son and I once looked out of our van window and were surprised to see an unidentifiable silent aircraft that looked as though it came from the twenty-fifth century or a comic book. As a former Naval Reserve Intelligence analyst, I've been trained to recognize most military aircraft, and this was not one of them. We got out of the van to get a closer look and it was gone; we continued about our business—it was just another day in the Southwest. There is so much beauty, history, and strangeness afoot here that one scarcely knows where to begin.

Let us go back in time to a younger and newer Earth. Four billion years ago, a great fire appeared in the sky and a sound like 10,000 freight trains filled the air; in one incandescent moment, 1,000 square miles of what is now Arizona were rearranged forever. A mere 50,000 years ago, according to our best reckoning, another meteor blazed down. This one struck east of Flagstaff and north of Sedona, creating a crater 1 mile wide and 600 feet deep with an explosion many times larger than that of the first fateful atom bomb test at Trinity, New Mexico. It is now a tourist destination. The multiple craters of the first ancient touchdown, however, can only be seen today from high altitude photographs. The circles created by the meteors are so ancient as to be nearly obliterated but modern cities and towns in Arizona such as Flagstaff, Phoenix, and Sedona, were founded on lands shaped by the stars.

Today, another circle of events is celebrated in the Southwest. Nine hundred miles of desert, lost cities, abandoned mines, and ghost towns in New Mexico and Colorado, and vast Lake Powell (1,960 miles of shoreline) make up what has come to be called the Grand Circle Tour. Within the Circle there are seven national parks: Bryce Canyon, Zion, Capitol Reef, Arches, Canyonlands, Grand Canyon North-Rim, and Mesa Verde. There are also seven national monuments in the area: Navajo, Natural Bridges, Cedar Breaks, Pipe Spring, Canyon de Chelly, Hovenweep, and Rainbow Bridge. The magnificent Monument Valley Navajo Tribal Park and Glen Canyon National Recreation Area round out the Circle, which is just north of, and includes small parts of, the ancient impact zone of the 4 billion-year-old meteor strike. As you look at the map, the Grand Circle looks like a vast bull's eye. The Grand Circle is, however, only part of the story.

The Southwest, or what we commonly think of as the Southwest, includes the states of Arizona, Nevada, New Mexico, and Utah. It also traditionally includes parts of Southern California, Southern Colorado, Southwestern Oklahoma, West Texas, and the northern reaches of Mexico. This is a land that has been torn by the forces of wind, water, and geology for millions of years. Oceans and rivers have risen and disappeared, leaving coral reefs at the top of the Grand Canyon and maritime fossils at the bottom of other canyons all over the Southwest. Hoodoos and other wind- and water-sculpted formations at Bryce and Zion National Parks in Utah, along with the fantastic Arches at Moab and Arches National Park, attest to enormously long periods of erosion and stability.

The four major deserts of the Southwest—Great Basin, Mojave, Sonoran, and Chihuahuan—were created by the rain shadows of great mountain ranges, themselves the product of ancient tectonic plate movements that have been spreading the continents apart since the Earth was young. The Sangre de Cristo Mountains, the Panamints, the Superstitions, the Sierra Nevada, the Hieroglyphics, the Guadalupes, and the Chocolate Mountains, all are desert builders and ancient ocean keepers on their leeward sides. Parts of

Nevada and Utah, like the vastly ancient sea bottoms of Edgar Rice Burrough's Mars, seem eroded beyond time's keeping.

There is something deeply appealing about ancient landscapes that silently endure all manner of geologic chaos. This unearthly patience of the desert is what has drawn generations of adventurers, outlaws, poets, painters, and writers to its secret Bedouin heart. They come to soak up the fierce romance of desert, wind, and sun. The timeless duration of this land lends itself freely to the thoughts of those who wish to meditate on its history and vistas. Frederick Remington perhaps said it best: "...the wild riders and the vacant land were about to vanish forever, and the more I considered the subject, the bigger Forever loomed." Forever is always just beyond the horizon and for Americans, forever is tied to the lands of the Southwest in the uniquely American images of cowboys and Indians that are so aptly described in *Travelers' Tales American Southwest* by the Rosebrook father-and-son team in their story, "John Ford's Monument Valley."

Alex Shoumatoff, in his excellent book, *Legends of the American Desert*, refers to the Southwest as "a tongue, the northernmost projection of Latin America." This is not an inaccurate assessment. The red and gold banners of Spain were flying in America long before the landing of the Pilgrims at Plymouth Rock.

But of course the Spaniards themselves were newcomers. The Hisatsinom (the ancient people), as they were called by the Pueblo, or Anasazi (ancient enemy), as they were called by the Navajo, were the ancestors of many of the Indian tribes of the Southwest. They explored, settled, and built small towns throughout the Southwest many centuries before the arrival of the Europeans. The influence of the Spanish, however, cannot be overestimated in the cultural formation of the Southwest and that influence is now reasserting itself. There are enormous numbers of Spanish-speaking people in the Southwest doing an extraordinary amount of work. Construction and business growth is at an all-time high in the region, and much of it can be attributed to hard-working folks from Mexico and Central America. They are, as Shoumatoff notes, part of the 50 million people who traveled and moved to the lands west of the Mississippi during the twentieth century.

Shoumatoff also aptly describes the Southwest as being one of the "four classic meccas" for people on quests. The other three classic meccas are the Amazon, Africa, and Tibet. Henry Shukman, on a modern day quest to the Southwest, echoes this sentiment in his book *Savage Pilgrims*. He describes travel as "bringing in the stores," and he notes, "It would be a long time before this voyage's nourishment wore off and might never wear off."

As I have traveled throughout this torn and parched landscape, I can only affirm this—the stores that my wife, young sons, and I have brought back have been sustaining in a way I sometimes feel I only marginally understand but immediately appreciate. Whenever I leave the agitated sphere of consciousness that comprises the likes of cities such as Albuquerque or Phoenix, and the mountains barrier themselves behind me, I feel a breath of fresh air moving in my soul. My entire being resonates with clarity, spaciousness, and a hint of sweetness—a quest already fulfilled.

My younger sister Maggie, a reluctant Easterner, wrote after a recent visit: "The desert must echo something of eternity with it restful intensity, for I can pull the memory of it into my mind's eye and it calms me. Funny, but the desert seems to be an oasis for me." The desert will do that to you. It is as if an enormous and moving consolation has been made out of emptiness and wonder. People come to the desert for many reasons (including low-cost housing) but many come because something in the desert calls them to come and be broken, like the prophets of old, and made whole again with wonder. And there are so many things to wonder at in the Southwest.

I have been constantly surprised, for example, at ancient evidence, visibly present, of a lot of water moving through parts of the Southwest. The Guadalupe Mountains, which run along the Texas Panhandle and the New Mexico border, are connected to a ridge, the petrified remnant of the ancient Capitan Reef. Where there are now deeply eroded mesas, in many places there were once oceans. A mere 10 million years ago in Arizona, north of Interstate

40 and west to the Grand Canyon, there was an ancient lake, once the size of Lake Erie. Lake Bidahochi, as it is called, lasted for nearly 4 million years before it finally dried up. Huge circular mounds of dirt and mud that could have only been deposited by enormous rivers of water are also found on the roads leading from Canyon de Chelly all the way to Monument Valley. I often ask myself, "What could this possibly mean in terms of our recent history?" Scientists say that the Grand Canyon and its even larger cousin to the south, Copper Canyon in Mexico, were created by millions of years of water erosion and "other earth changes." It is those other earth changes over the short run that bother me. There is still an awful lot we don't know about Mother Earth.

Oceans of water also seem to haunt the collective imagination of those who live here. Lake Powell, one of the largest man-made lakes in the world, is almost surely the reincarnated image of ancient waterways such as Lake Bidahochi, where prehistoric creatures made their daily pilgrimage. How else might one explain the odd fact that the highest percentage of boat owners in the United States live in the middle of the desert in Arizona? I could take a full-size submarine for days into the depths of Lake Pleasant, another large and growing man-made lake just north of Phoenix, and no one would know it was there.

The ancient sea bottoms of the American Southwest have conceivably influenced the fantasies and thinking patterns of more human beings than any other landscape on the planet. Who has not galloped into black canyons rimmed by fiery sunsets and chased outlaws into the purple sage with Zane Grey, John Wayne, and other heroes of the imagination? Who does not have a little bit of the cowboy or cowgirl branded into their souls? The West is the real thing for America and the Southwest is as real as it gets.

Come with us and you will discover the truths of the Navajo with Douglas Preston, Alex Shoumatoff, and Tony Hillerman. Descend with us into the Grand Canyon and explore the heat of the Southwest until thirst stops you. In *Travelers' Tales American Southwest* you will uncover the history of Acoma, America's oldest unsung city with Timothy Egan, and explore the vast staircase of Utah's new Escalante National Monument with Jeff Rennicke. You will taste the richness of the land with Barbara Kingsolver in Tucson as she makes a pact with wild javelinas, and explore barely marked trails with John Annerino as he trys to run like an Apache. You will also have a few wild adventures with Terry Tempest Williams, Patrick Pfister, and the Mad Monks.

Do not be alarmed if you discover yourself smelling the sweet odor of sage after a desert rain while you are reading or, suddenly find yourself on the way to Moab, Phoenix, Santa Fe, Las Vegas, or even Area 51. Hit the road friend, the desert is calling.

—SEAN O'REILLY
PEORIA, ARIZONA

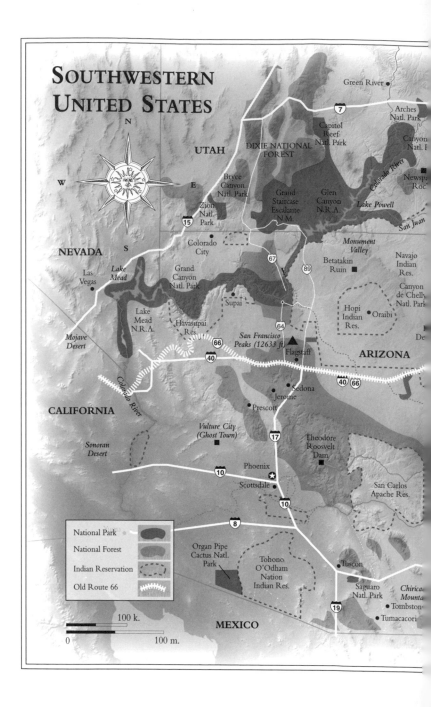

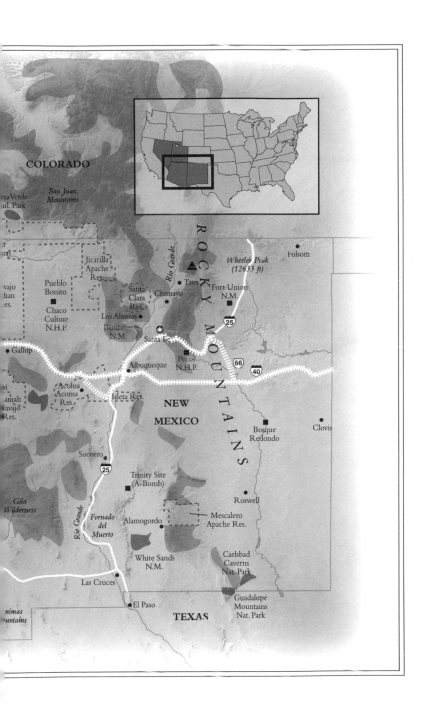

PART ONE

ESSENCE OF THE SOUTHWEST

DOUGLAS PRESTON

Land of the People

Enter the Southwest and be changed.

A LARGE STORM IS APPROACHING. AS WE REMOUNT OUR HORSES, a glittery light breaks through the clouds, turning the landscape the color of beaten silver.

As we set off, Acomita comes tearing out of somewhere, yelping, her muzzle filled with porcupine quills. We stop to pull them out. She endures the operation in whimpering gratitude.

We ride through the twisty little cedars, following a curve of exposed sandstone, where erosion has carved a slot through the rock. It is no more than a seep, dripping water drop by drop onto a sandstone ledge. A faint, chiseled channel in the sandstone directs the trickle to a pothole, which holds about two gallons. We tie the horses up and collect all the water in our canteens. When we finish, I watch as the spring drips water into the channel, drop by drop, where it trickles back into the empty pothole with infinite slowness. In five or ten hours there will be another two gallons. I wonder how old the tiny channel in the sandstone is: A hundred years? A thousand? It speaks of the eternal preciousness of water.

Just as we remount to head back to camp, the silvery light is abruptly snuffed out. The cloud has covered the sky and the land begins to blacken, and blacken, until the darkness is like midnight, swallowing trees and mountains alike in the murk.

Then we hear, rising in the east, a tremendous roaring sound, like a great waterfall or an approaching train. The horses prick up their ears and I can feel Redbone tensing with fear along his flank. I instinctively shorten the reins.

"What the *heck* is *that?*" Selene asks.

We are engulfed in an explosion of ice. Fat white hailstones come winging out of the sky and whacking the backs and heads of the horses and ourselves. The horses twitch, rear, and kick, and we quickly dismount and tie them under piñon trees, whose stiff branches and thick bundles of needles break the momentum of the hail. We ourselves retreat under the protection of the piñons.

I have never seen such large hailstones, some close to an inch in diameter. They rattle down through the trees like pinballs and ricochet across the ground, bringing with them a thick shower of twigs and needles. Once in a while a hailstone will strike my hat with a loud whack and go flying off down the mountain. An intoxicating smell of crushed and bruised piñon rises in the air, sharp and icy in the nose. Speech is impossible; we cannot make ourselves heard above the roar.

In ten minutes the hail ceases as suddenly as it began, and the darkness lifts.

"Look at this!" Selene cries, holding two hailstones up, one in each hand. They look like golf balls. "Have you ever seen any so big?"

"No," I say.

"Boy, they *hurt*! How can something as big as this come out of the sky?"

"Powerful updrafts of wind in a thunderhead," I say, "keep them aloft and they just grow bigger and bigger."

"I'd hate to own a greenhouse up here," she says, tossing the hailstones behind her. "This is a *really* weird place."

"I feel the same way," I say. The surreal light and the intense fragrance of resin in the air make me feel as if I have stepped outside reality, as if the world beyond the rising curtains of mist has disappeared. Everything is smoking; the wet black branches of the trees, the dark red clay, the horses' backs, our hats. The mist is an infusion of light, as if we are drowning in liquid silver. Christine wraps her arm around me and we huddle under the dripping trees.

"I can hardly remember what it's like to live a normal life anymore," Selene says. "It seems like years ago that we left. I think about my friends and school, and it doesn't seem real anymore."

"It's like we're starting life over again," Christine said. "On a new planet."

"Let's call it *Selene's* planet," Selene says. "Where everything is magical, and ghosts and witches exist but aren't mean, and there are dark forests and beautiful streams and the animals talk just like people, and where there are no televisions or malls."

"And where a slice of strawberry rhubarb pie costs five cents," Christine says.

"Mom! On Selene's planet there is no money!"

"How are people supposed to pay for things?"

"People trade everything. Nobody is hungry or poor. And all the mountains and rivers are alive, and you can talk to them too."

"Glug, glug, burble," says Christine.

"That sounds like a great place," I say. "Let's go there."

"We *are* there," Selene says.

I hold out my bare hand. A plume of steam drifts off my skin and rises into the air. "We're being transformed," I say, "into some other life form."

Selene takes off her wet glove and holds out her hand. It is also smoking. "It's happening to me too," she says.

"Maybe we can bring the magic and beauty of Selene's planet back home," I say. "We'll roll it all into a little stone and carry it back in the horse panniers."

Selene picks up a pebble and breathes on it. "Here's a good stone."

"The world will be totally different from now on," I say, rubbing the pebble and putting it into my pocket.

"Yeah," Selene says.

"Do you feel changed by this trip?" I ask.

Selene is silent for a moment. "I guess so...but I really don't know how. I feel so *different*. Now I know you're really my *Dad*. You're not like Mom's other boyfriends."

"Other boyfriends?" Christine says, sitting up.

"You know," Selene says, "easy come, easy go."

"*What!*" Christine cries. "You make it sound like I had all these boyfriends!"

"Aha!" I say. "The truth finally comes out."

Christine splutters in embarrassment. "I've only had *two* boyfriends since you were born. You're making me out to be a—!" She didn't finish the sentence.

"Easy come, easy go," Selene giggles, delighted to have struck a nerve.

"You're just trying to make me mad."

Selene jumps up and starts pelting us with hailstones. "Easy come, easy go!"

Christine chases her around a tree. "You rascal, I'm going to tickle you as a punishment."

She grabs the tail of Selene's duster and reels her in.

"Help!" Selene shrieks. "There's no tickling on Selene's planet! It's against the law! I order you to stop!"

An immense raven, startled by the sound, detaches itself from the shadow of a tree and disappears into the mist, croaking softly. I can hear the sound of its wings, like silk being brushed.

When everything settles down we pull our irritated horses out of the trees and brush the twigs and hailstones off. I help Selene into the saddle and we're off again.

We ride past an ancient Navajo sweat lodge, a skeletonized tent of juniper branches. The light struggles through the clouds. As the hail begins to melt, streamlets start trickling off Kinusta Mesa and running down the arroyos, making a pleasant sound of gurgling water. The mist fills the hollows like pools of smoke, eddying around our horses' feet as we walk down the trail. The world really does look different.

We continue to gain altitude, passing across Mexican Cry Mesa and riding up onto Cove Mesa, a sacred mesa known to the Navajos as *Chooh Dínéeshzhee'*, Where Animals Are among the Wild Roses. The fog lifts. At the top of the mesa we come out on a high plateau with endless views in all directions. Virtually the entire *Diné Bikeyah* is spread out before us, the four sacred mountains, the mesas, canyons, and deserts, all vanishing into vast blue distances where earth and space dissolve together. On either side, the mountainsides are riddled with enormous red canyons, a thousand feet deep, penetrating inward from east and west until they almost meet at a bridge of land a mere thirty feet wide. This is a sacred place, a stopping point on the Journey for Knowledge and Power described in the Navajo Wind Way chant. The landscape here is crisscrossed with the tracks of the gods.

*D*iné means "people" in Navajo and *Diné Bikeyah* means "land of the people."
—SO'R and JO'R

I have never really in my life seen such a place, the beauty of which, truly, cannot be rendered in words. We have broken through into another world.

At the edge of the trees stands a little Navajo hogan with a red bandanna shading the one window. Past the hogan, high on the side of a grassy hill, an old man is wandering through the sagebrush, peering into the red canyons with a pair of battered army binoculars.

Selene gives a shout and gallops over the crest of the hill, followed by everyone else. I ride up to the old man.

The man lowers the binoculars and watches me approach. He wears two shirts, one on top of the other. The outer shirt, of an indeterminate plaid, only has one button left and it is buttoned crooked, shirttails hanging down unevenly. His pants were once, it appears, a khaki color, but now they are dark with the dust and soil of the mountains. His K-Mart work boots have acquired the ancient patina of the earth. He wears no hat, only a bandanna with his hair tied in a traditional bun. His back is hunched and he moves with great deliberation, as if every motion were painful. He looks at me with a small, extraordinarily animated face, a face that crinkles and uncrinkles with great rapidity. When I stop and dismount he grins, exposing a single tooth.

"*Yá'át'ééh*," I say.

He says something in Navajo, slowly raising his arm to point off into the canyons. I can only shrug in ignorance.

"Goats," he says. "See goats?"

"You lost some goats?" I say.

He nods. "Lost goats," he repeats. "You see?"

"No," I say, "we haven't seen any lost goats."

He holds up eight fingers.

"Lost," he says again. He pantomimes, putting the binoculars to his eyes, looking around. "Lost." And he holds up eight fingers again.

"You lost eight goats," I say. "What do they look like?"

"White. One blue."

"I'm sorry, but we haven't seen any," I say. "If we see any, we'll come back here and tell you."

His face uncrinkles and he looks stricken. "No see?" he asks.

"No. How long have they been lost?"

"Week," he says. "Maybe coyote kill. Eat."

"I'm very sorry," I say. I can see from his face that the loss of eight goats is a terrible blow.

"You go where?" he asks, gesturing sideways with the flat of his hand.

"We're riding toward Shiprock," I say.

He leans forward, not understanding.

"*Tsé bit'a'í*," I say, pointing to the great pinnacle rising from the desert, visible to the east.

He scrunches up his face in puzzlement, and then suddenly understands.

"*Tsé bit'a'í!*" he cries, pointing and nodding. He is delighted.

"We started our journey at *Naatsis'áán*," I say. "Navajo Mountain."

"Ah! *Naatsis'áán!*" He points to the northwest. I am as delighted as he is that I can be understood.

I point to Roof Butte, one of the sacred mountains created by

First Woman, the home of Old Man and Old Woman Poverty. I try
to speak its name, "*Dzil dah neeztíinii.*"

"Heh?" he asks, leaning forward again.

"Roof Butte," I say. "*Dzil dah neeztíinii.*"

"*Dzil dah neeztíinii!*" he cries out, nodding vigorously.

Then he points to the Carrizo Mountains.

"*Dzil nahoozilii,*" he says. He swings around and points to another
mountain, a low flat peak, also sacred, called Beautiful Mountain.
"*Dzilk'ihózhónii,*" he says.

I point to Black Mesa.

"*Dzil Yíjiin!*" he cries out.

I point to a prominent mesa in the northwest called Waterless
Mountain.

"*To ádin dah'azká!*" he says.

I point down to Los Gigantes.

"*Tsé álts' óóz íí'áhí!*"

I point to the mountains south of us.

"*Lók'aach'égai leeshch'iihdeesgai!*" he cries.

In the remote distance I can just see Agathla pointing up.
"*Aghaalá,*" I say.

He nods again. "*Aghaalá. Aghaalá!* Good!"

I feel a chill going up my spine. We are naming the sacred
landscape of creation in the Navajo language, something that is
not done lightly or without
some purpose.

"*Tsoodzil,*" I say, pointing at
Mount Taylor, the Sacred
Mountain of the South.

He stops for a moment,
looking intently at me, and
then turns to look southeast.
"*Tsoodzil,*" he repeats, slowly,
his dark eyes reflecting the
blue of the sky.

Then he slowly points
west: "*Dook'o'oosłííd.*" He

> "You know, we Indians
> regard ourselves as the
> plumbers and electricians of
> the universe. All we're doing
> is trying to keep things from
> falling apart."
> —Melanie McGrath, *Motel
> Nirvana: Dreaming of the
> New Age in the Desert*

points northwest: "*Dibé nitsaa*." He points northeast: "*Sisnaajiní.*"

He names the sacred mountains with a simple, quiet reverence that I find unbelievably moving. Then he falls silent. I notice his rheumy eyes have suddenly filled with tears. His lips are wet, and he smacks them a few times, looking down at the ground. I am embarrassed.

"I guess this place where you live is about the most beautiful on earth," I say.

He looks at me kindly but says nothing, and then turns back toward the horizon. Moisture escapes through one of the creases around his eyes and creeps down his face. He stands at the edge of the hill, above the canyons, an old man weeping silently. Is he weeping for his goats? I wonder. But in my heart I know that is not why he is crying.

From the top of the rise, I hear Selene's shrill voice calling down to me. I look up. She is sitting on her horse, silhouetted against the sky, shouting and waving her hat.

"Hey *Dad*, gallop up here! Go as fast as you can! It's fun! There's tons of water over here in the rocks! We can go swimming!"

There is an awkward silence. I tell the old man that I will watch for his goats, and I swing into the saddle. I turn back once and he is still standing there, looking eastward into the distance. I spur Redbone and gallop to the top of the rise and over the crest, reining to a halt. Ahead stretches a slick-rock bench ending in an immense double canyon. A thousand feet deep and three miles across, cut into the great wrinkled upthrust of the Carrizo Mountains.

Selene rides alongside me and takes my hand, and we walk our horses together through the wet sagebrush, toward the vast red canyons of eternity.

Douglas Preston is a writer whose books include the acclaimed Cities of Gold, *the best-selling novel* Jennie, *and the thriller* Relic. *He has also written for* The New Yorker, Smithsonian, Harper's, Natural History, *and* Audubon. *In addition to the journey described in* Talking to the Ground: One Family's Journey on Horseback Across the Sacred Land of the Navajo, *from which this story was excerpted, he has explored other remote* trails on horseback. These include a crossing of the dreaded Jornada del Muerto ("Journey of Death") desert of southern New Mexico, and a retracing of the mysterious 1,000-year-old roads of Chaco Canyon. He lives in the mountains with his wife, Christine, who is a professional photographer, and their three children.

Making Peace

Living in the desert takes a different kind of patience.

JUNE IS THE CRUELEST MONTH IN TUCSON, ESPECIALLY WHEN IT lasts till the end of July. This is the season when every living thing in the desert swoons south toward some faint salt dream of the Gulf of Mexico: tasting the horizon, waiting for the summer storms. This year they are late. The birds are pacing the ground stiff-legged, panting, and so am I. Waiting. In this blind, bright still-June weather the shrill of the cicadas hurts your eyes. Every plant looks pitiful and, when you walk past it, moans a little, envious because you can walk yourself to a drink and it can't.

The water that came last winter is long gone. "Female rain," it's called in Navajo: the gentle, furtive rains that fall from overcast skies between November and March. That was weather to drink and to grow on. But not to remember, anymore than a child remembers last birthday's ice cream, once the months have passed without another drop. In June there is no vital sign, not so much as a humid breath against a pane of glass, till the summer storms arrive. What we're waiting for now is male rain. Big, booming wait-till-your-father-gets-home cloudbursts that bully up from Mexico and threaten to rip the sky.

The Tohono O'odham have lived in the Sonoran Desert longer

than anyone else who's still living; their answer to this season is to make frothy wine from the ripe saguaro fruits, and drink it all day and all night in a do-or-die ceremony to bring down the first storm. When it comes, the answer to a desert's one permanent question, that first storm defines the beginning of the Tohono O'odham new year. The storms themselves are enough to get drunk on: ferocious thunder and raindrops splatting so hard on the cooked ground you hear the thing approaching like mortar fire.

I saw my first of these summer storms in 1978. I hadn't been in Arizona long enough to see the calendar open and close, so I spent the early summer in a state of near panic, as the earliest people in any place must have done when they touched falling snow or the dry season's dust and asked each time: This burning cold, these dying plants—is this, then, the end of the world?

I lived in a little stuccoed house in a neighborhood of barking dogs and front-yard shrines to the Virgin of Guadalupe. One sweltering afternoon I heard what I believed must be kids throwing gravel at the houses, relentlessly and with feeling. It was hot enough so that the neighborhood, all of it, dogs and broken glass on the sidewalks included, had murder in mind. I knew I was risking my neck to go outside and scold kids for throwing rocks, but I went anyway. What I saw from the front stoop arrested me in my footprints: not a troop of juvenile delinquents, but a black sky and a wall of water as high as heaven, moving up the block. I ran into the street barefoot and danced with my mouth open. So did half my neighbors. Armistice Day.

Now I live on the outskirts of town, in the desert at the foot of the Tucson Mountains, where waiting for the end of the drought becomes an obsession. It's literally 110 degrees in the shade today, the kind of weather real southwesterners love to talk about. We have our own kind of Jack London thing, in reverse: Remember that year (swagger, thumbs in the belt) when it was 122 degrees and planes couldn't land at the airport?

This is actually true. For years I held the colorful impression that the tarmac had liquefied, so that aircraft would have plowed into it like mammoth flies bellying into ointment. Eventually an engineer gave me a pedestrian, probably accurate, explanation about heat interfering with the generation of lift above the wings. Either way, weather that stops modern air traffic is high drama in America.

We revel in our misery only because we know the end, when it comes, is so good. One day there will be a crackling, clean, creosote smell in the air and the ground will be charged and the hair on your arms will stand on end and then BOOM, you are thrillingly drenched. All the desert toads crawl out of their burrows, swell out their throats, and scream for sex while the puddles last. The ocotillos leaf out before your eyes, like a nature show on fast forward. There is so little time before the water sizzles back to thin air again. So little time to live a whole life in the desert. This is elemental mortality, the root of all passion.

Since I moved to this neighborhood of desert, I've learned I have other writers for neighbors. Unlike the toads, we're shy—we don't advertise our presence to each other quite so ostentatiously. In fact, I only found out I'd joined a literary commune when my UPS man—I fancy him a sort of manly Dorothy Parker in uniform—began giving me weekly updates. Visitors up at Silko's had been out looking for wild pigs. And Mr. Abbey had gone out in his backyard and shot the TV, again. (Sad to say, that doesn't happen anymore. We all miss Ed.)

I imagine other neighbors: that Georgia O'Keeffe, for example, is out there walking the hills in sturdy shoes, staring down the UPS man with such a fierce eye that he will never dare tell.

What is it that draws creators to this place? Low rent, I tell my friends who ask, but it's more than that. It's the Southwest: a prickly land where mountain lions make bets with rabbits, and rabbits can win. Where nature rubs belly to belly with subdivision and barrio. And coyotes take shortcuts through the back alleys. Here even the rain has gender, the frogs sing *carpe diem*, and fast teenage girls genuflect quickly toward the door of the church, hedging their bets, as they walk to school in tight skirts and shiny high heels.

When I drive to the post office every few days to pick up my mail, it's only about twelve miles round trip, but I pass through at least half-a-dozen neighborhoods that distinguish themselves one from the other by architecture and language and even, especially, creation myth. First among them is the neighborhood of jackrabbits and saguaros, who imperiously tolerate my home, though I can't speak their language or quite understand their myths.

Then, just inside the city limits, a red cobble of just-alike roofs—paved air—where long strands of exurban condominiums shelter immigrants from Wisconsin, maybe, or Kansas, who dream in green and hug small irrigated lawns to their front doors.

Next I cross the bridge over the Santa Cruz, whose creation story bubbles from ephemeral springs in the mountains of southern Arizona and Mexico. In these lean days she's a great blank channel of sand, but we call her a river anyway, and say it with a straight face too, because in her moods this saint has taken out bridges and houses and people who loved their lives.

Then I pass under the artery of Interstate 10, which originates in Los Angeles or Jacksonville, Florida, depending on your view of destiny; and the railroad track, whose legend is a tale tasting of dynamite, the lives and deaths of immigrants who united a continent and divided in twain the one great original herd of American bison.

Then without warning I am smack in the middle of a Yaqui village that is fringe-edged and small like a postage stamp, and every bit alive. Despite its size, Pascua Yaqui is a sovereign world; I come here every Easter to watch an irresistible pageant combining deer dances with crucifixion. Like the Tohono O'odham singing down the rain, the masked Yaqui dancers listen for the heartbeat of creation, and keep a promise with every vernal equinox to hold the world to its rightful position. On this small patch of dusty ground, the religion of personal salvation is eclipsed by a faith whose question and answer are matters of order in the universe. Religion of that kind can crack your mind open the way lightning splits a pine, leaving the wind to howl through the scorched divide. I can hardly ever even drive through here, in my serviceable old Toyota, without biting my lip and considering immensity.

Calle Ventura marks the entrance to another state, where on a fine, still day your nose can compare the goods from three tortilla factories. From here the sidewalks roll, the walls crumble and shout with territorial inscription, brown dogs lie under cherry Camaros and the Virgin of Guadalupe holds court in the parking lot of the Casa Rey apartments.

Across the street stands the post office, neutral territory: mailboxes all identical, regardless of the keyholder's surname, as physically uniform as a table of contents. We are all equals in the eyes of the USPS, containing our secrets. I grab mine and scuttle away. The trip home takes me right back through all these lands again, all these creation stories, and that's enough culture for one day, usually.

I close the door, breathless, and stare out my window at a landscape of wonders thrown together with no more thought than a rainstorm or a volcano can invoke on its own behalf. It's exactly as John Muir said, as if "nature in the wildest extravagance held her bravest structures as common as gravel-piles."...

> Until 1848, the land we call the Rocky Mountain West, the Southwest, and California was the Mexican Northwest. The Treaty of Guadalupe Hidalgo, which ended the war against Mexico, changed all that by ratifying the seizure of present-day California, Nevada, and Utah, most of New Mexico and part of Wyoming, Colorado, Kansas, Arizona, and Oklahoma. Five years later, with the Gadsden Purchase, the U.S. bought from Mexico a sliver of New Mexico's southern edge and its boot heel, and all of Arizona south of the Gila River.
>
> —Tom Miller, *Arizona: The Land and the People*

When I left downtown Tucson to make my home in the desert, I went, like Thoreau, "to live deliberately." I think by this he meant he was tired of his neighbors. For me the problem wasn't specifically my neighbors, whom I loved (and it's a good thing, since our houses were so close together we could lean out our bedroom windows and shake hands), but the kids who spilled over from—and as far as I could see, never actually attended—the high school across the street. They liked rearranging the flowers in my front yard, upside down. They had art contests on my front walk, the point being to see whether a realistic rendition of the male sex organ could be made to span the full sweep from sidewalk to front porch. When my brain was jangled to the limits of reason, I would creep from my writing desk to the front door, poke my head out, and ask if they could turn the music down. They glared, with "So What" eyes. Informed me this was a party, and I wasn't invited.

The school's principal claimed that kids outside the school grounds were beyond his jurisdiction; I was loath to call the city police, but did (only after the porch party ratified a new sport involving urination), and they told me what I knew they'd say: the principal ought to get those kids in school. My territory was up for grabs, by anyone but me.

After some years had passed and nobody seemed to be graduating, I struck out for Walden. My husband and I sold our house, collected our nerve, and bought four acres of rolling desert—a brambly lap robe thrown over the knees of the Tucson Mountains, a stone's throw beyond the city limits. There was a tiny cabin, which we could expand to suit our needs. I anticipated peace.

Like a pioneer claiming her little plot of prairie, I immediately planted a kitchen garden and hollyhocks outside the door. I inhaled silence, ecstatic with the prospect of owning a place that was really my own: rugged terrain, green with mesquite woods and rich in wildlife. No giant penises waiting to impale me when I threw open my front door. Only giant saguaros. Only bird song and faint hoofprints in the soil, evidence of wild creatures who might pass this way under cover of darkness.

Sure enough they came, the very first night: the javelinas. Woolly pigs. They are peccaries, technically, cloven-hoofed rooters of the New World, native to this soil for much longer than humans have known it—but for all the world they are pigs. I pressed my face to the window when I heard their thumping and rustling. Their black fur bristled as they bumped against one another and snuffled the ground with long, tusked snouts. I watched them eat my hollyhocks one by one.

Pioneering takes patience. I thought maybe that first visit was some kind of animal welcome-wagon tradition in reverse, and that over time we could reach an accord. Night after night, they returned. The accord seemed to be: you plant, we eat. The jackrabbits were hungry too, but I discovered that they shun the nightshade family—which conveniently includes tomatoes and eggplants—and that I could dissuade them from my flowers with chicken wire (although a flower bed that looks like Fort Knox is a doubtful ornament). Not so picky, the pigs. With mouths of steel and cast-iron stomachs, they relished the nightshades, and in their eagerness I swear they even ate chicken wire. Over the weeks I tried the most pungent flowers I could think of: geraniums, marigolds. They ate everything. Rare is the epicurean pig who has feasted at such a varied table as the one I provided.

I tried to drive them off. Banged on the windows, shrieked, and after a goodly amount of accomplishing nothing whatsoever through those means, cautiously opened the door a crack, stuck my head out, and hollered.

"Shoo, pigs!" said I.

"Not by the hair of my chinny chin chin," thought they, apparently, in what passes for thought within those bony skulls. They ignored me profoundly, inciting me to extremes. I stooped to throwing rocks, and once by the wildest of chances, so help me God, I hit one, broadside. With a rock the size of a softball, and a respectable thud. The victim paused for half an instant midgobble and sniffed the air as if to ask, *Was that a change in the weather?* Then returned to the hollyhocks at hand. On the He-Man Scale of Strength, my direct hit scored "Weenie." I seethed between the four walls of my house like Rochester's mad wife in the attic.

In a fit of spite I went to a nursery that specializes in exotics, and brought home an *Adenium obesum.* This is the beautiful plant whose singularly lethal sap is used by African hunters to poison their darts. Javelinas understand spite: they uprooted my *Adenium obesum,* gored it, and left it for dead.

Over the months our house slowly grew, with javelinas watching. We framed up an extra room, which we would eventually connect to the old house by tearing out a window, once it was sealed to the outside. We laid out sheet-metal ductwork, which would go into the ceiling, for heating the new addition. In the middle of the night we woke to the sound of the devil's own celebration: hellacious hoofs on tin drums. The pigs had found their way into the new room and were trampling the ductwork, sending their tinny war cry to the stars above....

It did not take me long in the desert to realize I was thinking like a person, and on that score was deeply outnumbered. My neighbors weren't into the idea of private property, and weren't interested in learning about it, either. As Kafka frankly put it, when it's you against the world, bet on the world.

So I dispensed with lordship, and went for territoriality. I turned a realistic eye on my needs. I don't really have to have hollyhocks outside my door. But I'd like some tomatoes and eggplants. Oak-leaf lettuce on crisp fall days, and in the spring green beans and snowpeas. Maybe a *little* bed of snapdragons. It wouldn't take much. Since I had no plans to raise a huge brood, sixty square feet or so of garden space would serve me very well.

I revised my blueprints and looked hard at Pueblo architecture, which shuns the monumental for the more enduring value of blending in. The Pueblo, as I understand their way of life, seem to be more territorial than proprietary, and they've lived in the desert for eight centuries. Between the javelinas and me it had come down to poison darts in about eight days. Enough with that.

I settled on a fairly ancient design. The wings of my house enfold a smallish courtyard. My territorial vireo song is a block wall, eight feet high. Inside the courtyard I grow a vegetable garden, a few fruit trees, and a bright flag of flowerbed that changes its colors every season. The acres that lie beyond the wall I have left to cactus and mesquite bramble, and the appetites that rise to its sharp occasion.

Life is easier since I abdicated the throne. What a relief, to relinquish ownership of unownable things. Engels remarked at the end of his treatise that the outgrowth of property has become so unmanageable that "the human mind stands bewildered in the presence of its own creation." But he continues on a hopeful note: "The time which has passed since civilization began is but a fragment of the past duration of man's existence; and but a fragment of the ages yet to come.... A mere property career is not the final destiny of mankind."

Indeed. We're striving hard to get beyond mere property career around here. I've quit with the *Adenium obesum*, and taken to leaving out table scraps for the pigs. I toss, they eat. I find, now that I'm not engaged in the project of despising them, they are rather a hoot to watch. On tiny hooves as preposterous as high-heeled pumps on a pirate, they come mincing up the path. They feel their way through the world with flattened, prehensile snoots that flare like a suction-cup dart, and swivel about for input like radar dishes. When mildly aroused (which is as far as it goes, in the emotional color scheme of the javelina), their spiky fur levitates into a bristly, spherical crown—Tina Turner laced with porcupine. I don't even mind that they come and eat up our jack-o'-lanterns at Halloween; it's worth it. They slay me every time with their hilarious habit of going down on their foreknees and walking along, pious supplicants in awe of life's bounty, pushing whole pumpkins before them.

Meanwhile, in the cloistered territory of the courtyard, so many things come and go it would feel absurd to call it mine: I've seen an elf owl picking through the compost pile; Gila woodpeckers fighting over the tree trunks; hummingbirds at the flowers; doves who nested in the grape arbor; a roadrunner who chased off the doves and gulped down their eggs; a pair of cardinals and a Pyrrhuloxia couple who nested in adjacent trees and became so confused, when the young fledged and flew to the ground, that they hopped around frantically for a week feeding each other's kids. A pair of Swainson's thrushes stopped in for a day on their migratory flight from Canada to Peru; to them this small lush square in a desert state must have appeared as Moses' freshet from the rock.

The cardinals, of course, eat the grapes. In some years the finches peck a hole in every single apricot before I get around to throwing a net over the tree. A fat, clairvoyant rock squirrel scales the wall and grabs just about every third tomato, on the morning I decide that tomorrow it will be ripe enough to pick.

So what, they all declare with glittering eyes. This is their party, and I wasn't exactly invited.

Barbara Kingsolver was trained as a biologist before becoming an award-winning writer. She lives with her husband and family in southern Arizona and in the mountains of southern Appalachia. This story was excerpted from High Tide in Tucson: Essays from Now or Never.

PATRICK PFISTER

The Recruiter

You never know who or what you'll meet in the desert.

ALL PRAYER IS ASKING BUT CERTAIN PRAYERS ROCKET UPWARD ON the fuel of desperation.

The dirty coins deep in my pocket totaled less than two bucks—my fortune in the world—and the flaming Mojave sun now setting had blazed on my unprotected head since dawn. Thirsty, hungry, and badly burned, I was stuck somewhere east of Palm Springs, too dizzy and road-drugged to know if I had crossed the Colorado River yet or not. Cars and semi trucks blasted past whistling death tunes as I tried to keep my thumb raised over Interstate 10, a friendly hitchhiker's smile pulled tight on my wind-whipped face.

Just then a red Oldsmobile wheeled off onto the road shoulder up ahead. I stumbled toward it, thinking it had to be a mirage. But the door handle was real, hot in my palm. I gave a tug and the door came open. The driver leaned across onto the dashboard and stared at me with bright, religious eyes.

"Where to, sir?" he asked.

It should have been a clear warning. Not only was he just a year or two younger than I, but anybody else, anybody half-interested in reality, would have told me to get a job or a haircut, or at least demanded to know if I was going to rob them. But too dazed and relieved to even think about it, I fell forward into the car and pulled the door shut behind me.

We exchanged names—he was Rod—then talked a bit about what we did. My end was easy—I did nothing—but his required a yellow t-shirt to puff out at chest level—he was a Marine.

"I used to be like you too," he said, fixing me with his bright eyes. "But then I signed up. I joined the best club in the world. Maybe you should think about doing it too."

I told him I would and then eased back against the worn upholstery. Desert landscape swirled past in a blur of sagebrush colors. For a few minutes I think I dozed off. I blinked my eyes open feeling slightly refreshed. At least my scalp was no longer on fire. I looked around. Traffic was light, a few semis, one or two cars. The westbound lanes were almost empty.

We drove through Blythe, crossed the Colorado River and entered western Arizona. A few minutes later we passed the ghost town of Ehrenburg. Strange region, I thought. Desolate, mysterious. The Chocolate Mountains are just to the south. Further on comes a petrified forest, some radium hot springs and then a territorial prison down by Yuma. All of it north of the

Desert. Mountain. Canyon. Arizona is contained in these three words. In the south and west lie the three great biological divisions of the desert: Mojave, Sonoran, and Chihuahuan, ecological provinces equivalent to the geologic province known as Basin and Range—low, hot, naked plains spread between sharp, fierce desert mountains. Northward stands the Colorado Plateau, the land of dry mesas and slickrock canyons climaxing at the Grand Canyon. A transition zone of mountains unites desert and plateau in a confusing and unique jumble that combines plants, animals, and landscapes from both north and south. Other isolated mountains stand throughout the state, islands of coolness and forest, sky islands.

—Stephen Trimble, *Arizona: The Land and the People* edited by Tom Miller

Mexican border in clear cowboy-and-Indian land: bobcat, coyote, bighorn sheep, and fox roam here. The wings of falcons and golden eagles slice the skies. Mountain men and riverboaters, gold miners, and gunslingers, Kit Carson and other big names all marched through. That's what makes it so hard to believe that eighty camels and their drivers from the Middle East were once here too. The Army imported them with ideas of facilitating desert transportation. Most of the drivers got homesick and left. One stayed, Hadji Ali (called "Hi Jolly" by the soldiers), and is buried near Quartzsite beneath an exotic pyramid-tomb bizarrely topped by a camel icon. It has to be the only one of its kind on the entire continent. After the Civil War the Army dropped their project and set the camels free. They went wild and wandered the desert for years, like ancient angry *jinn* spirits, destroying crops and terrorizing stock.

Strange region. Once the rear tire of my Triumph 500 blew into pieces near here and I spent two days without food or water, trying to hitch a ride out of hell. At night I curled up in my sleeping bag, stared into the blackness and listened to the sounds of the wasteland, perhaps not the bleating of wild camels, or the *jinn,* but creepy all the same.

But this time I had cheated fate. There would be no nights out in the cold. I had a ride straight through to Phoenix. I smiled.

"So what do you think?" Rod asked.

"Think?" I swung my head around. "Think about what?"

"The Marines."

"The? Ah! Well, you know, it's an…an idea. I'm not sure I'm exactly the right type but…"

"You are."

I nodded and sat up a little. He was staring straight at me, his eyes glowing as bright as two laser beams. His unshaven face would have looked fiercer without the peach fuzz but his long neck, fibrous limbs, and out-of-control gaze were still enough to ring my alarm bells. I quickly checked the speedometer and, surprised, found we weren't hurtling toward death. His hands had a choke hold on the steering wheel and both his arms were rigid but we were cruising along at moderate speed. He glanced at the road, then fixed his eyes on me again.

"The Marines are a first-class outfit," he began feverishly. "Top first class. Sure, I used to think they were just a bunch of grunts like you do, but they're not. Some of the best friends you'll ever make are right there on that bunk next to yours. And you know why? Because the Marines are the best, that's why. They teach you from day number one how to…"

The desert rolled past. Five, ten, twenty minutes and Rod went on hammering out his story, his eyes shooting over at the end of every sentence to nail down my reaction. The front seat of the car became an interrogation cell. I stared at the broken left hinge of the glove box—it looked as if the door had been torn off in a rage—dumbly nodding, agreeing with everything he said. My head began to ache so much it felt like the sun was blazing on it again.

The chrome grill of a semi, dazzled by a last ray of light, came rumbling towards us from the east and blew past in a roar. Across the rugged landscape shadows lengthened toward dusk. Rod went on about the Marines. They were the best, they were top first class, they weren't just a bunch of grunts. I tried to put my mind on something else, anything else. "Is it possible," I wondered, "to travel out here, even zooming along in an air-con Mercedes, without thinking of the pioneers bouncing toward the unknown in their flimsy covered wagons?"

"You're the only one who can make the decision," Rod said forcefully. "You and nobody but you. It's the biggest decision of your life, believe me. But the Marines are waiting and when you say yes they'll be there to help you along. The Marines are always there when you need them and nobody…"

It was no use. I had thought I was bound for Phoenix but I was headed straight for the sharp horns of a moral dilemma. A wrong word and I was out in the night. But silence all the way to Phoenix would be impossible. Sooner or later I would have to tell him to shut up.

It was a lesson. One must give humble thanks. My prayers answered, I had patted myself on the back for cheating fate. Now how high a price would I pay for pride?

"People respect a Marine," Rod continued. "They know what it takes to be one and they respect it. Just think how proud you'd feel with that kind of respect."

He went on to describe Marine life from the food served at Camp Pendleton where he was based to the female fruit he had for the picking in Tucson where he was heading. The Marines had made his life. They had given him all he had ever wanted, all anyone could ever want, and now they could do the same for me. His every word, every phrase was a verbatim quote from a recruiting bible. My stomach's flexor muscles contracted into steel knots and my breathing fell ten beats off rhythm as he went on and on. The Marines were this, the Marines were that. His father and grandfather had been Marines, so had his brother and two of his uncles. They all felt exactly like him: the Marines were top class.

Just then a cloud of steam came shooting over the hood and up the windshield. The temperature gauge jumped to red. Rod looked surprised, then at me. I knew the answer without asking. He hadn't checked the water. What would the pioneers think of this modern-day soldier whose covered wagon could cross the vast Mojave in hours but he himself lacked the common sense to inspect his supplies before leaving?

We stood together beneath the raised hood, staring down at a fizzle of water and air escaping the pressurized radiator cap. For a moment I enjoyed it—at least it had nothing to do with the Marines—but then I glanced up at the darkening sky, out across the sagebrush wasteland and at the lone car whizzing past (the driver struggling hard not to notice us) and I began to recall my two days and nights out here. We were in trouble.

I told Rod I would hitchhike to the first gas station and bring back water as soon as possible. I made it sound as though it would be easy, but I was certain only a miracle would save walking there and back. I cut off thinking about how many miles it might be. But suddenly Rod stood up straight, his yellow t-shirt puffed out.

"I'll go," he announced. "I'll put on my uniform. When these drivers see a Marine they'll stop right away."

Before I could laugh out loud he hurried back to the trunk and took out his suitcase. He opened it on the ground next to the car.

Two perfectly pressed, perfectly folded Marine uniforms, one tan, the other blue, lay on either side of a plastic hinge. The tan model had a few shiny trinkets over the shirt pocket. He selected it, then took off his t-shirt and jeans. His white boxer shorts flapped in the breeze of a passing truck. He put on his uniform as if I were a drill sergeant scrutinizing his every move. He bent out the side view mirror of the car and methodically ran a comb through his hair, wetting his fingers every few seconds to pat down strays. He took himself so seriously he ended up charming me. Maybe he was only playing soldier but he had a real uniform.

He marched out toward the road, put his hands on his hips and craned out his long neck to look east, then west.

"I've never hitchhiked before," he said. "Is it better to stand in one place or to walk?"

I came up next to him.

"Everybody's got their own theory," I began, "but it's twilight now and visibility's bad so I'd say—"

A maroon Cadillac pulled off onto the shoulder twenty yards in front of us, blowing up a small dust cloud. An old couple sat in the front seat. Rod ran forward. I trotted after him certain they were having problems as well, probably with their own radiator. Rod heaved open the rear door. I glanced in as the elderly man driving spoke to him.

"Trouble, soldier?"

"Car overheated, sir."

"Welcome aboard!"

The door slammed shut and pebbles sprayed my calves as the powerful Caddie surged out onto the road. A few minutes later the rear bumper threw off a last glint of silver and vanished into the distance. I went back and leaned against the Oldsmobile to begin the wait. Sand particles hopped about out on the road as cars and trucks shot past. The sky turned black and stars came out. I had never seen anything like it. A Cadillac?

In less than forty-five minutes Rod returned with a three-gallon plastic container full of water. A gas station attendant had given it to him free-of-charge because he was a Marine. Rod moved to the radiator. It was to be my only moment. I quickly warned him to stop.

"You can crack the block pouring water into an overheated engine," I told him. "You've got to start the car first."

The bright, religious light went out of his eyes. He blinked twice.

"I didn't know that," he said. His voice had a strange whine, as if he were really saying, "Why don't they ever tell you these things?"

But once he had changed clothes and we were back in the car cruising along into the Arizona night his chest again puffed out against his t-shirt.

"It's what I was telling you before," he said. "The Marines are first class all the way. You were scared when that thing happened with the radiator but I knew my training would do the job. I knew the uniform would be the ticket. Those old folks saw it and they came to help. People respect a Marine uniform because..."

He went on non-stop. I thought it couldn't possibly get any worse, but then it did: he began to ask questions. Why was it exactly that I had never before thought about enlisting? Did I have something against the Marines? Something personal? Or did I just think I was hot stuff, too hot for a ground unit?

I looked out the window at the black expanse. Were the *jinn* out there? Tall, humpbacked shadow-forms gliding across the wasteland? I imagined them alone, not only lost but without any hope of being found. Miles, oceans from home. Losing the way is easy, finding it again always difficult.

A plane skimmed the horizon blinking red landing lights. The Mojave should always be crossed at night. But in silence. At the most a little rock 'n' roll pulled in magically from some distant radio broadcast. But none of this yammering. I began to breathe heavily again.

"Even if you think you might not have the guts," Rod was saying, "the guts to be a first-class gyrene, and I mean a real ass-kicking dogface—"

"Rod, drop it for a second," I said suddenly. "Let's change the channel, O.K.?"

Instantly his right foot backed off on the accelerator. The car slowed down. Betrayal twisted his face into a grimace.

"I pick you up and give you a ride," he said, spluttering, "and— and you can't even listen when I talk a bit about what's important to me...?"

There was real pain in his voice. In thirty seconds I'd be out in the night.

"I meant about boot camp," I said quickly. "Change to that. Everybody says it's real rough. I just wanted to know if—"

"Oh, that!" He laughed with relief. "Sure, it's rough. But once you're through it, once you've made the grade and you know you've got the stuff to be a first-class Marine then all the rest is just... "

The desert rolled past. Headlights came toward us and shot by. The plane on the horizon shifted positions. The red lights turned to green. Rod went on to explain how much I would like life in the barracks, the comradeship and sense of duty. *"Semper fidelis,"* he intoned, pronouncing it horribly. He fixed his eyes on me again and talked about combat readiness, the advantages of re-upping, about weapons training and sentry duty. I sent up a small prayer for silence.

"A first-class leatherneck, that's what you could be," Rod said. "And you'd never regret it. Never. I never have. Never."

He was hysterical. I looked back out my window. For a moment I couldn't find the plane. Then I spotted it. It had moved southeast. I tried to judge the distance. It seemed impossible that it had gone so far in so short a time. But it was there, looking the same, except that now it didn't seem to be moving.

"Rod, look at that plane," I said.

"Huh? What about it?"

"Just watch it for a second."

He eyed me distrustfully, but then looked at the horizon. Every so often he checked the road. After a moment his forehead bunched into folds.

"It's just sort of floating there," he mumbled.

We talked about the possibility of nearby military airports but there was only the Yuma Proving Grounds and that was all the way down past the Chocolate Mountains, almost back to the California border.

"Maybe he's in trouble," Rod said.

At that moment a hill of sand and sage rose off the roadside and blocked our view. Rod stepped on the accelerator. The car sped forward but it took thirty seconds to get past the hill. I looked out again at the horizon. It was black. No lights, no sign of anything. I twisted sideways and scanned the full length of desert behind us. No lights at all. Chills went up my backbone. Rod slowed down. Just then a dark Dodge pickup pulled alongside Rod's window, a twenty-year-old blonde girl riding shotgun yelled something and pointed ahead. Her boyfriend lifted a hand off the steering wheel, waved it crazily in the same direction and then zoomed forward.

"There it is!" Rod cried.

A large oval shape of red and green lights was coming at us from one o'clock. It had radically changed direction. Dips in the road made it hard to judge its altitude. The pickup swerved into our lane thirty yards in front of us.

"It—it must be some kind of helicopter," I said.

"Too big," Rod replied excitedly. "And copters don't look nothing like that."

We were about to overshoot it. Rod cut our speed in half. For a full minute it kept coming directly at us. The pickup had also slowed down. Then the red and green lights went out. A moment passed. The desert was completely black. Suddenly the lights came back on. The angle had changed again. Rod hit the brakes and yanked sharply on the steering wheel. The car skidded to a stop on the gravel road shoulder.

I threw open the door and scrambled out. A second later Rod came racing around the front end. We stood side by side, his body trembling against mine. Across the road a half dozen cars had pulled off. Two of the drivers ran over to our side. The pickup was parked just ahead, the blonde girl and her boyfriend stood in the truck bed. A semi pulled off the road twenty yards back. Emotion pumped through my body like starlight.

For two or three minutes the green and red lights came toward us, retreated, came again. Twice they blinked off and reappeared at different angles. Then they began to move toward the southwest. In a minute only a faint glow lingered on the horizon and then that winked off into the darkness too. The semi truck driver gave a long, blast on his air horn.

Rod and I talked frantically. So did everybody else. People began to walk back to their cars. Rod and I climbed into the Oldsmobile still chattering. The couple in the pick-up tooted their horn and waved good-bye. We waved back. Suddenly I turned sideways to Rod.

"Hey, aren't we supposed to report it?" I asked, my emotions still ablaze. "You know, to the Air Force or something?"

He let out an unguarded snort.

"What's the use?" he said. "I know them fuckers. They never do nothing. They just laugh in your face, is all."

He caught himself just then and his head jerked around. I didn't look away. For a long moment we stared at each other. Then he shrugged and started the engine. He set his eyes on the road.

The rest of the ride to Phoenix went by nicely. Every so often Rod hummed a tune. For a while we listened to some rock 'n' roll on the radio, then we fell into a pleasant silence. I stared out the window and watched the desert night roll past, thinking of the *jinn* and giving humble thanks for the gift of redemption.

Patrick Pfister was born in Detroit and now lives in Barcelona, and is the author of Pilgrimage: Tales from the Open Road, *from which this story was excerpted.*

✶

High-tech-weapons staging areas are scattered throughout the Southwest. Aircraft such as the mysterious hydrogen-fueled hypersonic Aurora, tanks that move at ninety miles an hour, and experimental remote-controlled aircraft, fly out of or are tested at Area 51, the Yuma Proving Grounds, Edwards Air Force Base and other less well known bases. Area 51, a day trip from Las Vegas, is home to some of the military's cutting-edge flight technology. Military and civilian officials are notoriously close-mouthed about what goes on there; the Air Force still refuses to publicly state that Area 51 even exists. And yet every day an unmarked plane flies to Area 51 laden with civilians who work there and then commute back to Las Vegas. A fighter aircraft is said to have landed there several years ago with engine problems. A bag was promptly place on the pilot's head. My favorite line, in regards to this sort of insane and expensive secrecy, came from Clarence Kelly, former director of Lockheed's famous Skunk Works, who said, "We have some new things...." No shit.

—Sean O'Reilly, "Notes from the Southwest"

ALEX SHOUMATOFF

The Navajo Way

Here the land is a holy book written in stone.

ONE OF THE MOST REMARKABLE THINGS ABOUT THIS REPUBLIC IS
that there exists within its borders a parallel universe known as
Dinetah, a nation of more than 155,000 souls who subscribe to a
mind-set completely different from the modern American belief
that everything in nature is there for the taking. Dinetah is the
ancestral homeland of the Diné, more commonly called the Navajo,
a misnomer perpetrated by the Spaniards, as are many of the names
for the native tribes of the Southwest. An area larger than West
Virginia that sprawls out of Arizona into New Mexico and Utah,
Dinetah is bounded by four sacred mountains—North Mountain
(Debe'nitsaa), in the La Plata Mountains of Colorado, South
Mountain (Tso Dzil), or Mount Taylor, near Grants, New Mexico,
East Mountain (Sis Naajin'i), or Sierra Blanca, in Colorado, and
West Mountain (Dook Oslid), in the San Francisco Peaks, near
Flagstaff, Arizona—and four sacred rivers (the Colorado, the Little
Colorado, the San Juan, and the Rio Grande). It is some of the
starkest, most magically open-to-the-sky country anywhere—a
sagebrush steppe spotted with juniper and ancient, gnarled piñon
trees, occasionally gashed by a yawning canyon or thrust up into
a craggy, pine-clad mountain range, a magenta mesa, a blood-

red cliff, a tiara of lucent, stress-fractured tan sandstone.

"The land is our Bible," a Navajo woman named Sally once explained to me. Every feature has a name and a story and is sacred, just as every animal and plant has a "way," its own particular means of contributing, its right to be there, which must be respected. Much of a traditional Navajo's energies are devoted to keeping on good terms with the elements and one's fellow creatures, to "being in harmony with everything—yourself, mainly, all the living things, the air, Father Sky, the moon, and on and on," Sally continued. This state of *hozho*—or walking in beauty, as it is often translated—is the goal of the Navajo religion.

"You can be in harmony and sailing along just fine when suddenly you run into something disharmonious, and there's always a reason for it," she went on. "Like my brother Roy, who drowned. He got on bad terms with the Water People. Or my sister Lavine, who got bitten by a rattler when she was little. Her arm got big and bloated, and after that, every time I saw a snake I would kill it. Snakes see everything purple, and one day at noon when I was out with the sheep, everything suddenly turned purple. A snake slithered up and asked 'Why are you killing all our brothers?' I explained because my sister got bitten. So the snake said, 'Let's make a deal: Don't kill us, and we won't bother you.'"

A few years ago, Sally's husband, Kee Richard, started having nosebleeds. It turned out there was a tumor in his nose. The doctor in Flagstaff said it was cancer and zapped it with radiation, but Sally's aunt, who was a medicine woman, took one look at Kee Richard and asked him "Did you ever kill a porcupine?" "Well, yes," Kee Richard said. "When I was ten, I clubbed a porcupine with a stick from the fire. It went off to die with blood pouring out of its nose." Sally's aunt told him he had to offer turquoise and abalone to the porcupine and make a confession to ask forgiveness.

According to archaeological evidence, the Navajo were part of a migration from Siberia somewhere between 11,000 and 16,000 years ago. The Navajo themselves, however, say the People emerged from Navajo Lake, in northeastern Arizona.

"Don't tell me you're falling for that Bering Strait stuff," Sally's cousin Tom, a traditionalist, chided me. Glottochronological evidence suggests that the Navajo split off from the Athabascans of the Pacific Northwest within the past 1,000 years and began to drift south in loose, highly mobile bands. Their religion was an animism that evolved from their exceptional ability, as hunters, to "get inside the skulls of the animals," as one elder put it, a detailed understanding of the way of each species. Between 900 and 1,500 years ago, they arrived in the Southwest, where the Anasazi—ancestors of the Hopi—had lived for centuries in cliff dwellings and communal mud pueblos. The Anasazi had learned to grow maize from their Mexican cousins, a practice the Navajo adopted, along with the Anasazi's elaborate mysticism surrounding the plant. The Hopi, whose name for the Navajo means "Skull-Bashers" (while the Navajo call the Hopi "Cliff-Shitters" and "Hopeless"), still live on their four Tibet-like mesas in the middle of Dinetah.

While the Hopi were their favorite prey, the Navajo also incorporated a lot of core Hopi beliefs: that the clouds are ancestors who have to be prayed to and harangued to let down their liquid essence in the form of rain, that this is the fourth world (the Navajo call it Glitter World, the previous ones—Black, Blue, and Yellow—having been destroyed because of wickedness of their inhabitants). When they weren't raiding the Anasazi, the

The *Hopituh Shi-nu mu*, "the peaceful little people" of northeastern Arizona, have a beautiful word to describe the way change is introduced into our live. *Tunátyava* means "comes true, being hoped for," an expression of gratitude and confidence in the way the Great Spirit brings to us what we feel in our hearts. This humble acceptance of what is and what has been honors the interconnectedness of all things without questioning or measuring the time required for change to occur.

—Cynthia S. Larson, "Comes True, Being Hoped For," *Parabola*

Navajo would appear at the pueblos with game to trade for pro-
duce. The Anasazi were in decline, weakened by years of drought.
By 1519, when Cortés arrived in Mexico and with astonishing ease
conquered the Aztec empire of Montezuma II, the Anasazi disappeared. The Navajo moved into the vacant niches and thrived,
developing a complicated, lyrical, and witty religion based on fifty-
eight ceremonials, or "sings," chanted by *hataali*, medicine men
who specialize in one or two of them.

Nightway, for instance, which initiates boys and girls aged seven
to thirteen into the ceremonial life of adults, takes nine days to sing
and consists of 576 subsongs that must be intoned perfectly, word
for word, before the first frost and the first thunderstorm, while the
snakes are hibernating. The slightest mistake can result in self-hex-
ing: crippling, paralysis, loss of sight. Enemyway, a healing ceremony,
was sung for Navajo soldiers returning from the killing in Vietnam,
to purge their souls. A couple of years ago, I attended a four-day-
long Beautyway for Sally's son, who had just served a nine-year
sentence at Fort Leavenworth. "Maybe if I had Beautyway done for
him before he went to boot camp, he wouldn't have gotten into
trouble," she told me. Waterway, nearly extinct, is for people who
survive drowning or flash-flooding, or who dream of drowning;
for sickness from, among other things, rain and thunder, or from
eating the meat of lightning-struck sheep or horses.

There is a high degree of paranoia in Dinetah because the
Navajo live with many realities, not just the material plane. Evil is
not just something down in the underworld, it's out there all the
time; it's in your face. If you see an owl, it means somebody's going
to die. If you see a coyote headed north, you have to make a prayer.
Coyote sickness—brought upon by transgressing, even inadver-
tently, the way of the coyote—is something you would wish only
on your worst enemy: one side of your mouth droops permanently,
you become unable to remember anything, or you take to the bottle and, if you're a woman, you give yourself to all comers.

One morning as Tom and I sat outside his hogan, way out in the
Arizona desert, we noticed a skinny black dog with a white beard
slinking behind a rise, 200 yards off. I asked if it was a stray. Tom

said it was a skinwalker. "He's been here a couple of days." Skinwalkers are witches—*chindi*—who can take the form of animals, particularly wolves or coyotes, and can inflict illness or death on those they have it in for. They are believed to be people who want to become rich and have gone through an elaborate ceremony that includes the sacrifice—by untraceable magic means—of a relative. When a skinwalker is identified, he is often beaten to death and mutilated beyond recognition, so he won't come back. Every so often a forensic pathologist in Albuquerque told me, the Navajo Police bring in the pulverized cadaver of a suspected skinwalker from the rez, as everybody calls the part of Dinetah that the Great White Father designated as a reservation for the Navajo.

Maybe the Navajo are more aware of death and evil than your average suburban-Anglo-American because they live in the desert, which, as Georgia O'Keeffe put it, "knows no kindness in all its beauty." In any case, their paranoia is tempered by a rollicking sense of humor, an irrepressible love of puns and wordplay. Their nickname for Hitler, for instance, is (He Who) Smells His Mustache. The way to break the ice with a Navajo is to make him laugh. In my first trip through Dinetah with my family, in 1985, we pulled over to check out some rugs a group of men had strung up under a brush ramada. While I was having a rather forced conversation with one of the men—the rugs worked out to be about $1,000 a square yard—there was a sudden explosion of laughter behind the ramada. My two boys, aged five and six, had gathered the other men around them and were putting on a little show with their Gobots, with a few twists transforming them from trucks into robots, which for some reason was killingly funny.

A lot of Navajo humor is derived from their language, which is tonal and full of prefixes that subtly shade the meanings of words and is virtually impenetrable to a non-Navajo. There are, for instance, thirty ways to say "wind." The Japanese were never able to decipher the messages of the famous Navajo code-talkers in the Pacific Theater, who were actually just speaking Navajo. The humor spills over into the whole Navajo psyche. All you have to do is graze a Navajo's funny bone—tell him a good joke and he will practically die laughing.

The way to turn off a Navajo is to ask a lot of questions. One time, after I had been bombarding Tom with questions, he finally snapped: "If you quit acting like Harry Reasoner, maybe you might learn something." Another time I was talking with a group of Navajo about how tourists should behave. "Don't ask questions," one woman told me. "What is that for? Why do you wear that? What does that mean? Just step back and bite the Albuquerque bullet. Don't try to understand us in one day. You Americans are always looking for instant religious satisfaction, like instant mashed potatoes. But it's a lifetime thing. We live it every day."

"Do you have any special word for 'tourist?'" I asked. There I was, doing just what the woman had said not to do.

"I call them 'moon children,'" she said. "They must have come from the moon 'cuz they have no respect for the earth, and they're so pale."

Roxana Robinson, an O'Keeffe biographer, told me about a woman tourist who'd walked into a trading post on the rez and tried to start a conversation with a black-haired Navajo woman holding a redheaded baby. "Was the father red-haired?" the tourist asked. "I don't know," the mother retorted. "He never took off his hat."

"For us, every day is a thanksgiving day, a prayer in the cycle of life," Tom observed one time. "But for you whites, every day is a slogan. 'Give me liberty or give me death.' 'The Uncola.' 'I've just begun to fight.'"

Tom had built his hogan with the help of his cousin brothers. It was the six-sided "male" hogan with adobe-chinked log walls, a dome-shaped roof of cribbed, mud-smothered logs, and a hole in the center for smoke to exit. The door must face east, so you can greet the rising Father Sun. The woman is the keeper of the hogan. She tends a fire for her family. If a person dies in the hogan, or if the hogan is struck by lightning, it is abandoned. Navajo traditionally live in extended-family compounds known as outfits. These days the hogans are mixed with trailers, shacks, and prefab ranch houses. The sheep corrals—of which there are many—are circles of entwined piñons that look like giant crowns of thorn.

★

The converging Canyon de Chelly and Del Muerto Canyon are the spiritual heart of Dinetah. According to Navajo legend, they were made by hippopotamus-like creatures wallowing in the mud of what was then a vast quagmire. After the creatures had gouged out the canyons, they sent Hummingbird, who was monument-sized, to see if the walls were dry, which explains why some of them are scored with stuttering parenthetical gashes that look like the imprint of huge wings. The canyons have been inhabited for more than 2,000 years. The ruins of long-departed Anasazi are still preserved in scalloped alcoves under the 600-foot-high walls, which are decorated with hundreds of pictographs. On one sandstone panel is the masterpiece of some unknown Navajo Michelangelo, a mural portraying a cavalcade of Spanish soldiers in cloaks and flat-brimmed hats. With muskets held aloft—the Narbona Expedition of 1805, sent to take care of "the Navajo problem." Ninety Navajo men and twenty-five women were gunned down by these "caballeros" as they huddled in a cave on the rim of what would become known as the "canyon of death."

The canyons were a focus of resistance in 1863, when General James H. Carleton launched a campaign to round up the Navajo. Most of the men were killed outright; the women were marched 300 miles to an internment camp at Bosque Redondo, in south-eastern New Mexico. Many died on the Long Walk, and many more during the four years they spent in the Place of Confinement. Carleton's idea was that if you took the Navajo "away from their haunts and hills and hiding places" to a reorientation center and "teach their children how to read and write; teach them the arts of peace; teach them the truths of Christianity," they would become model citizens. "Fair Carletonia," as the camp was called, fell tragically short of its utopian mandate. In fact, it became a model for Hitler's concentration camps.

The leader of the 1863 Navajo campaign was fifty-three-year-old Kit Carson, the renowned Indian fighter. This was his last hurrah. The Navajos called him "Rope Thrower" because he lassoed them and marched them into captivity. By the winter of '63, Rope Thrower's tactics had left the People starving. Entering Canyon de

Chelly with a detachment of bluecoats, he met fierce resistance from a cult founded by Hashkenneniinii, the Angry One, who thought he could enlist the supernatural being Monster Slayer. The Navajo taunted Carson. Occasionally they would attack and then scamper up the cliffs using secret handholds. Peach orchards were torched; a wrinkled grandmother was shot in the head as she chanted a witch-craft song. Finally, the People realized they had to submit. The few thousand survivors were released from the Place of Confinement in 1867, including Tom and Sally's then-twelve-year-old great-grand-father, Old Gold Tooth. From them the People rebounded. Now they're the largest Native American nation in the country.

A lot of the reason for the Navajo's extraordinary regeneration has to do with their capacity for adaptation, with their cultural fluidity. "The Navajo are the beggarly nomads, the sponges of American Indian culture," a University of Arizona anthropologist told me. "If they saw something good in another culture, they took it. They took sheep from the Spaniards and became the great-est sheepherders in the world. They took silversmithing and carried it to new artistic levels. They took horses and became the preemi-nent cowboys of the Southwest."

They also took the rifle and the pickup, the junk food, the TV, and the booze of Anglo culture. While juggling these cosmologies, they continued to adhere to the Navajo Way, but many of them stumbled, and stumble. At this point it is no longer accurate to say there is one Navajo culture. There are born-again Navajo, peyote "roadmen," dope-smoking hippies, gung-ho vets who listen reli-giously to Rush Limbaugh, heavy metal freaks, even Satanists. Teenage drinking, fetal alcohol syndrome, domestic violence, and infant-mortality rates are all elevated on the rez. Five hundred Indians freeze to death or are hit by cars in New Mexico every year. Most of them are drunk, and most of them are Navajo. Some have been seduced by Anglo values, by what Tom calls "the almighty dollar and the ownership thing."

Two years ago, I played golf with Albert Hale, then the chairman of the Navajo Nation, who was in Dutch for allegedly taking his secretary to Paris on the tribe's tab and for playing in a pro-am in Albuquerque. He showed up with a large entourage at Piñon Hills, a municipal course in Farmington, just off the rez. Hale was a progressive who had as much in common with Tom as Donald Trump has with the Dalai Lama. "The council accused me of wasting Navajo money," he complained. "Our people are very traditional. They don't understand that golf courses are where a lot of business is done and that I was schmoozing corporate types." He was hoping to get Chi Chi Rodriquez to help build a course at Window Rock, the tribal headquarters. "We need to get everybody to see we are introducing a new game," he argued. "All they know is basketball and rodeo; they see golf as not useful. But golf teaches honesty, discipline, and good ethics. It teaches a code."

> The Indians make more sense of nature than white men do. They accept and use it, even if they can't explain it. They go up in the mountains and sit there and watch the gods walk through the trees. I used to run a trading post in Navajo country, so I know them well. They don't respect the white man. There's nothing to respect, when you really get down to it.
> — Barry Goldwater

I observed that the state of mind you need to be in to play optimal golf, the state of harmony with yourself and your surroundings, is not unlike *hozho*, walking in beauty. Hale told me the Navajo used to play a game where they slapped around a feather-stuffed rawhide ball with a crooked stick. Hale had a good hand-eye coordination. He played golf with zest, spitting on his palms and letting her rip. A few days later, I played with Notah Begay, the top Native American golfer, whose father is Navajo. Notah was Tiger Woods's teammate at Stanford. In 1998 he shot an almost-inconceivable fifty-nine on the Nike tour. He told me that his religion is an important part of his game.

On the back nine we were alone in the vastness of the desert steppe. Only the occasional jack rabbit would hop out of the brush and sit motionless along the fairway, frozen with nervous attentiveness. From the thirteenth tee, Notah smacked a drive that went forever. The wind took it 380 yards, and as we were walking to it he remarked, "It's so silent out here it hurts your ears."

Alex Shoumatoff was born in Mount Kisco, New York in 1946. Formerly a staff writer for The New Yorker *and now a contributing editor of* Vanity Fair, *he has been hailed for his profiles of personalities from Chico Mendes to Dian Fossey, and for his reporting from the farthest-flung reaches of the world, from Africa to Tibet. He is the author of many books, including* Legends of the American Desert: Sojourns in the Greater Southwest. *He lives in upstate New York with his wife and four sons.*

★

The enduring and popular image of the Southwest is one of desert and slick rock country but the other side of this coin are the mountains and the high country of Arizona, southern Colorado, New Mexico, and Utah. Mountains form the backdrop of many cities including Albuquerque, Las Vegas, Phoenix, Santa Fe, Taos, and Tucson. The most dramatic of these desert ranges are surely the Sangre de Cristo Mountains that form the ramparts of Taos and Santa Fe. There is an aura around these mountains that can only be approximated by the word holy. One intuitively understands why the Indians still think of them as sacred places.

—SO'R and JO'R

JEB J. ROSEBROOK AND
JEB STUART ROSEBROOK

* * *

John Ford's Monument Valley

This is the West that the movies have
engraved in all our minds.

SOMEWHERE WITHIN 1,500 MILES OF A LAND THE NAVAJOS CALL TSE
Bii Ndzigaii, "clearing or plain among the rocks," where prominent
sandstone outcrops known as Ear of the Wind, Three Sisters, and
Bear and Rabbit rise high above the arid landscape, the station
wagon approaches a movie set and its waiting crew and actors. A
small man with an accordion plays "Red River Valley." Director
John Ford, forty-four years old, has arrived for a day's work making movies in the place he calls "my lucky spot"—Monument
Valley. It is 1938.

"You're ten years too late," a Hollywood studio executive had
told Ford in 1937, referring to the death of Western films in the
talkie era. "People don't make Westerns anymore."

Two years before, Ford won his first Academy Award for *The
Informer*, a story of the 1922 Irish rebellion. Now Ford had a vision
for a Western film based on the *Colliers'* magazine story "Stage to
Lordsburg" by Ernest Haycox. Ford and screenwriter Dudley
Nichols expanded the tale of a stage traveling from Tonto, Arizona,
to Lordsburg, New Mexico, through hostile Apache country. They
shaped it into the story of a disparate group of characters: the
crooked banker, an Army officer's pregnant young wife, the vain,

failed Southern aristocrat, the whiskey salesman, the prostitute with a heart of gold, and the escaped prisoner–gunfighter facing a showdown in Lordsburg. Ford titled it simply *Stagecoach*.

The director shopped the screenplay at nearly every studio, and was rejected. Ford's luck changed when *Stagecoach* found a home with producer Walter Wanger and independent United Artists Films. And his luck would continue.

In late September, 1938, Harry and Leone "Mike" Goulding, owners of a struggling trading post in Monument Valley between Kayenta and Medicine Hat, heard on the radio that a major Western film by John Ford was in preproduction. The Gouldings had come to Monument Valley as newlyweds in 1924. They were aware portions of two Western films, Zane Grey's *The Vanishing American* (1925) and *Lone Star Ranger* (1929), had been filmed there. The Gouldings and their neighbors, the Navajos, many of whom faced starvation, were desperately trying to survive the Great Depression. Using their last sixty dollars, and armed with photographs of Monument Valley, Harry and Mike drove to Hollywood to convince Ford to use their beloved landscape as the location for his film.

When the determined couple arrived at Ford's office, a secretary attempted to put them off. In Linda Upton's unpublished history, *Monument Valley Stories from Goulding's Trading Post*, Mike Goulding recalled what happened next: "Well," Harry said, "I've got plenty of time to wait, just like any old Navajo. Why, I've wintered in littler places than this. I'll just go and get my bedroll and bed down right here." With Mike remaining in the lobby, Harry Goulding met John Ford, spreading out dramatic photographs of the valley before the director. Upton wrote: "The slow-talking trader gave the sales pitch of his life."

Before the Gouldings drove home, the inspired Ford flew to Monument Valley and, moved by the stark but magnificent landscape, he made his decision to film there. By early October, makeshift tents were set up near the trading post to house extras and the crew. The cast stayed at what nearby accommodations could be found. Navajos were hired (together with their horses) at Hollywood wages as extras, wranglers, and stuntmen. And Navajos, like the Bradley brothers, acted as interpreters to the mostly non-English speaking Indians while the Stanley brothers and Son of Many Mules would become regulars as actors in Ford's Monument Valley films.

Another Navajo, a medicine man called Hastiin Tso, would get the director's attention in a most unusual way. Harry Goulding claimed Tso could summon up any weather Ford needed. Legend has it Ford challenged Goulding by asking for snow. The next morning, snow graced the valley. From then on, Hastiin Tso was on Ford's Monument Valley payroll as his "weatherman." Ford said if he could believe in "the little people of Ireland," there was no reason for him to ever doubt Hastiin Tso.

Stagecoach previewed in Los Angeles on February 2, 1939. Made for $531,374, it grossed $1 million its first year. Against competition from *Gone With the Wind* and the *Wizard of Oz*, the film was nominated for seven Academy Awards, including Best Director. The popular Western won for music and Best Supporting Actor, Thomas Mitchell. More importantly, *Stagecoach* began a personal and professional relationship with Monument Valley that would affect Ford's life as well as the Gouldings and hundreds of Navajo families for the next twenty-five years. And change the career of thirty-one-year-old B-Western star John Wayne. Like Ford, Wayne would become forever identified with Monument Valley.

In its vast isolation—a ten-hour drive from Flagstaff often over treacherous dirt roads—Monument Valley became an ironic yet perfect complement to Ford, who, by virtue of his Maine childhood, close by the Atlantic, was a man of the sea. Born Sean Aloysius O'Feeney in 1895, he was the eleventh and last child of immigrants John, a saloonkeeper, and Barbara O'Feeney. Young Sean, a scrapper, was never one to back down from a fight. But he also loved reading, especially American history, and possessed a near-photographic memory. Turning down an athletic scholarship to the University of Maine, he followed his older brother Francis, an actor, across the country to the Pacific and a moving-picture boomtown called Hollywood. The brothers Americanized O'Feeney to Ford. Sean became John or "Jack" and found a champion rodeo cowboy, Nebraskan Hoot Gibson, for a roommate. By

1920 Francis had acted in nearly 400 silent Westerns, while Jack, rising from stuntman-actor to writer-director, was under contract to Universal, making Westerns with Gibson and, later, Tom Mix.

By 1934, as his older brother's career slowed, Jack Ford was directing some of Hollywood's biggest stars. His success earned him his beloved seagoing yacht, *Araner*, named for the islands off Ireland's coast. But in Monument Valley, Ford had discovered another ocean, remote and stunning away from Hollywood, with one skipper in command. "For Ford, Monument Valley was not only a location," producer-agent Martin Jurow told a writer, "it was his dream of the America he loved."

By 1946, after having won two more Academy Awards (*The Grapes of Wrath* in 1940 and *How Green Was My Valley,* 1941) and serving with distinction in the Navy during World War II—during which he filmed the Japanese attack on Midway Island—Ford returned to his favorite valley to film *My Darling Clementine.* The story of Tombstone and the legendary gunfight at the O.K. Corral starred Henry Fonda, one of Ford's favorite leading men (*Young Mr. Lincoln*, 1939, *Drums Along the Mohawk*, 1939, *The Grapes of Wrath*), as Wyatt Earp.

"I saw Tombstone pop out of the desert like a rabbit from its hole," Mike Goulding recalled. Twentieth Century Fox spent $250,000 re-creating 1881 Tombstone. According to author Upton, "the forty-seven buildings constructed for the film doubled as warehouses, work rooms, dining halls, and housing for approximately 600 of the cast and crew." Additionally, the Navajos were paid to supply 1,500 head of cattle to be used in the filming. To the Gouldings, the cast, crew, and Navajos, "Tombstone" was dubbed "Fordville."

By 1950 Ford directed four more films in Monument Valley, his cavalry trilogy, starring John Wayne: *Fort Apache, She Wore a Yellow Ribbon* (his first to show the valley in color), and *Rio Grande*, as well as portions of *Wagonmaster*, the westward tale of a Mormon wagon train. Fords films now featured an ensemble cast that included Victor McLaglen, Ward Bond, Harry Carey Jr., Ben Johnson, and the director's brother Francis.

Through his years in Monument Valley, Ford left no doubt who was in charge. Called "Mr. Jack" by Harry Goulding and characterized by his slouch hat, the dark glasses, the inevitable chewing on his handkerchief, and the cigars, Ford constantly pushed his actors to the limit to achieve the performances he expected of them.

At Goulding's Trading Post, there was assigned table seating, with Ford at the head table. Mike Goulding related to Upton that after dinner the Ford company often "danced to old-fashioned waltzes, and the clink of silver dollars punctuated Ford's lively card games with John Wayne, Ward Bond, and others."

Wayne's son Michael recalls the nightly card games while spending time on location with his father. "They played pitch, hi-lo, jack-in-the-boot." Ford made sure he won, because he would change the rules as they played. One Halloween the director suggested a costume party to Mike, which he attended dressed as an Irish policeman. Ford's patriarchal monarchy did not rest on Sundays, when he brought in a priest to say Mass for everyone, regardless of religion, with all expected to contribute to the collection.

Although he won his fourth Oscar with *The Quiet Man* in 1952

I have been a fan of everything Western for as long as I can remember. From John Ford's *She Wore a Yellow Ribbon* to television's *Maverick, Bonanza,* and *Gunsmoke,* a part of me has longed to live for a few moments as Miss Kitty booting some drunken tinhorn out of the saloon, or as a pioneer woman riding horseback alongside a covered wagon. So when all the cowpoke-type adventure vacations started springing up all over the American West, I was the first one on my block to sign up. Visions of howling wild beasts, moonlit campfires, and spitting tobacco juice into tin pots danced in my head. I thought, what better time to test my mettle and live out my fantasy than my fortieth birthday? So what that my idea of exercise is taking a shower.

—Mary Elizabeth Morrison,
"Old West Adventure"

Ford was, within three short years, badly in need of his "lucky spot," Monument Valley. "I think I'm going blind," Ford wrote a friend in 1953, after filming *Mogambo* in Africa. The resultant cataract surgery caused permanent weakness in one eye, forcing him to wear an eye patch. In 1954, due to illness and creative differences with star and longtime friend Henry Fonda, he was replaced on *Mister Roberts*. There was a gall-bladder operation. His beloved home was razed to enlarge a parking lot for the Hollywood Bowl. Once again, Ford was in need of a change of luck.

Then there was a novel by Alan LeMay, *The Searchers*.

Now sixty, John Ford returned to Monument Valley. He approached filming *The Searchers* with a seriousness none had seen in him before. If he believed his career was on the line he said nothing. But "it was a different movie than anything I'd seen Ford do," Harry Carey Jr., a veteran of many Ford films, said in his autobiography, *Company of Heroes*. "From the first day of shooting, it had a mood about it."

It also was a family affair. Ford's son Patrick served as associate producer, and Wayne's son Patrick (also Ford's godson), was part of the cast.

With medicine man Hastiin Tso once more acting as Weather Provider, Ford filmed throughout the summer in sandstorms and temperatures that soared to 115 degrees. Released in 1956, *The Searchers* was hailed by critics as a "visual masterpiece." John Ford, in concert with John Wayne, had brought forth an American classic. According to Michael Wayne, rock-and-roll legend Buddy Holly was inspired to pen his classic song "That'll Be the Day" after hearing John Wayne's signature line in *The Searchers*. In Hastiin Tso's third decade working with Ford, the film also proved to be his finest moment. He would die two years later.

In *Sergeant Rutledge* (1960), Ford set out to tell the story of the African-American Buffalo Soldiers, to be followed in three years by what he believed would be the final chapter of his Westerns. *Cheyenne Autumn*, based on Mari Sandoz's book, told the plight of 300 Northern Cheyenne Indians who fled an Oklahoma reservation in an attempt to return to their ancestral lands in the Dakotas.

"I've killed more Indians than Custer, Beecher, and Chivington put together," Ford told director Peter Bogdanovich. "There are two sides to every story, and I wanted to show their [the Indians'] side for a change."

"It was a subject I had long wanted to do," says Richard Widmark, the film's star, who had approached Ford with a similar project some years before. But according to Widmark, the director "didn't want to do it at the time."

Unfortunately the autumn of John Ford's career had arrived.

With the road to Monument Valley now paved, its spectacular buttes had become a magnet for tourists. Isolation was a thing of the past. The rigorous location schedule of eighteen-hour days, six days a week challenged Ford's age and stamina. Skies were often overcast, compounded by windstorms and unseasonable rain. Ford fell behind schedule. He became ill with chills and fever. John F. Kennedy, an Irish-Catholic president, was assassinated. Ward Bond had died of a heart attack two years before. In one telling moment, Ford told actor George O'Brien, whom he had known since silent picture days: "It's just no fun anymore."

Despite the difficulties of the production, Widmark, who played a cavalry officer, remembers Ford as "vigorous

Geronimo, kept a prisoner of war until his death, never relinquished the hope of being returned to his native deserts. One day at Fort Sill, pointing to the west, he solemnly declared: "The sun rises and shines for a time, and then it goes down, sinks, and is lost. So it will be with the Indians. When I was a boy, my father told me that the Indians were as many as the leaves on the trees, and that in the north they had many horses and furs. I never saw them, but I know that if they were once there they have gone. The white man has taken all they had. It will be only a few years when the Indians will be heard of only in the books which the white man writes."
—Ross Calvin, *Sky Determines*

and [he] had many future plans." Widmark also remembers the good times at Goulding's Lodge. "We were like an extended family. We had dinner with Ford and the group in the lodge every night. It was a close relationship, with Ford as 'Daddy.'"

Similarly, in her autobiography *Baby Doll*, Caroll Baker, who played a Quaker schoolteacher in *Cheyenne Autumn*, also has fond memories of Ford. "I felt that he thought of me as a daughter, and I knew that I was his pet on the film unit. While we were on location, I always ate lunch and dinner by his side. He used to watch my plate and never allow me dessert or bread and butter or potatoes."

Unfortunately, critics greeting *Cheyenne Autumn* were generally unkind, even cruel.

At seventy-six, Ford found the strength to return to his "lucky spot" one last time, in 1971, to appear in director Peter Bogdanovich's documentary, *Directed by John Ford*.

His greatest tribute from this valley he loved came from his friends and working companions, the Navajos. On the Fourth of July 1955, during filming of *The Searchers*, he was presented with a sacred deerskin and made a member of the Navajo tribe. He was given the name Natani Nez, meaning "tall soldier."

This message was inscribed on the deerskin:

"In your travels may there be beauty behind you, beauty on both sides of you, and beauty ahead of you."

John Ford died of cancer at his home in Palm Springs, August 31, 1973. He was seventy-eight. "Again, I'm sorry to say 'adios,'" he once wrote in the Gouldings' guest book. "My thanks to Hastiin Tso, who gave us such wonderful weather."

But there will never be an "adios" to the personal legacy the Tall Soldier left to the Navajos and to Monument Valley.

Scottsdale-based Jeb J. Rosebrook, a film and television writer, became acquainted with John Ford in the late 1960s. Jeb Stuart Rosebrook, Jeb J.'s son, is a historian of the American West and also serves as research editor at Arizona Highways.

★

Once I had a trip into the Valley of Tsay Bege [near Monument Valley] with a man who is, you might say, a spiritual sexton of the place. He is a white man, a cowboy, but he belongs there because he has an old affinity with the valley, and with its spirits.

We walked across the sand, among the cactus and the desert bushes. Finally we stopped before a pile of brush. My friend said: "There is an old man buried under here, and he was a man I respected. He was a leader among the Indians. See what they sent with him."

We looked closely, and found the brush-pile littered with the utensils of man. There was a coffee pot with a hole in the bottom; an old saddle, hacked with an ax; the bones of a horse. Everything had been damaged in some way.

"They knocked the horse in the head," said my friend, "so its spirit could escape and go with the old man, to provide him with comforts in the next world. Everything was knocked in the head, so its spirit could get out. See the shovel there, with the broken handle. The old man might need a shovel, so they knocked it in the head."

—Ernie Pyle, *Arizona Highways* (1946)

News from Nowhere

There is no place quite like it in the world.

THE DAM

Park full of people in blue overalls and khaki shirts—low flimsy white town with greenery…. Barren mountains full of silver, iron, gold, aluminum, Aztec turquoise, sulphur, that looked as if they would ring if you hit them with a hammer…the landscape "all heaved up and then baked again"—flat basin of deep red, with whitish expanse that looked like water—gray and blue mists—blue inky clouds, as if for a storm.

By 2:30 in the afternoon the temperature in the little desert railroad town of Las Vegas, Nevada, peaked. A hundred ten, a hundred twenty degrees. Edmund Wilson noted in his journal that men and women and children were milling around the only two patches of green there were, the lawns in front of the courthouse and the depot.

Victor Castle was one of the hundreds of people who slept out on those lawns at night. The morning after he got in, Castle and three friends drove out to Boulder City. They looked at the housing the Six Companies consortium was slapping together for the workers at the dam. It would be months before the town could be occupied. Then they went on to the camp called Rag City, where whole families of squatters had thrown up a huddle of tents and crude shelters of wood and cardboard and flattened tin cans. In Rag City, Las Vegas water was going for two gallons for fifteen cents, five gallons for a quarter. Most of the Rag City people dipped their supply from the gritty brown water of the hole someone had dug in the riverbank.

Castle got a job working in the road gang boarding house, where four waiters served 350 sweating, half-naked men at a stretch, scarcely clearing the plates from one batch when another came along. After two days he quit.

He wrote that he'd rather mooch on the main stem than work in 140-degree heat for $2.00 a day and meals, and even then have $1.50 a month taken out of his pay for insurance that didn't even cover heat exhaustion. At the dam site itself it was so hot that the gas tanks on the equipment exploded by spontaneous combustion. If a man was dumb enough to try to pick up a crowbar without gloves he could end up with second-degree burns. In the two days Castle was in camp he'd seen two men brought in unconscious from the heat. One was dead before they could even drive him to the hospital in Las Vegas.

By the spring of 1932

The Industrial Workers of the World, or Wobblies, as they later came to be called, were a radical workers' group started in 1905 in Chicago by one "Big" Bill Haywood of the Western Federation of Miners and Eugene V. Debs of the Socialist Party. Their stated goal was to bring down what they perceived to be an unfair labor system patronized by big business. They were hated by business groups and government officials alike who often referred to them as the scum of the earth and who used every means at their disposal, ethical and otherwise, to destroy them.

—SO'R and JO'R

Boulder City had been built, and the families of the dam workers poured in from the shanties of McKeeversville and Rag City. The new city was the ultimate company town: a little version of Calvin's Geneva out on the desert, run by a vice-hating puritan and one of the Six Companies thugs who had made his mark busting Wobbly heads in Las Vegas. As for the Wobblies, their drive to rebuild themselves had died in the heat and dust of the dam, killed by the Great Depression and their own brave illusions.

By December of 1934 Hoover Dam was virtually complete. It rose in the air of Black Canyon taller than the Empire State Building, the largest construction project the world had ever seen. Soon the giant generators would be in place, spinning out immense kilowattage to light Los Angeles and drive its new factories and to keep the lights burning all night long on Fremont Street in Las Vegas. Before long, the cribs of the Skidway and the road houses lining Boulder Highway would be gone and Las Vegas would become a place of increasingly rationalized sin. The two cities, the Puritan City on the road to Black Canyon and the City of Sin, were still connected by the power lines that rose out of the dam.

There is a story that deep inside the dam's four and a half million tons of concrete lies the corpse of a worker. No such accident ever happened. But this is of little account: we know the penalty we must pay for such monstrous works. We know a worker lies buried in the dam.

And little by little the dam silts up. The water becomes sedimentary and brackish, more and more destroying the desert land it once irrigated. Slowly, inevitably, the Colorado River eats into the foundations of the dam.

The Philosopher

The Philosopher is making his way toward Las Vegas at eighty-five miles an hour. Outside the windows of the car the charred landscape wavers in the brutal light.

The Philosopher has a theory about the desert. The Philosopher has a mind, the desert is America itself. Weary of the embarrassment of culture, which hangs on him like a seedy bathrobe, the *not*-ness

of the desert fascinates him. He has been reading Tocqueville. But
instead of the institutions, societies, clearing in the woods, prisons,
workshops, courthouses, and counting houses his countryman
found in the new land, he finds the desert, leveling all values, making them all equally insignificant, and, thus, like the hummocks of
brush and the outlines of the Joshua trees set against in the clear,
hard light, equally original. In his mind the desert spreads outward
from its center, swallowing everything. He sees it as a movie, an
infinite panning shot. The Philosopher's map of America is like
those nineteenth-century atlases that found at the continent's heart
a Great American Desert, featureless, almost impassable, a blank
space between two coasts. Driving into a kind of vortex, he surrenders himself to the imploding tunnel of his description of the land.

The desert doesn't think, therefore doesn't understand that it
exists. It holds no mirror up to its strenuous beauty. Says nothing.
Knows nothing. Transparent as glass, what can one make of it? It
becomes another text. (One doesn't cruise this one: one zooms
into it, inscribing one's description of it on its transparency.) The
United States is the oldest country in the world, Gertrude Stein
once said, because it has been in the twentieth century longest. It
is this ancient source of the future the Philosopher longs for, this
history-less, nostalgia-less place that he calls America. He himself is
afflicted with nostalgia—not for the past, with its cultural gim-
cracks, its tarted-up toga history, but for what he terms a nostalgia
for the future.

The Philosopher speaks to no one. Not to the joggers who repel
him with their manic hygiene, not the breakdancers on the corners
of the streets, not the truckers he sees briefly reflected in the
rearview mirror of his rental car as he zooms beyond them. The
Philosopher does not speak, nor does he listen. He only sees. Sight:
the most metaphysical of the senses. He notes the words stenciled
on his rearview mirror: *Caution: objects in this mirror may be closer than
they appear.*

Where Tocqueville slogged on foot through the mud if there
were no roads, and down rivers in rackety steamboats, lived in one-
room pioneer cabins and Indian villages, his notebook always by

him, his countryman in the Chrysler surrenders himself to the luxury of speed. And how convenient it is, after all, this an air-conditioned cocoon spun out of the articulations of theory. The Philosopher is a blast of heat and the acrid smells of sage and creosote. The Philosopher pushes the button and the window rises.

Signs

The Sign is everything here. It looms above the landscape, immense, aggressive, insistent. Even the familiar logos of gas stations and fast-food restaurants are Brobdingnagian, competing with the cries of those that front the casinos. A team of architects from the East drove down the strip and learned that you take in the Sign before anything else. For them Fremont Street was nothing but one immense neon false-front, casinos flowing into each other behind a single popping and sizzling façade in colors so intense they paled the daylight. You consume the sign here, not that to which it points. Beyond the sign is metaphysical darkness. A world that cannot name itself, that gropes in anguish in its inky chaos. When Jean Baudrillard, who is speeding across the desert to rendezvous with this predestined place, arrives, he will find in Las Vegas the ultimate tribute to his work: a city that imitates his categories. It is a simulacrum of the simulacra of his thought. Is this not, indeed, Utopia? Where the idea becomes the pure environment, a kind of gigantic bottle that shuts out anything but itself.

Treadmills to Oblivion

At Caesars Palace a moving sidewalk sucks the Tourist into some strange version of Rome, if Rome, as Fellini now and then suggested, were a movie set. But what movie would this be? In the enclosed shopping mall, the Tourist finds a faux Roman street, with fountains, a café, shops selling expensive leather jackets, reproductions of artifacts from museums around the world. On the domed ceiling, the clouds pick up the tints of dawn, then blaze to noon, then slowly fade into a gentle sunset. Twilight comes, the stars wink on, the cycle starts again. The pathos of a whole day has been canned in a few minutes of sadness. Ejected by the sidewalk, back on the featureless, blazing noon of the Strip, the Tourist is at a loss, until the treadmill of the Mirage sucks him into an indoor jungle, acoustically punctuated by the clash of a million slot machines' electronic distributions of fortune. City of treadmills! Even at the airport a moving sidewalk had taken him to his rental car. From hidden speakers somewhere the voices of comedians whose names are familiar only to those who go to the shows in the casinos had told him lame jokes and warned him to keep to the right and watch his step.

The Tourist is on vacation. To be on vacation is to taste, if only faintly, what it means to be free. Free of the sinister dictatorship of the calendar, of the everlasting burden of work, free above all, of the need to choose. The disembodied voices coming over the moving sidewalks give the Tourist his instructions, prompt his needs to see, to be stimulated, to consume. And everything is possible. The ambience of the casino's interior suggests this: the banquets of cheap food, the fictive luxuries of flocked wallpaper and mirrored ceilings, the floor shows where the nakedness of women is offered impartially to everyone. The Tourist stretches himself out, luxuriates. He has placed the world permanently on hold. Here all hierarchies melt, are reconstituted under the democratic nightstick of Luck. Devalued, stripped of moral significance, money becomes the universal solvent and the true democracy. Standing in line at the buffet, waiting for the topless revue to start, in silk shirts and tractor hats and message t-shirts and sport coats bought in Palm Springs, we know what the Tourist knows—that we are all one.

In the corridors of the Mirage, white tigers prowl in a white boudoir, surrounded by white trees, white cliffs, white rocks, while on a television monitor their tamers discourse in Teutonic accents on the tigers' rarity. Farther on is the dolphin habitat. An odd word, "habitat," the Tourist thinks. Isn't everything here a habitat, thermostatically controlled, sealed off? Outside the desert sizzles in heat. Inside the casino hums in its dark orbit, beyond time, beyond space. It is a country in itself. With its own flag, its own constitution, its own rules. Like some huge iron lung, the air conditioners endlessly recirculated the exhausted air from the lungs of the tourists, the

hum of their machinery drowned out by the pinging chatter of
the machines. This place, pretending to be so foreign, isn't it oddly familiar, after all? With its piped-in-music, its ostentatious displays of leisure, of food, of sexual availability, is this not a strange, mutant version of the worlds imagined by Bellamy and Fourier? This is Pleasure Industrialized. Back outside the Mirage, frequently spaced signs tell the Tourist of its main attraction:

> THE VOLCANO ERUPTS DAILY
> EVERY 15 MINUTES AFTER
> DARK UNTIL MIDNIGHT,
> EXCEPT IN INCLEMENT
> WEATHER. THE RED
> FLASHING LIGHT DENOTES
> INCLEMENT WEATHER.

The Cage

Even in the umbilical of the jetway the Gambler had noticed the sound, faint at first. Then louder, increasingly more familiar, cheerful. It was as if, walled up in some padded chamber, he could hear the blood corpuscles caroming through his arteries. Once inside the airport itself, the sound became a high, cheerful jangle and roar. This sound the Gambler

---

Before I'd ever been to Las Vegas, I was full of scorn for the place. Then, on my first visit, I went to a magic show. The magician—a gorgeous, poised, and energetic young woman—invited me to participate in her act. Up close, I could see that her heart was beating like a hummingbird's, and it was clear that she was performing just one step ahead of huge fear, yet still giving all she had to the show, and, no doubt, her dreams. She was a pure embodiment of human striving, and I was very moved by her. The next day, I visited Siegfried and Roy at their backstage apartment, where a live Siberian tiger paced a glass shower stall and a stuffed vulture brooded over the bed, and all the while the German magicians talked with great courtesy to a group of boys interested in magic. Experiencing these twin pinnacles of hope and improbability in two days—well, let's just say I had to reconsider my opinion of Las Vegas.

—James O'Reilly, "Not Just Fear and Loathing"

heard was the ringing of the slot machines. The machines were the first altars on the sands of the new country.

Before there was money, a man might gamble a bow, a blanket, a horse, perhaps his wife. Gambling is a magical form of barter, a transaction in which the exchange is always radically unequal. But the thing one gambles becomes subtly different the moment it is staked. It enters a magic realm in which it becomes charged with the energies, risks, possibilities of the game. Yet at the same time, it becomes oddly devalued. Now it represents only an abstract token, an emptiness waiting to be filled with hope, aggression, and desire according to the unforeseen opportunities of the game. So, in order to play, the Gambler must go to the Cage. It is the Cage that makes gambling possible.

You've heard the fairy tale of the princess who could spin straw into gold? Behind the imaginary bars of the Cage sit those postsexual antiprincesses, the cashiers who spin gold into straw. At the Cage the ordinary bills passed across the counter come back as ships, spill out in nickels and quarters into the little plastic buckets emblazoned with the casino crest, cornucopias of possibility. Liberated from the vulgar economies of the everyday, from its value in terms of work, or saving, or denial, money undergoes an awful transubstantiation at the Cage: now it represents not its ghostly missing part, all that is cost in effort and care, but a magical possibility.

The Gambler moves away from the Cage, a plastic container, disturbingly reminiscent of his last visit to a delicatessen, held chalicelike between his hands. Before staking a chip, he has entered a symbolic realm.

Gangsters

The Gangsters have left only a few visible traces. The vulgarity of their hotels and casinos (for they were the first Americans who, having lost their history, were replacing it with one taken over from Hollywood, which had turned them from off-book businessmen into tragic figures) has so familiarized itself that it no longer shocks or amuses or offends. What the movies offered in a ghostly version on the screen, was what Las Vegas promised in the flesh. Both

Hollywood and Las Vegas were not places but floating promises of liberation from the places we had come from, from family, history, class. Thus the Gangsters who founded contemporary Las Vegas saw its site as desert in a moral sense, as a blank slate, a landscape upon which to impose their visions, and as machine for extracting money from desire.

The only cameras allowed in casinos are those we never see. And we always know they are there. Above the false ceiling of the casino, behind peepholes and one-way mirrors, are the closed-circuit television networks that continually watch the action. The security system is a fossilized remnant of the nervous systems of those paleo-Gangsters. Ever alert to the card-counter who might jimmy the casino's edge, the dealer who might collude with a customer, the shill who might drop a hundred-dollar chip into the front of her dress, the security system externalizes the Gangsters' own paranoia. The complex operation of the casino's inner life is analogous to those signs blazing outside it which the architects Venturi and Brown and Izenour saw—signs that "shout their gorgeous cacophony, but hide their constraining order."

So the first generation of Gangsters founded the city with money from their crimes, leavened by the pension funds of Midwestern truck drivers, and the projections—so amply justified—of a constant infusion of dollars from the tourist suckers. Utopia is a country, after all, and all countries have their tax collectors. The Gangsters were nothing more than businessmen who had seized the privilege of collecting a tax on our desires for sex, for success, for action, for oblivion. How easily these rough men outgrew their ori-

> Las Vegas was the part-time home of one of the most reclusive and bizarre millionaires America has ever seen. Industrialist Howard Hughes, an outspoken racist and buyer of politicians, spun a web of political intrigue and corruption that has yet to be fully uncovered.
>
> —Sean O'Reilly, "Notes from the Southwest"

gins and settled into a comfortable sort of Chamber of Commerce of Vice existence! True, a few had to be iced off, kidnapped, taken out of the game—but how very few they turned out to be. And how easily they and their surviving associates were replaced in almost seamless transitions by their heirs, the corporate managers of pleasure. It is all part of the increasing gangsterization of American life. The taxes on our desires are now collected by corporations who advertise on network TV.

Liberace

When the winds blow once more through the empty corridors of these false-front mausoleums, we will know that there is something Egyptian about this place. We will know it by the monuments that rise, purposeless, out of the desert; we will know it when we discover that here is where the Celebrities have come to die, embalmed inside the temples of their own personae. The museum is difficult to find because it is part of a shopping strip, and looks, in fact, not like a museum at all but like a shopping strip building. Inside are his pianos, his automobiles, the glass cases filled with his costumes, his plaques, and trophies.

Grinning from the photographs on the walls, he hangs here distributed, the berdache of this place, magician of the casino stages, eternally camping behind that golden grin, entombed by the monstrous costumes loaded down with sequins and metallic thread, the leaden tail-coats, the seventy-five-pound capes. Even his cars, like ceremonial hearses, are laden with mirrors, with sequins. Is it true that he had so many plastic surgeries on his face that he could not close his eyes? Sleepless before his own image, he spent his long nights putting in the medicinal drops that took the place of tears.

Dancing on the Feet of Chance

There is a story everyone knows about Nick the Greek, when he was old and broke and reduced to playing for small change in the card rooms of Gardena. Someone asked him how it felt to have come from such heights to this. He turned on the questioner and said, "It's action, isn't it?"

Action is a locus, a point of charged energy, a void without a landscape, without history. It speaks of pure, liberating disconnection from anything but its own rhythms, its own surge. So you bet. You bet your lunch, you bet your pants, you bet your paycheck. You bet everything just to feel it. Moment by moment your life ticks away. But at the edge of this action you are never more alive. No one on the outside can understand it. Not your husband. Not your wife. Not your friends. Not your shrink. No one can understand the rush. Or the terror. But the moment has no duration. It has to be repeated again and again. From nothing (you are nothing here, just a person at a table) you have to create yourself. You have to create yourself again and again.

To gamble means to squeeze your life, card by card, into a story; to compress it to a point, a light blazing up at the last turn of the card that is action. Over and over again, dying and being reborn, you tell the story that is in your life but has become greater than that life, its envelope, its field.

What are the numbers the House is running against you? 0.6 percent? 5.26 percent? 20 percent? This is the true cost of gambling: this knowledge is the real price of the game. Because the game is rigged and you know it. Little by little the casino's edge eats into you. Little by little it chews you away. The ball that stutters around the frets of the roulette wheel has no memory; the Gambler is cursed with the inability to forget.

But for just this moment, this entry into the liberating territory of Luck, he must forget. That's the trick. The Gambler stares out over the green tables of the casino like Moses gazing over the Promised Land. The little tremors of anticipation race each other up and down the nerves of his legs. He is conscious only that he will win. He fingers the chips in his hand. He could laugh for joy.

The Philosopher and the Great Whore

Rising up before him in the night, all at once, "bathed in phosphorescent lights," is his true destination, "sublime Las Vegas." And yet, like some long-awaited assignation, the physical consummation seems anticlimactic. The city is too open to his categories, too shameless in its pandering to his terminology. Like some aging yet oddly inexperienced whore, who in her eagerness shows everything all at once, the town has no mystery. The Philosopher, who has invented the useful concept of hyperreality, has resurrected the notion of the simulacra, ideas whose very shadows Las Vegas pants to inhabit, finds the town, in spite of its sublimity, beneath contempt. The visit to the capital city of his vision of the future is, after all, less charming than incest, or a freeway in Los Angeles. A few mots tossed off as an afterthought, like a quick feel in a hotel corridor and he is gone. He drives out of Las Vegas with the window rolled up. He doesn't see, over the rim of the horizon, the vast wedge of concrete driven into the gorge, hear the hum of the dynamos that drive the power that lights the city. The Philosopher turns the air conditioner up a notch, and once more on the asphalt arrow of highway enters the abstraction of desert.

Learning from Las Vegas

The women keep coming up to the Gambler, proffering drinks, proffering Keno, proffering change. "Hi, I'm Krystal from Boise," the nametags say. "I'm Sheri from Sacramento." "I'm Debbi from Chicago." They all have name tags and they all have smiles and the horrible thing is that the smiles are genuine. The smiles detach themselves from their bodies. They float there, above their nametags, ready to be plucked. A kiss left by the Philosopher, who is no longer there.

Later, fuzzy with liquor, needing to piss, the Gambler loses his way in Caesars, finds himself in a little rotunda surrounded by boutiques. Above him looms the familiar marble shank of the *David* of Michelangelo, his cloak casually draped over his shoulder, surveying with his sightless marble eyes some scene of which only marble can dream. This *David*, the Gambler reads, is an exact replica of the one in Florence, carved from the same mother-stone. Standing there, under the shadow of a six-pound marble testicle, all history and time are canceled in the dark zone between this figure and his original. Between these two points, the world loses its orbit, wobbles crazily. What is the need for the original if it can be so facilely reproduced? Shaved down to a few primitive needs, can the Gambler himself be reproduced?

The Gambler finds the can and makes his way back to the casino floor. Later still, he comes to another heroic statue, one he's been searching for. It is of Joe Louis, the great boxer. His pedestal is low, the statue almost accidentally placed. The boxer crouches as if in the casino itself, his fists encased in their marble gloves. Since the Gambler last saw this statue a small television monitor has been added. It is as if television must testify to the reality of everything, the tigers in their cages at the Mirage, this gladiator. Again and again on the little screen Joe Louis pounds Max Schmeling to the canvas. The Gambler remembers the saddest photograph he knows, from Mario Puzo's book on Las Vegas. The photo has no caption: none is needed. It is of Joe Louis, broke, reduced to living on tips and the charity of the casinos. He stands outside one of the hotels, his sport shirt untucked, a cigarette casually held at his side, his eyes filled with something so terrible you don't want to know it.

The Gambler is a fake, like everything here except the green bills and hard coins the casino owners take to their banks. He has stolen titles to his musings from Fred Allen and from Friedrich Nietzsche, both of them dead, and from a group of smart-aleck architects and from everyone else, knowing full well that titles, like faces, can't be copyrighted. He has stolen ideas from a half-baked French philosopher. Now he has put a few quarters in a video poker machine. On the way out of the Showboat he tells someone that he came within one card of hitting a royal flush. Some casino wise guy overhears him. "And they didn't give you nothin' for that?" the wise guy says.

The Gambler looks back on the casino, the tables with their clacking dice and fluttering cards, the nags galloping across a dozen television screens while the horse players hunch in their carrels like scholars in the reading room of some museum, the cocktail girls negotiating the crowded floor with their trays full of drinks and aprons full of change. Everywhere machines are pinging and spinning, disgorging their hard little pellets of happiness, swallowing someone's life a nickel at a time. In a forlorn little alcove the Keno players are sitting at their desks like passengers waiting for the next ferry across the Styx. He has a vision of naked men squatting in the dust. It is the beginning of culture or its end. They are gambling.

Our Revels Now Are Ended…

Keep going. Past Fremont Street, past the garish casinos on the Strip, which by daybreak have lost their hold on the landscape. The neon signs, which imposed their blazing shouts on the darkness, now dimmed, show only the bizarre, oddly naked offers of the casino facades. Abruptly, the town ends. Only the zone of rusted beer cans that the architects who last surveyed the city found mediating between town and the vast, treeless expanse of the Mojave Desert mark this transitional space. Here the casinos "turn their ill-kept backsides toward the local highway." There is nothing else. Like the false fronts of some old western main street, built overnight atop a lode of silver or gold that ran out its course in a year or two, you know that Las Vegas itself could, overnight, blow away, the rough magic of gangsters and hoteliers disappearing like the trembling lines of heat mirage.

Casino magnate Steve Wynn has started to warn that something terribly wrong is happening in the fantasy city he helped to create. He says it is time to "slow down and think about what we're doing." These words—slow down, think— usually get checked at the Vegas airport. At Lake Mead, just a few miles from where the city draws its water, there are fish with twisted spines and mutated genes. The males have female egg protein in their blood plasma, making them unable to reproduce. If human embryos followed a similar pattern, extinction could be around the corner. Biologists theorize that the fish took in too much of the liquid waste of Las Vegas. In all their plumbing and engineering, the water czars made one monumental error. As it turns out, the people of this most daring of American cities draw their drinking water just six miles from the same spot where they dump their waste.

—Timothy Egan, *Lasso the Wind: Away to the New West*

★

The Meadows

Green grass. Willows. The little stream meandering through the valley. Thirty-two hours without water across the bleak desert from the Muddy, the oxen stumbling, about to give out. Then come the Meadows.

> The water of the springs is very clear: they are from twenty to thirty feet in diameter, and at the depth of two feet the white sand bubbles all over as tho it was the bottom, but upon wading in, there is no foundation there, and it has been sounded to a depth of sixty feet, without finding bottom, and a person cannot sink to the armpits, on account of the strong upward rush of water.

The third day was the Sabbath (honor it and keep it holy). They made a bower of willows to shield them from the brutal sun, prayed, and sang songs of Zion. That first summer they cleared the ground, planted oats, corn, peas, beans. When they looked at their well-watered plots they thought they could see the corn grow.

They made peace with the Indians, baptized them, hired them to help clear the brush and make adobes for the fort. Looked forward to the time when they could send for their women and children. But the soil turned out to be filled with alkali, and the crops died slowly all summer long. Still they kept working, preaching.

A band of miners came out, sent by the Prophet, Seer, and Revelator in Salt Lake. The miners hired the Indians to pack the lead ore down the steep trail to the improvised smelter. The Indians quit after one load. Later on, four Paiutes lugged ore alongside the mule train in exchange for pants. The Paiutes walked barefoot through the snow to save their moccasins

Then the miners and the settlers fell out with each other. There was too much foreign matter in the lead to smelt it properly in their primitive furnaces and they abandoned the diggings. (The foreign matter turned out to be silver. Later speculators lugged it out by the bushel basket.) A few days after the diggings were abandoned two miners came back with a cart to salvage their supplies. The Indians had already destroyed all the improvements. Then the colonists themselves were called home. A year after the last colonists left, an itinerant missionary came through the settlement. He spoke with the Indians. Of the colonists, their life, their improvements, there was scarcely a trace. "There seems to be but very little 'Mormon' in them," he wrote. "And they showed me on their fingernails how much."

Night and day at Las Vegas Boulevard North and Washington Avenue the cars go whizzing by. Out on the desert are rising the steel-girded walls of the Emerald City. There is no longer a fort, a green meadow. No gushing spring. No little stream, cold and clear as a millrace.

The Prophet

Before the whites came to the desert, a Paiute shaman with prophetic gifts foretold that a people from across the ocean would come to take the country. Every night, for one or two years, he named all the mountains and said the Indians would lose them. He was a very old man when the Mormons first came to settle on the Muddy River and the prophecy came true. And how many remember the names of the mountains anymore in Las Vegas?

Zeese Papanikolas teaches at the San Francisco Art Institute. He is the author of Buried Unsung: Louis Tikas and the Ludlow *and* Trickster in the Land of Dreams, *from which this story was excerpted.*

✳

"So," she said. "You heard something about the fate of the white man. And you want to know more."

I mumbled that, yes, I did. Did she know anything?

She looked at me with intensity. "The fate of the *Bilagáana*," she repeated.

"I keep hearing," I said, "about how we, I mean the white people, are going to suffer a fate similar to the Anasazi."

"And *I'm* supposed to know something?" she said, looking at Norman.

"Go ahead," Norman said. "Tell him."

There was a long silence. She sighed irritably.

"Well," she said, "a long time ago, when I was a little girl, my grand-father talked about that once. He was a medicine man. I guess it was a very important and sacred piece of information." She stopped and held her head in her hands for a moment.

"Oh, I *wish* I'd had more sense and asked him what he meant! I was just a kid and I wasn't thinking about things like that. I didn't know anything. And then he died before I grew up and I never did get a chance to ask him what he meant. He was very old and wise, and he knew a lot of sacred things. I never forgot what he said and when I got older I thought about it more and more. It seems like I'm thinking about it more and more these days. Wondering what he meant."

"What did he say?" I asked.

She looked at Norman.

"Well, he said that the white man was going to create an image of himself. And when that happened, the image would turn and destroy the creator."

—Douglas Preston, *Talking to the Ground*

COLIN FLETCHER

The House of Time

For a moment, live like a cliff dweller,
deep in the Grand Canyon.

I CLIMBED BACK TO MY PINK APARTMENT HOUSE, UNPACKED, AND
settled in.

Of the four little rooms, one of the center pair was so small that
I felt sure it had been built for a child. The other, rather less
cramped, looked as though it might have done for a reasonably
petite wife. The two end chambers were bigger, and the farthest
offered not only the widest part of the ledge as its front porch but
also a jutting section of wall that created a little alcove—the sort of
useful place in which any present-day man would unhesitatingly
dump his traveling bag when he had unpacked. I designated this
farthest chamber the "master cubicle."

When I had first looked inside the cubicle I had thought: "What
tiny people they must have been!" Yet when I crawled in through
the doorway and stretched out full length I found that there was
plenty of room for my 180-pound bulk. The cubicle showed every
sign of having been built for a man just about my size. Its floor
measured three feet by seven. The roof, at the point I needed to sit
up, seemed to have been chipped away to give a convenient three-
foot clearance.

Once I had grown used to the gloom and a slight stuffiness, I decided that my master bedroom was a distinctly comfortable place. It offered advantages that would roll easily off any realtor's tongue. It was cool, and quite free from the usual desert dust. And its picture doorway commanded, beyond the blue-and-white river, a breath-stopping sweep of curved rock—a view that would have added thousands of dollars to the value of any house built today.

I dwelt in my cliff dwelling for twenty-four hours. And, hour by hour—conscious of my vast ignorance, yet curiously confident—I began to focus on my cave dweller more sharply.

First I pictured him building his home. I saw him chipping patiently away at the roof of the cave, so that there would be headroom when he sat up in his cubicle. (If I was right in assuming that he had built this cubicle to fit his own person—and at the time I had no doubts at all—then he was a shade shorter than I am, butt to crown, though only by a bare inch.) I saw him chipping back the footwall at an angle, so as to make room for his legs. I saw him, next, choosing with unhurried care the material for the cubicle walls. I saw him cementing each piece of rock in place with pink mud-plaster that he had probably made from pounded rock. I saw him nod with satisfaction when, after fitting several oversize pieces near the place his head would come, he lay down full length and found, sure enough, that the protrusions formed neat little ledges in exactly the right convenient place for whatever he wanted handy little ledges for. (Not pen and notebook, like me, of course; but he wanted them for something, all right.) I saw him fashioning the doorway: neatly rectangular and just big enough for him to pass through once he had learned the proper jackknife technique (which I soon did). I saw him, next, making the door lintel: peeling the bark off a stick about an inch in diameter and three feet long, smoothing off its undersurface, and squaring off one side for about nine inches at each end so that when he cemented the stick in position it could not rotate. (Like most natural sticks, it was not quite straight, and if it had been free to rotate it would not have done its job.) Finally I saw my satisfied craftsman jackknifing through the doorway to make sure that the stick was in exactly the right position to warn him, by touching his bent back, that if he straightened a half inch more he would break the stick and the rough stone above the doorway would gouge into his bare skin. I found myself wishing he could have known that thanks to his meticulous work this same stick, protected from rain and direct sunlight and practically indestructible in such a dry climate, would also be brushing my back in timely warning, all these years further down the line.

I slept soundly through a warm night. Then it was day again. And as the hours passed I came to feel that slowly—not through conscious effort, but merely by living as he had lived—I was coming to know a little more about this man who had preceded me. Piece by untidily added piece, I explored new sectors of the life he had led. Or at least that I confidently imagined he had led.

It seemed reasonable to assume that fear of enemies had driven him up into the cliff. No other reason, in fact, made much sense. And he had chosen a superb defensive position. His rear and flanks were impregnable. And any frontal attack would smack of suicide. In daylight, enemies could approach no closer than the foot of the talus, 600 feet below, without being seen. And as soon as they began to scramble up the talus they became vulnerable to rolled rocks and thrown stones as well as plunging arrows. If the attackers managed to climb close enough to retaliate, the small doorways of the cubicles would protect the cowering women and children. Even the men, hurling rocks or firing arrows, would be quite well protected by the lip of the ledge. And in the final savage moments the defenders would hold every advantage as they swung their long clubs and as a last desperate resort kicked and punched at the breathless, precariously balanced invaders.

At night, the dice were hardly less loaded. Any intruder had to climb the last forty feet on small ledges he had never seen. And if he succeeded in creeping up to the first cubicle (which had a neat peephole overlooking the only approach) without awakening anyone (assuming that the family ever slept en bloc), he still had to make a mortal thrust through the small doorway before any kind of startled, clumsy push sent him cartwheeling back the way he had come, screaming and doomed.

Day or night, there was precious little doubt whose side I would rather be on.

In time of danger there would naturally be fear as you waited. But there always is, in any kind of warfare. And that unoutflankable ledge did not seem too bad a place to be frightened in, especially if you were squatting there with a comfortable stock of boulders poised ready to roll, and a mound of sling-size stones, and a bow and flint-headed arrows, and, as final reserve, a long and trusty club close at hand and held fast by stones to keep it from rolling down and away. A better place to be frightened in than a World War II pillbox, certainly. An incomparably better place than somewhere deep and anonymous with the firing button of an ICBM under your metaphorical thumb as you waited, waited, waited to be told at the hundredth remove that some distant member of the same demented species had just pushed his own terrible and impersonal button.

During my stay in the cliff dwelling I also kept company with my man in a few of his peaceful leisure moments and learned some of the little important things. I sat as he must often have sat, doing nothing in particular, outside his cubicle door. My bare butt occupied the same convenient little squatting-ledge that his must have occupied. My toes curled over the same rough lip of rock that his had curled over. My eyes saw what his had seen: river, rock, sky, space, and luminous light. My eyes heard what his had heard: silence; the roar of the river; the repetitive but liquid call of a rock wren; the tearing of air as a swift plunged past; the mewing of two hawks that had made their home in the cliff face, 100 feet higher than his. ("Were there really hawks nesting up above in his time?" I wondered.)

By now I had picked up some other facts too. I had discovered that bare feet are remarkably safe engines to use for climbing around on loose rock. Also that my man's soles were tougher than mine. I learned that when he belched, it echoed. And when, following up this revelation, I lay in our little cubicle and called out to his wife through the partition, I confirmed that we lived—he and I—in a natural echo chamber.

There was one thing about the life of this man and his wife that

I understood more clearly now than I had done in the beginning. The first time I looked inside the master cubicle I had thought not only what small people the occupants must have been but also how difficult it must be to beget children in such cramped quarters. After I had spent a night in the cubicle I knew better. There was plenty of room. It was a warm place too, and snugly private. You could do much worse.

Many details of my cliff dweller's domestic life still puzzled me, of course. The family no doubt tossed their garbage down the cliff. But what, I wondered, about toilet arrangements? And there was also the problem of how to keep the kids from falling downstairs.

Many such surface details of my man's life remained a blank. But in the course of the second morning I began to feel that I was learning things of a quite different kind.

It seemed clear to me by then that my man was blessed with an insight that we modern men tend to lose, walled in as we are by our complexities (or do I mean walled *out*?). Living his simple life— eating breakfast with his wife and children on the ledge, watching the swifts plunge past and snap up their insect breakfasts, watching the hawks come mewing back to their upper story home with breakfasts for *their* children—he could hardly help but understand, clearly and steadily, that man is an integral part of everything that goes on around him. More particularly, because the rock was a part of everything he did—sitting, seeing, hearing, cooking, fighting, making love—he understood it. Naturally, his understanding was different from mine. Even his questions were different. When he lay in our master cubicle and looked up at the chipped gray limestone above his head—at the same chip marks that I looked up at—he probably did not wonder why the rock was gray inside and red on its surface. He almost certainly did not conclude that it was stained by long ages of rainwater from the red rocks above. And yet (it seemed contradictory at first, but I don't think it really was) I felt that he knew something about the rhythm of the rocks. Not in a logical way, of course, that he could have talked about. But I had an idea that when he looked at a partly detached slab of pink rock down near the kitchen and wondered how long before it would fall,

he would have known in his own way that it would still be standing partly detached when I passed by, centuries later, to take his
place for a day and a night.

Because this man lived in a different age, the surface of his
answers would clearly be different from mine. He could not pon-
der on the marvel and mystery of a Redwall that had been built by
the remains of countless tiny organisms that are in a tenuous sense
our ancestors. He would undoubtedly think in terms of some kind
of a god. And his god, I felt sure, was the Spirit of the Rocks.

Today, we no longer believe in the Spirit of the Rocks. Or if we
do, we put the idea rather differently. But we all, willy-nilly and in
spite of our conscious selves, have to believe in something.

*Colin Fletcher was born in Wales and educated in England. He lived in
Kenya, Zimbabwe, and Canada before moving to California in 1956.
Soon afterward he spent a summer walking from Mexico to Oregon across
California's deserts and mountains. Later he became the first man known
to have walked the length of Grand Canyon National Park within the
Canyon's rim. Each of these feats generated a book:* The Thousand-Mile
Summer *and* The Man Who Walked Through Time, *from which
this story was excerpted. He continues to explore and write books:* The
Complete Walker *(revised four times),* The Secret Worlds of Colin
Fletcher, *and* River: One Man's Journey Down the Colorado, Source
to Sea.

EDWARD ABBEY

Water

The true value of water can only be
appreciated when it is scarce.

"THIS WOULD BE GOOD COUNTRY," A TOURIST SAYS TO ME, "IF ONLY you had some water."

He's from Cleveland, Ohio.

"If we had water here," I reply, "this country would not be what it is. It would be like Ohio, wet and humid and hydrological, all covered with cabbage farms and golf courses. Instead of this lovely barren desert we would have only another blooming garden state, like New Jersey. You see what I mean?"

"If you had more water more people could live here."

"Yes sir. And where then would people go when they wanted to see something besides people?"

"I see what you mean. Still, I wouldn't want to live here. So dry and desolate. Nice for pictures but my God I'm glad I don't have to live here."

"I'm glad too, sir. We're in perfect agreement. You wouldn't want to live here, I wouldn't want to live in Cleveland. We're both satisfied with the arrangement as it is. Why change it?"

"Agreed."

We shake hands and the tourist from Ohio goes away pleased, as I am pleased, each of us thinking he has taught the other something new.

The air is so dry here I can hardly shave in the mornings. The water and soap dry on my face as I reach for the razor: aridity. It is the driest season of a dry country. In the afternoons of July and August we may get thundershowers but an hour after the storms pass the surface of the desert is again bone dry.

It seldom rains. The geography books credit this part of Utah with an annual precipitation of five to nine inches but that is merely a statistical average. Low enough, to be sure. And in fact the rainfall and snowfall vary widely from year to year and from place to place even within the Arches region. When a cloud bursts open above the Devil's Garden the sun is blazing down on my ramada. And wherever it rains in this land of unclothed rock the runoff is rapid down cliff and dome through the canyons to the Colorado.

Sometimes it rains and still fails to moisten the desert—the falling water evaporates halfway down between cloud and earth. Then you see curtains of blue rain dangling out of reach in the sky while the living things wither below for want of water. Torture by tantalizing, hope without fulfillment. And the clouds disperse and dissipate into nothingness.

Streambeds are usually dry. The dry wash, dry gulch, *arroyo seco*. Only after a storm do they carry water and then but briefly—a few minutes, a couple of hours. The spring-fed perennial stream is a rarity. In this area we have only two of them, Salt Creek and Onion Creek, the first too salty to drink and the second laced with arsenic and sulfur.

Permanent springs or waterholes are likewise few and far between though not so rare as the streams. They are secret places deep in the canyons, known only to the deer and the coyotes and the dragonflies and a few others. Water rises slowly from these springs and flows in little rills over bare rock, over and under sand, into miniature fens of wire grass, rushes, willow and tamarisk. The water does not flow very far before disappearing into the air and under the ground. The flow may reappear farther down the canyon, surfacing briefly for a second time, a third time, diminishing in force until it vanishes completely and for good.

Another type of spring may be found on canyon walls where

water seeps out between horizontal formations through cracks thinner than paper to support small hanging gardens of orchids, monkeyflower, maidenhair fern, and ivy. In most of these places the water is so sparingly measured that it never reaches the canyon floor at all but is taken up entirely by the thirsty plant life and transformed into living tissue.

Long enough in the desert a man like other animals can learn to smell water. Can learn, at least, the smell of things associated with water—the unique and heartening odor of the cottonwood tree, for example, which in the canyonlands is the tree of life. In this wilderness of naked rock burnt to auburn or buff or red by ancient fires there is no vision more pleasing to the eyes and more gratifying to the heart than the translucent acid green (bright gold in autumn) of this venerable tree. It signifies water, and not only water but also shade, in a country where shelter from the sun is sometimes almost as precious as water.

Signifies water, which may or may not be on the surface, visible and available. If you have what is called a survival problem and try to dig for this water during the heat of the day, the effort may cost you more in sweat than you will find to drink. A bad deal. Better to wait for nightfall when the cottonwoods and other plants along the streambed will release some of the water which they have absorbed during the day, perhaps enough to allow a potable trickle to rise to the surface of the sand. If the water still does not appear, you may then wish to attempt to dig for it. Or you might do better by marching farther up the canyon. Sooner or later you should find a spring or at least a little seep on the canyon wall. On the other hand you could possibly find no water at all, anywhere. The desert is a land of surprises, some of them terrible surprises. Terrible as derived from terror.

When out for a walk carry water; not less than a gallon a day per person.

More surprises. In places you will find clear-flowing streams, such as Salt Creek near Turnbow Cabin, where the water looks beautifully drinkable but tastes like brine.

You might think, beginning to die of thirst, that any water however salty would be better than none at all. Not true. Small doses will not keep you going or alive and a deep drink will force your body to expend water in getting rid of the excess salt. This results in a net loss of bodily moisture and a hastening of the process of dehydration. Dehydration first enervates, then prostrates, then kills.

Nor is blood, your own or a companion's, any adequate substitute for water; blood is too salty. The same is true of urine.

If it's your truck or car which has failed you, you'd be advised to tap the radiator, unless it's full of Prestone. If this resource is not available and water cannot be found in the rocks or under the sand and you find yourself too tired and discouraged to go on, crawl into the shade and wait for help to find you. If no one is looking for you write your will in the sand and let the wind carry your last words and signature east to the borders of Colorado and south to the pillars of Monument Valley—someday, never fear, your bare elegant bones will be discovered and wondered and marveled at.

A great thirst is a great joy when quenched in time. On my first walk down into Havasupai Canyon, which is a branch of the Grand Canyon, never mind exactly where, I took with me only a quart of water, thinking that would be enough for a mere fourteen-mile downhill hike on a warm day in August. At Topocoba, on the rim of the canyon, the temperature was a tolerable ninety-six degrees but it rose about one degree for each mile on and downward. Like a fool I rationed my water, drank frugally, and could have died of heatstroke. When late in the afternoon I finally stumbled—sun-dazed, blear-eyed, parched as an old bacon rind—upon that blue stream which flows like a miraculous mirage down the floor of the canyon, I was too exhausted to pause and drink soberly from the bank. Dreamily, deliriously, I waded into the waist-deep water and fell on my face. Like a sponge I soaked up moisture through every pore, letting the current bear me along beneath a canopy of overhanging willow trees. I had no fear of drowning in the water—I intended to drink it all.

In the Needles country high above the inaccessible Colorado River there is a small spring hidden at the heart of a maze of fearfully arid grabens and crevasses. A very small spring: one drop per second, over a lip of stone. One afternoon in June I squatted there for an hour—two hours? three?—filling my canteen. No other water within miles, the local gnat population fought me for every drop. To keep them out of the canteen I had to place a handkerchief over the opening as I filled it. Then they attacked my eyes, drawn irresistibly by the liquid shine of the human eyeball. Embittered little bastards. Never have I tasted better water.

Other springs, more surprises. Northeast of Moab in a region of gargoyles and hobgoblins, a landscape left over from the late Jurassic, is a peculiar little waterhole named Onion Spring. A few wild onions grow in the vicinity but more striking, in season, is the golden princess plume, an indicator of selenium, a mild poison often found in association with uranium, a poison not so mild. Approaching the spring you notice a sulfurous stink in the air though the water itself, neither warm nor cold, looks clear and drinkable.

Unlike most desert waterholes you will find around Onion Spring few traces of animal life. Nobody comes to drink. The reason is the very good one that the water of Onion Spring contains not only sulfur, and perhaps selenium, but also arsenic. When I was there I looked at the water and smelled it and ran my hands through it and after a while, since the sampling of desert water is in my line, I tasted it, carefully, and spat it out. Afterwards I rinsed my mouth with water from my canteen.

This poison spring is quite clear. The water is sterile, lifeless. There are no bugs, which in itself is a warning sign, in case the smell were not sufficient. When in doubt about drinking from an unknown spring, look for life. If the water is scummed with algae, crawling with worms, grubs, larvae, spiders and liver flukes, be reassured, drink hearty, you'll get nothing worse than dysentery. But if it appears innocent and pure, beware. Onion Spring wears such a deceitful guise. Out of a tangle of poison-tolerant weeds the water drips into a basin of mud and sand, flows from there over sandstone and carries its potent solutions into the otherwise harmless waters of the creek.

There are a number of springs similar to this one in the American desert. Badwater Pool in Death Valley, for example. And a few others in the canyonlands, usually in or below the Moenkopi and Shinarump formations—mudstone and shales. The prospector Vernon Pick found a poison spring at the source of the well-named Dirty Devil River, when he was searching for uranium over in the San Rafael Swell a few years ago. At the time he needed water; he *had* to have water; and in order to get a decent drink he made something like a colander out of his canteen, punching it full of nail holes, filling it with charcoal. How much this purified the water he had no means of measuring but he drank it anyway and although it made him sick he survived, and is still alive today to tell about it.

There are rumors that when dying of thirst you can save your soul *and* body by extracting water from the barrel cactus. This is a dubious proposition and I don't know anyone who has made the experiment. It might be possible in the Sonoran desert where barrel cactus grows tall as a man and fat as a keg of beer. In Utah, however, its nearest relative stands no more than a foot high and bristles with needles curved like fishhooks. To get even close to this devilish vegetable you need leather gloves and a machete. Slice off the top and you find inside not water but only the green pulpy core of the living plant. Carving the core into manageable chunks you might be able to wring a few drops of bitter liquid into your cup. The labor and the exasperation will make you sweat, will cost you dearly.

When you reach this point you are doomed. Far better to have stayed at home with the TV and a case of beer. If the happy thought arrives too late, crawl into the shade and contemplate the lonely sky. See those big black scrawny wings far above, waiting? Comfort yourself with the reflection that within a few hours, if all goes as planned, your human flesh will be working its way through the gizzard of a buzzard, your essence transfigured into the fierce greedy eyes and unimaginable consciousness of a turkey vulture. Whereupon you, too, will soar on motionless wings high over the ruck and rack of human suffering. For most of us a promotion in grade, for some the realization of an ideal.

In July and August on the high desert the thunderstorms come. Mornings begin clear and dazzling bright, the sky as blue as the

Virgin's cloak, unflawed by a trace of cloud in all that emptiness bounded on the north by the Book Cliffs, on the east by Grand Mesa and the La Sal Mountains, on the south by the Blue Mountains and on the west by the dragon-tooth reef of the San Rafael. By noon, however, clouds begin to form over the mountains, coming it seems out of nowhere, out of nothing, a special creation.

The clouds multiply and merge, cumuli-nimbi piling up like whipped cream, like mashed potatoes, like sea foam, building upon one another into a second mountain range greater in magnitude than the terrestrial range below.

The massive forms jostle and grate, ions collide, and the sound of thunder is heard over the sun-drenched land. More clouds emerge from empty sky, anvil-headed giants with glints of lightning in their depths. An armada assembles and advances, floating on a plane of air that makes it appear, from below, as a fleet of ships must look to the fish in the sea.

At my observation point on a sandstone monolith the sun is blazing down as intensely as ever, the air crackling with dry heat. But the storm clouds continue to spread, gradually taking over more and more of the sky, and as they approach the battle breaks out.

Lightning streaks like gunfire through the clouds, volleys of thunder shake the air. A smell of ozone. While the clouds exchange their bolts with one another no rain falls, but now they begin bombarding the buttes and pinnacles below. Forks of lightning—illuminated nerves—join heaven and earth.

The wind is rising. For anyone with sense enough to get out of the rain, now is the time to seek shelter. A lash of lightning flickers over Wilson Mesa, scorching the brush, splitting a pine tree. Northeast over the Yellowcat area rain is already sweeping down, falling not vertically but in a graceful curve, like a beaded curtain drawn lightly across the desert. Between the rain and the mountains, among the tumbled masses of vapor, floats a segment of a rainbow—sunlight divided. But where I stand the storm is only beginning.

Above me the clouds roll in, unfurling and smoking billows in malignant violet, dense as wool. Most of the sky is lidded over but the sun remains clear halfway down the west, shining in under the storm. Overhead the clouds thicken, then crack and split with a roar like that of cannonballs tumbling down a marble staircase; their bellies open—too late to run now—and the rain comes down.

Comes down: not softly not gently, with no quality of mercy but like heavy water in buckets, raindrops like pellets splattering on the rock, knocking the berries off the junipers, plastering my shirt to my back, drumming on my hat like hailstones and running in a waterfall off the brim.

The pinnacles, arches, balanced rocks, fins and elephant-backs of sandstone, glazed with water but still in sunlight, gleam like old gray silver and everything appears transfixed in the strange wild unholy light of the moment. The light that never was.

For five minutes the deluge continues under the barrage of thunder and lightning, then trails off quickly, diminishing to a shower, to a sprinkling, to nothing at all. The clouds move off and rumble for a while in the distance. A fresh golden light breaks through and down in the east, over the turrets and domes, stands the rainbow sign, a double rainbow with one foot in the canyon of the Colorado and the other far north in Salt Wash. Beyond the rainbow and framed within it I can see jags of lightning still playing in the stormy sky over Castle Valley.

The afternoon sun falls lower; above the mountains and the ragged black clouds hangs the new moon, pale fragment of what is to come; in another hour, at sundown, Venus too will be there, planet of love, to glow bright as chromium down on the western sky. The desert storm is over and through the pure sweet pellucid air the cliff swallows and the nighthawks plunge and swerve, making cries of hunger and warning and—who knows? maybe of exultation.

Stranger than the storms, though not so grand and symphonic, are the flash floods that follow them, bursting with little warning out of the hills and canyons, sometimes an hour or more after the rain has stopped.

I have stood in the middle of a broad sandy wash with not a trickle of moisture to be seen anywhere, sunlight pouring down on me and on the flies and ants and lizards, the sky above perfectly clear, listening to a queer vibration in the air and in the ground under my feet—like a freight train coming down the grade, very fast—and looked up to see a wall of water tumble around a bend and surge toward me.

A wall of water. A poor image. For the flash flood of the desert poorly resembles water. It looks rather like a loose pudding or a thick dense soup, thick as gravy, dense with mud and sand, lathered with scuds of bloody froth, loaded on its crest with a tangle of weeds and shrubs and small trees ripped from their roots.

Surprised by delight, I stood there in the heat, the bright sun, the quiet afternoon, and watched the monster roll and roar toward me. It advanced in crescent shape with a sort of forelip about a foot high streaming in front, making hissing sucking noises like a giant amoeba, nosing to the right and nosing to the left as if on the spoor of something good to eat. Red as tomato soup or blood, it came down on me about as fast as a man could run. I moved aside and watched it go by.

> A flick of lightning to the north
> where dun clouds grumble—
> while here in the middle of the wash
> black beetles tumble
> and horned toads fumble
> over sand as dry as bone
> and hard-baked mud and glaring stone.
>
> Nothing here suggests disaster
> for the ants' shrewd play;
> their busy commerce for tomorrow
> shows no care for today;
> but a mile away
> and rolling closer in a scum of mud
> comes the hissing lapping blind mouth of the flood.
>
> Through the tamarisk whine the flies
> in pure fat units of conceit

as if the sun and the afternoon
and blood and the smells and the heat
and something to eat
would be available forever, never die
beyond the fixed imagination of a fly.

The flood comes, crawls thickly by, roaring
with self-applause, a brown
spongy smothering liquid avalanche:
great ant-civilizations drown,
worlds go down,
trees go under, the mud bank breaks
and deep down underneath the bedrock shakes.

A few hours later the bulk of the flood was past and gone. The flow dwindled to a trickle over bars of quicksand. New swarms of insect life would soon come to recover the provinces of those swept away. Nothing had changed but the personnel, a normal turnover, and the contours of the watercourse, that not much.

Now we've mentioned quicksand. What is quicksand anyway? First of all, quicksand is *not*, as many think, a queer kind of sand which has the hideous power to draw men and animals down and down into a bottomless pit. There can be no quicksand without water. The scene of the sand-drowned camel boy in the movie *Lawrence of Arabia* is pure fakery. The truth about quicksand is that it is simply a combination of sand and water in which the upward force of the water is sufficient to neutralize the frictional strength of the particles of sand. The greater the force and saturation, the less weight the sand can bear.

Ordinarily it is possible for a man to walk across quicksand, if he keeps moving. But if he stops, funny things begin to happen. The surface of the quicksand, which may look as firm as the wet sand on an ocean beach, begins to liquefy beneath his feet. He finds himself sinking slowly into a jelly-like substance, soft and quivering, which clasps itself around his ankles with the suction power of any viscous fluid. Pulling out one foot, the other foot necessarily goes down deeper, and if a man waits too long, or cannot reach something solid beyond the quicksand, he may soon find himself trapped. The depth to which he finally sinks depends upon the depth and the fluidity of the quicksand, upon the nature of his efforts to extricate himself, and upon the ratio of body weight to volume of quicksand. Unless a man is extremely talented, he cannot work himself in more than waist-deep. The quicksand will not *pull* him down. But it will not let him go either. Therefore the conclusion is that while quicksand cannot drown its captive, it could possibly starve him to death. Whatever finally happens, the immediate effects are always interesting.

My friend Newcomb, for instance. He has only one good leg, had an accident with the other, can't hike very well in rough country, tends to lag behind. We were exploring a deep dungeon-like defile off Glen Canyon one time (before the dam). The defile turned and twisted like a snake under overhanging and interlocking walls so high, so close, that for most of the way I could not see the sky. The floor of this cleft was irregular, wet, sandy, in places rather soupy, and I was soon far ahead and out of sight of Newcomb.

Finally I came to a place in the canyon so narrow and dark and wet and ghastly that I had no heart to go farther. Retracing my steps I heard, now and then, a faint and mournful wail, not human, which seemed to come from abysmal depths far back in the bowels of the plateau, from the underworld, from subterranean passageways better left forever unseen and unknown. I hurried on, the cries faded away. I was glad to be getting out of there. Then they came again, louder and as it seemed from all sides, out of the rock itself, surrounding me. A terrifying caterwauling it was, multiplied and amplified by echoes piled on echoes, overlapping and reinforcing one another. I looked back to see what was hunting me but there was only the naked canyon in the dim, bluish light that filtered down from far above. I thought of the Minotaur. Then I thought of Newcomb and began to run.

It wasn't bad. He was in only a little above the knees and sinking very slowly. As soon as he saw me he stopped hollering and relit his pipe. Help, he said, simply and quietly.

What was all the bellowing about? I wanted to know. I'm sorry, he said, but it's a horrible way to die. Get out of that mud, I said, and let's get out of here. It ain't just mud, he said. I don't care what it is, get out of there, you look like an idiot. I'm sinking, he said.

And he was. The stuff was now halfway up his thighs.

Don't you ever read any books? I said. Don't you have sense enough to know that when you get in quicksand you have to lie down flat? Why? he asked. So you'll live longer, I explained. Face down or face up? he asked next.

That stumped me. I couldn't remember the answer to that one. You wait here, I said, while I go back to Albuquerque and get the book.

He looked down for a moment. Still sinking, he said; please help?

I stepped as close to him as I could without getting bogged down myself but our extended hands did not quite meet. Lean forward, I said. I am, he said. All the way, I said; fall forward.

He did that and then I could reach him. He gripped my wrist and I gripped his and with a slow steady pull I got him out of there. The quicksand gurgled a little and made funny, gasping noises, reluctant to let him go, but when he was free the holes filled up at once, the liquid oozing into place, and everything looked as it had before, smooth and sleek and innocent as the surface of a pudding. It was in fact the same pool of quicksand that I had walked over myself only about an hour earlier.

Quicksand is more of a menace to cattle and horses, with their greater weight and smaller feet, than it is to men, and the four-legged beasts generally avoid it when they can. Sometimes, however, they are forced to cross quicksand to reach water, or are driven across, and then the cattleman may have an unpleasant chore on his hands. Motor vehicles, of course, cannot negotiate quicksand; even a four-wheel-drive jeep will bog down as hopelessly as anything else.

Although I hesitate to deprive quicksand of its sinister glamour I must confess that I have not yet heard of a case where a machine, an animal or a man has actually sunk *completely* out of sight in the stuff. But it may have happened; it may be happening to somebody at this very moment. I sometimes regret that I was unable to perform a satisfactory experiment with my friend Newcomb when the chance presented itself; such opportunities come but rarely. But I needed him; he was, among other things, a good camp cook.

After the storms pass and the flash floods have dumped their loads of silt into the Colorado, leaving the streambeds as arid as they were before, it is still possible to find rainwater in the desert. All over the slickrock country there are natural cisterns or potholes, tubs, tanks and basins sculptured in the soft sandstone by the erosive force of weathering, wind and sand. Many of them serve as little catchment basins during rain and a few may contain water for days or even weeks after a storm, the length of time depending on the shape and depth of the hole and the consequent rate of evaporation.

Often far from any spring, these temporary pools attract doves, ravens and other birds, and deer, and coyotes; you, too, if you know where to look or find one by luck, can slake your thirst and fill your water gourd. Such pools may be found in what seem like the most improbable places: out on the desolate White Rim below Grandview Point, for example, or on top of the elephant-back dome above the Double Arch. At Toroweap in Grand Canyon I found a deep tank of clear sweet water almost over my head, countersunk in the summit of a sandstone bluff which overhung my campsite by a hundred feet. A week after rain there was still enough water to fill my needs; hard to reach, it was well worth the effort. The Bedouin know what I mean.

The rain-filled potholes, set in naked rock, are usually devoid of visible plant life but not of animal life. In addition to the inevitable microscopic creatures, there may be certain amphibians like the spadefoot

> In [the West], mere land is of no value. What is really valuable is the water privilege.
> —John Wesley Powell (1877)

toad. This little animal lives through dry spells in a state of estivation under the dried-up sediment in the bottom of a hole. When the rain comes, if it comes, he emerges from the mud singing madly in his fashion, mates with the handiest female and fills the pool with a swarm of tadpoles, most of them doomed to the most ephemeral existence. But a few survive, mature, become real toads, and when the pool dries up they dig into the sediment as their parents did before, making burrows which they seal with mucus in order to preserve that moisture necessary to life. There they wait, day after day, week after week, in patient spadefoot torpor, perhaps listening—we can imagine—for the sound of raindrops pattering at last on the earthen crust above their heads. If it comes in time, the glorious cycle is repeated; if not, this particular colony of *Bufonidae* is reduced eventually to dust, a burden on the wind.

Rain and puddles bring out other amphibia, even in the desert. It's a strange, stirring, but not an uncommon thing to come on a pool at night, after an evening of thunder and lightning and a bit of rainfall, to see the frogs clinging to the edge of their impermanent pond, bodies immersed in water but heads out, all croaking away in tricky counterpoint. They are windbags: with each croak the pouch under the frog's chin swells like a bubble, then collapses.

Why do they sing? What do they have to sing about? Somewhat apart from one another, separated by roughly equal distances, facing outward from the water, they clank and croak all through the night with tireless perseverance. To human ears their music has a bleak, dismal, tragic quality, dirgelike rather than jubilant. It may nevertheless be the case that these small beings are singing not only to claim their stake in the pond, not only to attract a mate, but also out of spontaneous love and joy, a contrapuntal choral celebration of the coolness and wetness after weeks of desert fire, for love of their own existence, however brief it may be, and for joy in the common life.

Has joy any survival value in the operations of evolution? I suspect that it does; I suspect that the morose and fearful are doomed to quick extinction. Where there is no joy there can be no courage; and without courage all other virtues are useless. Therefore the frogs, the toads, keep on singing even though we know, if they don't, that the sound of their uproar must surely be luring all the snakes and ringtail cats and kit foxes and coyotes and great horned owls toward the scene of their happiness.

What then? A few of the little amphibians will continue their metamorphosis by way of the nerves and tissues of one of the higher animals, in which process the joy of one becomes the contentment of the second. Nothing is lost, except an individual consciousness here and there, a trivial perhaps even illusory phenomenon. The rest survive, mate, multiply, burrow, estivate, dream and rise again. The rains will come, the potholes shall be filled. Again. And again. And again.

More secure are those who live in and around the desert's few perennial waterholes, those magical hidden springs that are scattered so austerely through the barren vastness of the canyon country. Of these, only a rare few are too hot or too briny or too poisonous to support life—the great majority of them swarm with living things. There you will see the rushes and willows and cottonwoods, and four-winged dragonflies in green, blue, scarlet and gold, and schools of minnows in the water, moving from sunlight to shadow and back again. At night the mammals come—deer, bobcat, cougar, coyote, fox, jackrabbit, bighorn sheep, wild horse and feral burro—each in his turn and in unvarying order, under the declaration of a truce. They come to drink, not to kill or be killed.

Finally, in this discussion of water in the desert, I should make note of a distinctive human contribution, one which has become a part of the Southwestern landscape no less typical than the giant cactus, the juniper growing out of solid rock or the red walls of a Navajo canyon. I refer to the tiny oasis formed by the drilled well, its windmill and storage tank. The windmill with its skeleton tower and creaking vanes is an object of beauty as significant in its way as the cottonwood tree, and the open tank at its foot, big enough to swim in, is a thing of joy to man and beast, no less worthy of praise than the desert spring.

Water, water, water.... There is no shortage of water in the desert but exactly the right amount, a perfect ratio of water to rock, of water to sand, insuring that wide, free, open, generous spacing among plants and animals, homes and towns and cities, which makes the arid West so different from any other part of the nation. There is no lack of water here, unless you try to establish a city where no city should be.

The Developers, of course—the politicians, businessmen,

bankers, administrators, engineers—they see it somewhat otherwise and complain most bitterly and interminably of a desperate water shortage, especially in the Southwest. They propose schemes of inspiring proportions for diverting water by the damful from the Columbia River, or even from the Yukon River, and channeling it overland down into Utah, Colorado, Arizona and New Mexico.

What for? "In anticipation of future needs, in order to provide for the continued industrial and population growth of the Southwest." And in such an answer we see that it's only the old numbers game again, the monomania of small and very simple minds in the grip of an obsession. They cannot see that growth for the sake of growth is a cancerous madness, that Phoenix and Albuquerque will not be better cities to live in when their populations are doubled again and again. They would never understand that an economic system which can only expand or expire must be false to all that is human.

So much by way of futile digression: the pattern is fixed and protest alone will not halt the iron glacier moving upon us.

No matter, it's of slight importance. Time and the winds will sooner or later bury the Seven Cities of Cibola—Phoenix, Tucson, Albuquerque, all of them—under dunes of glowing sand, over which blue-eyed Navajo Bedouin will herd their sheep and horses, following the river in winter, the mountains in summer, and sometimes striking off across the desert toward the red canyons of Utah where great waterfalls plunge over silt-filled, ancient, mysterious dams.

Only the boldest among them, seeking visions, will camp for long in the strange country of the standing rock, far out where the spadefoot toads bellow madly in the moonlight on the edge of doomed rainpools, where the arsenic-selenium spring waits for the thirst-crazed wanderer, where the thunderstorms blast the pinnacles and cliffs, where the rust-brown floods roll down the barren washes, and where the community of the quiet deer walk at evening up glens of sandstone through tamarisk and sage toward the hidden springs of sweet, cool, still, clear, unfailing water.

⋆

Edward Abbey was born in Home, Pennsylvania, in 1927. He was educated at the University of New Mexico and the University of Edinburgh. He died at his home in Oracle, Arizona, in 1989. This story was excerpted from his classic book, Desert Solitaire: A Season in the Wilderness.

✳

The extraordinary rock formations of Bryce and Zion canyons (both national parks) are slices of earth cutting deep into time. More than 200 million years ago, this color-saturated sandstone—part of the Colorado Plateau—was drifting desert dunes. Then seas encroached, compacting the sand and cementing it with calcium carbonate and other mineral compounds (iron oxide produced the canyons' brilliant oranges and reds). Volcanic uplift raised the tableland 12,000 feet above sea level, and during the dinosaur era rivers began to slice through the vast prehistoric cake, exposing layers that range from bloody reds to sun-bright yellows to pastel blues.

From the heights of the plateau, you can look downs at the spires of Bryce, then descend 4,000 feet in a few hours of highway time and look up at the sheer walls of Zion.

Water is the artist here. When it falls on the plateau and begins its journey down toward the Colorado River, sediments come along for the ride. Some water penetrates limestone and other soft rocks until it hits a less permeable layer. Then it moves sideways, often appearing in seeps high up the canyon walls. The softer rock above is carried away or undercut until if falls in slabs, leaving the sturdier stuff as arches, pinnacles, and fluted walls. Although the wearing of rock into oddly shaped hoodoos—as the locals call them—may have happened faster in wetter times, even today you can see the process of erosion in the muddy tumult of a spring stream....

These natural works of art have awed mankind since the days when bands of Paiute Indians traveled through the canyons sometimes carving their signatures in the form of petroglyphs and pictographs. The Indians had their own names for the canyons (Zion was originally called Mukuntuweep National Monument), but Mormon explorers and pioneers such as Ebenezer Bryce are largely responsible for the biblical names that now abound.

— Geoffrey O'Gara, "Gardens of Stone," *Travel & Leisure*

PART TWO

SOME THINGS TO DO

ALETA GEORGE

Vertigo

*A journey into the Grand Canyon
has unintended results.*

THIS TRAIL, BETTER SUITED FOR MOUNTAIN GOATS THAN HUMANS, ascends so steeply that within ten minutes of climbing, the people back at camp are as small as my fingernail. All sixteen of us who are floating down the Colorado River are taking the side hike to Thunder River today, but Dave and I got a head start and are taking off alone. After breakfast, I noticed Dave watching me as I watched him.

"Are you ready to head up the mountain?" he said casually, with a canteen around his neck and in his hand a camera with a lens as long as my hiking boots.

"Just about," I say, lacing up my shoes and standing. "Let's go."

The first part of the trail to Thunder River climbs and hugs the canyon walls before it drops back down in the side canyon of Tapeat's Creek, a tributary of the Colorado. As we climb the precipitous and narrow trail, I explain to Dave that I need to go slowly. "I never knew I had vertigo until this trip," I tell him.

I never felt dizzy climbing the gently sloping coastal range of my native California, but these dizzying drops in the Grand Canyon are on an entirely different scale. To stop my head from spinning I pause and look across the chasm to the clay-pink cathedral walls, still shadowed with mauve in the early morning light: a humming Van Gogh painting. My legs are shaking from trying not to slip on the loose rocks underfoot.

My brother Lanny invited me on this trip when his best friend had to cancel. An old friend from his wilder, extreme-sports days who had a private permit invited him. We didn't know anyone else on the trip until the planning meetings.

Since I had never been rafting before, Lanny took me on a one-day commercial rafting trip on the American River. We were supposed to help paddle but on a few of the rapids Lanny whooped and hollered and lifted his arms as if he was on a roller coaster.

"She's so serious," Lanny said when our guide scolded him for not paddling.

I appreciated that she took her job and our lives seriously. But I also appreciated that my brother was trying to show me the lighter side of river running. Rapids can be fun.

But the American River is a baby compared to the Colorado—the mother of all rivers. I admit I was nervous. I asked around. I heard and read the stories about Crystal, Lava Falls, and the other rapids on the Colorado that were rated IXs and Xs when the rest of U.S. rivers didn't have any run-able rapids above a V. But people did survive. A few people that I talked to said that the experience changed their lives. Having just graduated from college, I was ready for a life-altering experience. Little did I know.

The day came for Lanny and me and three other people to hike down to the river where we would meet the boats at Phantom Ranch. Our boating party had already been on the river for seven days. Five people were hiking out and we were taking their places for the remaining two weeks of the trip. We started down the Kaibab Trail at 6 A.M., each of us carrying at least forty pounds on our backs and a gallon of water each because there wasn't any water on this seven-mile trail that drops 7,260 feet from the rim of the canyon to the river. The trail was narrow and the drop made my head spin.

Almost immediately I slipped on some loose rocks, my feet flew out from under me, and I landed hard on my bottom with my heavy pack pulling me back. My heart beating fast, I slowly got to my feet and realized that this was very serious and I had better pay attention. It was the middle of August and by ten o'clock it was 100 degrees. Last week they closed the trail because a young Boy Scout died of heat exhaustion.

At what seemed the steepest of drops, my brother put his arm around me for a brother-sister moment of enjoying the scenery. There was an ease and confidence in his body that belied our situation and made it seem that we were on a leisurely stroll through the English countryside looking at swans on a lake. He went into detail about the colors, the rocks, the grandeur, as we hung precariously to the side of a mountain that wouldn't know if we lived or died on its sides

"Isn't it beautiful?" he sighed.

"This isn't a good angle for me," I'd reply trying not to look into the quivering oblivion. I concentrated on carefully putting one foot in front of the other. My goal was very simple: to get to the bottom alive.

Five hours later at Phantom Ranch, I was sitting in the weak shade of a tamarisk tree digging my feet into the cool sand when I saw a scraggly-looking guy walking to the boats carrying full ten-gallon water containers in each hand. His long-sleeved tie-dye shirt was faded and torn, and his purple parachute pants were stained reddish-brown like the river and the canyon walls. His head was covered with a red-stained white hat that had a flap in back to protect his neck. His glasses were in the style of the 1950s with the square, thick black lenses. I said to myself, "Now there's a river rat with a few stories to tell."

After carrying the water containers to the boats, he approached each of us who had hiked down, hand extended, and said, "Hi, I'm Dave." He was the last-minute replacement for a boatman who had to cancel so I didn't meet Dave until we got on the river.

The first time Dave looked out for me was on the third day of the trip. There were two inflatable kayaks and my brother convinced me that I should try them with him. We looked at a map and there were no big rapids ahead. I agreed, though I had never been in a kayak before. He gave me a few lessons on shore and then we got ready to go. Standing by my kayak, I watched with dread as the other boats left. My brother got in his kayak, entered the current, gave me a parting "Good luck!" and never looked back.

Oh, great.

All the boats had left. I had to do this. I pushed myself into the river. Dave was ahead of me in his yellow cataraft, and he kept turning around to check on me. With him was Linda, his passenger for the day. We riders rotated spots on the boats, but Linda seemed to like Dave's boat and they got on well, I noticed. She was tall and slim with long brown hair. Last summer she backpacked for three months on the John Muir Trail all by herself. I admired her, but I found her intimacy with Dave increasingly annoying. After all, she had a boyfriend. He was one of the five who hiked out at Phantom Ranch.

I practiced a few moves with my paddle. I tried not to dwell on the fact that the river was as wide as a football field, as deep as a...who knows what...and full of freezing, hypothermia-inducing, dam-release water. I came to a riffle, which wouldn't scare an experienced kayaker, but to me it was as bad as approaching Niagara Falls in a barrel. I knew I was going over. Dave was half a football field ahead of me, pointing river left, which means "stay to the left."

"I can do this. I can do this. I can do this. La-la-la. Here I am a capable woman. I can...I can..." I repeated to myself.

Seconds into the riffle, a small wave hit me broadside and I flipped over into the big water. My breath contracted sharply from the cold. When I fell out of the kayak, it wasn't like the harrowing white-water spills that you read about where you don't know which way is up and the tumultuous waves slam you into rocks and keeper-holes until the river decides to spit you out. There was no such drama for me, only a graceful blip over the side of the kayak and into the freezing big water. If the water wasn't so cold, I might have enjoyed being part of the current, which this time of year carries 22,000 cubic feet per second (compared to the American River which runs at 1,200 cubic feet per second). If it wasn't so cold, I might have floated on my back, feet first, and relaxed into the current while gazing at the blue skies and the epoch-marked canyon walls. But it was freezing, and you can lose the ability to function in water this cold. I grabbed onto the kayak and watched while Dave rowed upstream to get me. When Dave's boat pulled alongside me, Linda reached down and without hesitation, pulled me straight out of the water by the lapels of my life jacket. Dave tied the kayak to his boat. There I was, rescued by Dave and Linda. My brother was downstream and didn't even know I had flipped. So much for a brother/sister bonding moment.

I sat shivering in the warm sun. Dave asked me if I wanted a beer. I said sure. He pulled his yellow mesh drag bag out of the water and fished out a couple of cheap beers. He threw one to me and I took a long pull. There is nothing better than a cheap beer on the river. I'm not entirely sure why, but for some reason it tastes better than the microbrews that I usually prefer. He opened his, took a small sip and spit out a stream expertly, long and far.

"Did you get some sand in your mouth?" I asked.

"No," he said. "That's for the river gods."

He was starting to look like a blond Jeff Bridges.

On the trail to Thunder River, Dave and I drop into the cool canyon of Tapeat's Creek where the trail levels off and we are in a terrain of barrel and prickly pear cactus, which Dave tells me the Anasazi Indians harvested for food. The fast, clear, clean running current of Tapeat's Creek tries to take my footing as we cross, but Dave offers his hand to steady me with his sure grip.

The river has made its mark on this canyon with fossilized water-currents on the white walls of the canyon. When the canyon narrows, I run my hand along the elaborate swirls and feel the powerful history of this watershed. The wall is cool to the touch. This place—the canyon—is so sensuous. Everything about it relaxes you: the heat emanating from the canyon walls, the pastel shades of the landscape, the age of the rocks. The water, the lack of all electronic communication devices: everything.

Our conversation is easy like the flow of water. Dave tells me about his kids (two teenagers), his work (he's a welding teacher), and his home (only an hour from mine). My legs are hitting their stride and we amble easily through the pleasant canyon. In the distance is a mountain that looks like its giving us a sideways raspberry. We laugh at its blubbering reddish-brown lips.

We start up the mountain switchback to Thunder River. All around is desert, making the coming oasis very sweet. My vertigo once again threatens my balance on the hot and dusty desert trail as Dave starts talking about the time he went bungee jumping.

Thunder River gushes out of the sheer-faced rock wall like a pressurized fire hose, supporting green moss, maidenhair ferns, and trees. The water is so sweet and pure that all comers carry as many empty containers up the mountain that they can manage to carry back down full of water. Pure, fresh water is a godsend on the Colorado River. In fact, the water of the Colorado becomes vital to your days: you float on top of it, making slow lazy circles driven by the current and eddies; you ride it down the rapids, breathing in and out with the rise and fall of the waves; you dip your hot body into it when you can no longer stand the heat and would rather stand the prickly cold; you wash your face and body with it, you drink it, and you pee in it.

Misted by the thundering oasis, Dave and I share a lunch of crackers, mustard sardines, and trail mix. We take some pictures and fill our canteens.

On the way back down the mountain, Dave says, "It's good to have someone to share this hike with. The last few times I was in the canyon, I came up here alone. The good thing about that was that I could take a nature walk."

"What's a nature walk?" I ask.

"I take off my clothes and walk naked. It feels great," he said.

"Well," I say, "don't let me stop you." He doesn't.

At one point, back in the cool canyon of Tapeat's Creek, nature walk over, the trail drops to the bottom of a twelve-foot rock that you have to climb down. Dave climbs down first and I hand him his camera and both of our canteens. I turn onto my belly and begin climbing down as he helps by leading my feet to footholds and talking me through the descent. When I am nearly down, I say, "Look out, I'm going to jump." Before he steps out of the way, his finger slides ever so lightly up the outsides of my thighs. I am wearing very short shorts. His touch is nearly imperceptible, but the tingle reverberates through every cell of my body and out the top of my head.

When we are nearly back to camp, and once again on the steepest part of the trail, Dave goes first while I take one small step at a time, making myself look down into the chasm of what seems my imminent death. He is going nice and slow and in really dicey parts he stops to watch me get through it. When we are almost down, I say: "Thanks for watching out for me."

"I'm not watching out for you," he says. "I just want to have a better view when you fall." We both laugh. I was to learn that this kind of humor was quite normal for my not-so-normal, soon-to-be husband.

Aleta George lives in Northern California with her husband and two step-teens. Her stories have appeared in California Wild, Passionfruit, Poetry Flash, *and the* Travelers' Tales *anthology,* A Woman's Passion for Travel.

GREGORY McNAMEE

✦

Nuclear Memories

Some of the heat in the desert
has been thermonuclear.

To judge by attendance records at the Titan Missile Museum in Green Valley, Arizona, near my Tucson home, plenty of regular folks from around the world feel a little lump in the throat when the atomic era comes to mind. Nearly fifty thousand of them come each year to this decommissioned missile installation, Complex 571-7 on the Pentagon's roster of death-dealing real estate, a stone's throw away from another piece of death-dealing real estate, the bustling retirement community of Green Valley. Deactivated on November 11, 1982, but still owned by the Air Force, the installation is the only place in the United States where the interested traveler can get a close-up look at the weapons that once troubled the sleep of millions of people around the world.

Eighteen such installations—glorified holes in the ground, 146 feet deep, once stuffed full of expensive computer equipment and rocketry—dotted the desert around Tucson during the Cold War's boom years. Built in 1961, this one, called the Copper Penny because of its proximity to a nearby copper mine, is the only one that remains. The others were blown up in 1982, following strategic-arms-limitation talks conducted by Ronald Reagan and a succession of Soviet leaders after much bellicose prelude. Here four-man crews would sit for twenty-four-hour shifts, awaiting the day when the Reds went a step over the line and all hell would break loose, in the meanwhile baby-sitting a 330,000-pound, 110-foot-long Titan II intercontinental ballistic missile targeted on one of three cities inside the former Soviet Union. Just which ones, no one outside the war room in Washington can say. "The targets," said a museum guide to me, "were known only as one, two and three. I don't think the boys inside really wanted to know what they were going to vaporize."

Most Americans of a certain age know these steel-case gray and institutional not-quite-lime-green bunkers, but only through films like *War Games, Fail-Safe, Seven Days in May,* and *Dr. Strangelove.* Fine though they are, those films do not do justice to the retro, paranoia-inducing weirdness of Complex 517-7. The nukeproof burn suites, the glass case full of ignition-switch keys that once promised holocaust, and the red phone, no longer connected, that once rang straight through to Strategic Air Command Headquarters are quite enough to make the visitor—again, if he or she is of a certain age—think of taking cover. Even the missile base's motto, *Peregrinamur pro pace*—"We are made to wander for peace"—can make sensitive souls feel uneasy.

As befits an excursion into the Cold War mindset, the Titan Missile Museum is rich with carefully posted statistics, factoids, time lines. A sign near the museum entrance proudly reports the details of construction: the underground silo and command center used 1,100 tons of rebar, 2,100 cubic yards of concrete, 120 tons of steel beams, 200 tons of electromagnetic lining, and 117 tons of steel rings. The sign announces, with weird pride, the statistics of the Titan II itself, a missile that, after attaining an apogee of 450 miles above the surface of the earth at a cruising speed of 17,000 miles per hour, could strike targets more than 5,000 miles away from its launch site.

Not many of the aptly named Titans were ever built. "We had fifty-four when we started," another guide remarked to me. "We had fifty-four when we were finished. We didn't have to use any of them. After all, we're still here, aren't we?"

The staff of old-timers who entertain questions with bemused and patient smiles are always good for such comforting sentiments, and even a few strange chuckles, as when one warrior replied, when I asked him whether I could photograph the place, "Absolutely, anything you want," all the while shaking his head from side to side in the near-universal gesture meaning no. The guide, a retired Strategic Air Command bomber pilot, then pointed out to me such regalia as the "maximum uncomfortable" rocket-fueling suits installation personnel had to wear when servicing the missile, and the retractable radio antennae designed to rise from a case-hardened underground bunker in the event that a Russian thermonuclear missile landed atop the site and knocked out above-ground communications. "Nuclear near miss?" he crowed. "Failure to respond? Don't look for that in this part of the world."

The high point of our tour came with a hands-on reenactment of the launch sequence that never came, in the case of my tour group commanded by a shy Australian housewife, a tour that comes complete with an eardrum-shattering sequence of bells and klaxons. During this reenactment, the guides shifted disconcertingly from the historical past to the narrative present. On my visit, a guide yelled, "A Soviet ICBM has

> I was walking down a dirt road in Chinle, Arizona. It was well after dusk. An old man approached. We stopped and talked. We listened to each other celebrate the night, as the Big Dipper rested on the western horizon.
>
> "You know the Milky Way is the path of souls…" he said.
>
> A crescent moon hung over a hogan and the stars seemed especially bright. I watched a satellite travel across the sky. Skylab had just fallen to earth somewhere in Australia. I thought about what the old man had just said so casually. I looked up to the sky once again. The Pleiades were as they had always been.
>
> —Terry Tempest Williams,
> *Pieces of White Shell:*
> *A Journey to Navajoland*

just obliterated the site above us. We have thirty days of food and water and air left down here. Let's just hope and pray there'll be a world left when we come out."

There was a world left. Stopping for a moment's rest in the shade alongside a radar-equipment trailer, my friend, rock musician and film editor Clif Taylor, grinned and said to no one in particular, "The combination of Cold War fear and modern humor in this place is really weird." A German sugar-beet farmer, born in 1966, rejoined, "In my country, we don't talk about war like this. Maybe things are different if you're the winner."

"This place cost 10 million dollars to build back in 1961," our guide, unimpressed by pacifist sentiments, interrupted to say. "It was supposed to be in operation for only ten years. Well, it stayed in service for more than twenty years. I call that a pretty cheap insurance policy."

Asked how much punch the fully armed Titan II packed by way of that insurance, he scratched his head thoughtfully and replied, "Well, the Air Force doesn't want us to discuss payload, but I can get you in the neighborhood of a megaton. A megaton. Compared with this baby, that little thing we dropped on Hiroshima was a firecracker. But that's all over now. People in Moscow can sleep soundly tonight."

Private mythologies are one thing. In the West we have woven the Cold War, uneasily, into our public mythology, and the man is right: people in Moscow, and in New York, and even in Gila Bend can sleep soundly, the night punctuated by the ticking of a Doomsday Clock now set at fourteen minutes to midnight. The cities remain standing, while the desert countryside of four continents bears the marks of the nuclear era. All appears well, at least on the surface. We can now shed our nihilism and go to church.

Or perhaps not. I think of the works of the critic Susan Sontag, who spent her childhood in southern Arizona and who conjured

a permanent modern scenario: apocalypse looms, and it doesn't occur.... Apocalypse has become an event that is happening, and not happening. It may be that some of the most feared events, like those involving the irreparable ruin of the environment, have already happened. But we don't know it yet, because the standards have changed. Or because we do not have the right indexes for measuring the catastrophe. Or simply because this is a catastrophe in slow motion.

A catastrophe in slow motion: that sounds about right. It has slowed down to a crawl, strangely so. Rockets are aimed at us from Moscow and Alma-Ata and perhaps Urumqi, but they no longer seem real; Pax Coca-Cola reigns over the world; and India and Pakistan are so far away.

But for those of us who grew up in its frightening, long shadow, the Cold War will go on forever, like a desert highway. It endures. It is built into the landscape of the desert, and into our minds: ground zero, like the kingdom of heaven, will be forever within us.

Gregory McNamee is the author or editor of many books, among them The Sierra Club Desert Reader *and* Gila: The Life and Death of an American River. *His work has appeared in such journals and online publication as* Outside, Orion, The Nation, Newsday, Discovery Online, *and* The Washington Post Book World. *This story was excerpted from* Blue Mountains Far Away: Journeys into the American Wilderness.

★

Pinned up on the corkboard at home is a picture of me at ground zero, the spot where the first atomic bomb went off, dwarfed by a sooty lava obelisk. I am holding one hand against my breasts while the other fends off the hair in my face. I am very thin and my eyes are screwed up against the sun. It must have been 100 degrees that day, but I am wearing a leather jacket which has caught the wind and ballooned outwards. You can't see it in the photo, but I have a piece of greenish trinitite in one hand. When the bomb when off at 5:29:45 on the morning of July 16, 1945, the heat from the blast turned the sandy topsoil into radioactive glass, or trinitite as it became known, and this is the only remaining evidence of the momentous transformations wrought by the bomb on the desert. The crater itself was filled in, the green lawn of trinitite bulldozed, the huts and buildings of the base and scientific outposts taken down and disposed of. If there is radioactive dust remaining, then it is indistinguishable from the other sort. Everything of the steel bomb tower but a single concrete sump evaporated away and fell as metal rain, somewhere over the Tulorosa Valley, along the Jornada del Muerto. The refashioning of history begins when the first most crucial evidence is blotted from the land. Eventually the story of the A-bomb test will simplify into archetype, like the gunfight at the OK Corral, the Seven Cities of Cibola, Bill Bolger's body, or the padre's gold, if, that is, it has not already done so.

—Melanie McGrath, *Motel Nirvana: Dreaming of the New Age in the American Desert*

JEFF RENNICKE

The Grand Staircase

*The author explores Utah's Grand
Staircase-Escalante National Monument.*

"Kaiparo...Plat...over there...Strai...Cliffs...there.... The
Gul...." Just like the wings of some great bird, the wind on W
Mountain is pummeling us, shredding the words Grant Johnson is
yelling in my ear. "Wolve...Ben...." I catch only stray fragments
before the wind snatches his voice and hurls it into the void. No
matter. I know what he's trying to say.

He's trying to say we can see forever.

From this peak, the views of southern Utah roll out like
"treacherous, endless seas," as poet Ann Weiler Walka has written.
To the west, Kaiparowits Plateau barrels for fifty miles like some
huge freight train made of stone. To the southwest, the sky is sliced
by the knife edge of the Straight Cliffs. There are cloud shadows
snagged in the mouth of the Gulch and along the serrated teeth of
Wolverine Bench. A single turn of the head takes in hundreds of
square miles of space—dizzying, breathtaking, leave-you-weak-in-
the-knees kind of space. And it's just a small corner of Grand
Staircase-Escalante National Monument.

At 1.9 million acres, Grand Staircase-Escalante is the largest
national monument outside of Alaska, and the wildest. In the entire
2,947-square-mile monument—an area nearly six times the size of

Grand Teton National Park —there are just two paved highways, a handful of axle-busting back roads, and one maintained hiking trail.

The rest is pure space, a monument to wilderness. There are wind-carved spires, nameless mesas, and sculpted buttes. There are grottoes and arches, springs and cliffs, mesas and rivers without end. And every one of them, if you hike with someone like Grant Johnson, seems to have a story.

"Come on, George!" Johnson says, cajoling a large chestnut horse to take the next step. It is a big one. The trail ahead disappears down a spiraling crack in the canyon wall, the third "pucker," or tight spot, on what Johnson calls "a five pucker trail" dropping a thousand feet off Spencer Flat.

A former uranium miner, amateur archaeologist, and dynamite expert turned wilderness guide, Johnson is a man pieced together from all his incarnations—blond pony tail, stubble of whiskers, chipped front teeth, intense blue eyes, and the splat of a hat left over from his mining days. He is a man with miles in him, and a love for canyon country.

For twenty-five years he's been exploring this landscape on foot, on horseback, and through the stories of the few old timers still roaming the hills. Watching George and the rest of the horses in our pack maneuvering through the pucker as if they had eyes in back of their heads reminds him of one of those stories.

"It was almost dark, in the middle of a blizzard. I was getting close to home, barely able to see," he says. "I'd made twenty miles and was feeling pretty good about myself when I heard a rider coming out of the dark. It was old Ivan Lyman, a rancher who has a camp way the hell down in Horse Canyon.

"I yelled, 'Ivan, you're not heading to camp. It's pitch black. How you gonna see?'"

"'If I can't see, my horse will be able to,' Ivan says. Twenty-some miles he was going, alone and in the dark." Johnson shakes his head as much out of respect as in disbelief. Tough country breeds tough people.

Our plan is not as ambitious. After a half-day hike in, Grant, wrangler/cook Tina Karlsson, photographer Tom Bean, and I will strike the Escalante River, cross and re-cross the jade green stream, and then set up a base camp deep in Escalante Canyon, one of the most popular sections of Grand Staircase-Escalante. From there we'll explore the northeastern portion of the monument in a series of long day hikes. As the raven flies we'll cover fewer miles in five days than ole Ivan Lyman could cover in two.

But it is enough. In national parks and monuments I've too often found myself rushing to every scenic turnout, gathering a few postcards, and going home with the foolish notion that I'd "seen" the place. It's a mirage to think you can see a place like Grand Staircase-Escalante in just one short trip. Here snowflakes take thousands of years to cut an arch. There are falls that whisper with water only once or twice in a lifetime, flowers that bloom only in the dark of night. Getting to know such a place does not come easy, or quick. And so we won't even try to see it all in one trip. Instead, we will look closely at one small part. Sometimes it is not how much you see, but how deeply you look.

It is early evening when we reach camp, a large flat where the river bends a slow, sensuous curve through the slickrock. The camp is fringed with cottonwoods, their leaves rattling like snapping fingers on the first evening breezes come softly up the canyon.

I am standing still, watching a kaleidoscope of light play across the canyon, when Grant comes up behind me, leading one of the horses. "I could stay in camp the whole trip and just watch this one wall," I say without looking at him.

"Yeah," he says. "When I first saw this country it haunted me. I saw it in my sleep. I couldn't believe there were places like this in the world, cliffs like that. And think how many more there are out there," he says, gesturing with his eyes toward the route of tomorrow's hike.

Under the first streaks of color, soft red, in the morning sky, we are making our way along that unmarked route. We will not be on the marked trail our entire trip. We will just wander, following the wind, or our whims. Unlike some parks or monuments there are no "beauty spots" here, no centerfold peaks or postcard geysers that everyone visits. This is not wilderness by the numbers. The beauty is everywhere, just as likely to be around the next bend as it is to be beneath your feet.

"Look at this," Grant says, picking up a stone—Arizona obsidian, blue-black and chipped to an edge as sharp as honed steel. Around us, the ground glistens with flakes—pieces of arrowheads, worked stone, charcoal from fires long cold.

This land wears time well. The dry air preserves artifacts, even down to thousand-year-old corncobs. We find shards of Hopi black-on-yellow pottery, petroglyphs of bear tracks and bighorn sheep etched into canyon wall—all clues that trace the tracks of human history at least 8,000 years in these canyons.

Holding an arrowhead nearly as weightless as a ray of light, I think about what remains and what disappears. I've always wished that shards of language could survive like pieces of pottery. "Wouldn't it be nice to hear their voices?" I say to Grant as we poke around. "To know their word for raven or beauty?"

There is a pureness about the Escalante. It is as poetic in its graceful vistas as it is in some of its most forbidding terrain. These places that hold the power to feed our souls and inspire our being are few and far between. Our children—and theirs—should be able to live in a world that includes the Escalante in its purest form.

As the great writer and advocate Wallace Stegner said in closing his 1960 essay *Wilderness Letter*, "We simply need that wild country available to us, even if we never do more than drive to its edge and look in. For it can be a means of reassuring ourselves of our sanity as creatures, a part of the geography of hope."

The question of what we develop for our survival and what we preserve for our survival is now more acute than ever before.

—Robert Redford

"Or for 'Hey, quit poking around in our stuff!'" Grant laughs as we set the artifacts back on the ground and continue on.

We crawl up a cottonwood branch to see panels of rock art, play on a mesa top clumped with boulders that look exactly like cauliflower, and shimmy under an immense box elder to find a spring jetting water, as sweet as sugar, straight from the rock.

Through it all, Grant is telling stories. About a storm on W Mountain—"It came first as a dust cloud, then hail, then rain. A bolt of lightning killed a golden eagle that's still up there." About a flash flood that broke over his head on horseback, "right at this bend in the river." About puddles on the flats above Deer Creek that "shine like pools of spilled mercury" after a sunset shower.

Then just before we turn for camp, Grant stops at a small canyon. "This is a special place," he says, his voice low and reverent. "It is a privilege to be here. Go up this canyon quietly, one at a time, so we can experience it that way."

And so we do. Walking into the canyon is like entering a cathedral in stone. The walls, swirled with patterns, rise dark and cool hundreds of feet. A pool at the end reflects the sky like a sacred eye. Years of thunderstorms have sculpted a now-dry falls into a swooping curve of rock. In what Grant calls "The Fern Room" the light is tinged green by rows of maidenhair ferns. There is no sound but the trilling of a canyon wren from somewhere up above and the slow *drip, drip, drip* of spring water seeping through the walls.

It feels…sacred. There is no other word for it, the kind of place where you find yourself whispering, hands folded as if in prayer. With no rush to race to another overlook, or to make miles, we sit quietly, looking, listening, letting the beauty seep into us the way spring water finds its way through solid rock.

"I'm just not going to tell you," Grant says, laughing. We are back at camp after another day of hiking, gathered around a campfire that sends sparks into the dark like constellations of orange stars. Grant is telling more stories—flash floods in the Gulch, rattlesnake fangs stuck in a pair of boots like porcupine quills. But I can't get him to tell us the names of the places we've been hiking the last few days.

"Most of those spots don't have names anyhow," he says, fire-light glowing on his face. "Sometimes the locals call it something, but it's nothing official. I like it that way. It has an uncharted feel. You feel like the first one to discover it.

"Even W Mountain," Grant says after a pause. "You know what the W stands for, don't you? It stands for 'Where the hell was that mountain again?'" He should know. He named it.

With the fire burning down, the talk turns to politics and the controversial creation of the monument. The presidential proclamation that set it aside in 1996 took many, including Utah's congressional delegation and even environmentalists, by surprise. Some saw it as unexpected, although overdue, recognition the land deserved.

Others did not.

In local towns, President Clinton and Secretary of the Interior Bruce Babbitt were hung in effigy, black balloons were released in mourning over the perceived land-grab and the loss of potential jobs at a proposed coal mine.

"Everybody sees it differently," Grant says poking at the fire. "One old rancher got disgusted when I said this canyon was pretty. 'It's just a bunch of damn rocks,' he said. But another one said that when God got done making the Earth he had a bunch of creativity left over and so used it all up here. Me, I'm about 50 percent in favor of the monument. We don't need a bunch of new regulations, but if that's what it took to save it from a coal mine, then I can live with it."

I watch the sparks rising again from the campfire and listen to the land, inscrutable as always, silent on it all.

Mornings come slowly to these canyons, softly. The first light touches the canyon rim and slides liquid-like down the walls. The sand is cool. The air sharp with the scent of wood smoke and coffee, sausage cooking. The horses' breath rises like smoke, their coats dusted to the colors of the canyon wall. We hug our mugs of coffee and linger, waiting for the weather to warm before setting off on our last full day of hiking. I have asked Grant to take us somewhere he's never been, to explore with us. His eyes light up.

"This country is made for poking around like that. When anyone asks where they should hike in Escalante, I just say 'pick any place and go explore.'"

That's just what we do. We ford the river and set off across a stretch of canyon with no name, no trails. All day we are loose in one of the last blank spots on the map. For hours we follow the starburst of cougar tracks in the sand, dry creeks, the swirls of color in a slickrock wall. We scramble down into a crack only as wide as our outstretched arms yet a hundred feet high and get stuck on tiny ledges as slick as glass trying to climb into a shadowy alcove.

Every step is a surprise. Once Grant suddenly stops in mid-stride as if he's stepped on a snake. At his feet is a tiny yellow flower. "Touch it," he says. "And smell your fingers." Lemon. Later, pulling myself over a canyon wall, I look down just in time to see dozens of piñon jays appear on the wing below us. They are dusty blue, the color of the sky against the butterscotch yellow of a canyon filled with cottonwoods. "Look," I say, but as Grant turns, the birds wheel and disappear from view, chattering as they go. Still, the vision stays with me for hours, like the scent of lemon on my fingers, a flash of beauty in the midst of beauty.

Some have questioned why the monument has to be so big. The reason is for days like this one. Space here is as much a part of the land as wind or rock. We need a few places with the feeling of endlessness still in them where horizons outstretch the reach of human eyes, if only for the way they remind us again and again of the immensity of the world we live in, and the humbleness of our place in it.

We sit on a ledge above the river and watch the evening throw shadows across the canyon, the river glowing silver with the last moments of light.

"It's funny," Grant says after a long silence. "Sometimes a view like this can make me almost melancholy."

"Why?" I ask him.

"Because every place I see brings back a memory of a great trip I did there once, or a story I could tell."

"Like what? Tell me one now," I say to him.

He sits quietly, scanning the distance, and then says, "O.K., like that mesa there—see the one with the shadowy cliff? Well, once, a couple years ago…"

Wisconsin-based Jeff Rennicke is a contributing editor to National Geographic Traveler.

✦

I was hiking way down deep in the Escalante one time when I saw this alcove up above. It was all rubble all the way up, a dangerous place to climb. "Ah, it's nothing," my friend said, but I just had a feeling about it. I climbed up there, the only way that seemed to make sense, and just as I topped out I came face to face with this huge boulder, eight feet by six feet. It was like a TV screen and on it was the strangest petroglyph I've ever seen in this country. It was a big fat guy with a huge belly and horns. He was holding a spear in his right hand. There were some dogs, and running away down in the corner of the rock were two hump-backed flute players—Kokopeli figures—and one had a spear right through its skull. It was an eerie place.

After I'd come back down, I was climbing around on the other side of the canyon, just exploring—I'm always looking for new ways in and out of the canyon. I came across an ancient ladder, juniper trunks jammed into a narrow crack in the cliff wall. As I climbed the ladder, I looked back and there was that petroglyph, again staring right at me, this time from across the canyon. It was as if it was guarding a secret route through the canyon walls. I climbed down, and I've never gone back there.

—Jeff Rennicke, "The Guardian," *National Geographic Traveler*

SUSAN HAZEN-HAMMOND

Riding with Apaches

She glimpses another world on the reservation.

I WANTED TO GO HORSEBACK RIDING ON THE SAN CARLOS APACHE reservation in east-central Arizona. So late one afternoon in June, I coaxed my little car through the axle-deep water at Highway Tank and bumped along a rocky road toward the Anchor Seven Cattle Association's ranch house at Hilltop. Harold Kenton, a licensed guide who also is a medicine man and the stockman for Anchor Seven, had agreed to take me riding in the high country nearby.

No one was home when I arrived dusty and sweaty at the small ranch house. The place looked deserted, and I wondered if Harold and I had misunderstood each other.

Hilltop consists of two houses, the other one uninhabited. There's no electricity, phone, or running water. It takes an hour and a half to drive to San Carlos, the nearest town. I pitched my tent behind the house and waited.

About dusk Harold and his cowboys drove up in a battered pickup, even sweatier and dustier than I was.

Harold, who has shoulder-length black hair, a gold cap on his front tooth, and a tattoo of an eagle on his left arm, adjusted his felt cowboy hat. He looked at my tent, and his dark eyes turned to slits in his round face. "Better move that around to the front," he said in a clipped accent full of glottal stops and dropped consonants. "There are things out there in the night we don't know about."

I assumed he was referring to Apache beliefs in the supernatural, but I didn't want to start out by saying the wrong thing.

"You mean, besides you and seven Apache cowboys?" I asked.

He laughed.

I moved the tent.

Before dawn someone in the house began singing in Apache. It was Harold. "People used to sing a prayer every morning. It's the old Apache way," he told me, as he fried eggs in bacon grease for the cowboys.

At first Harold seemed to have forgotten he'd agreed to take me riding. I suspected that meant I was still too much the outsider. I waited and watched.

Harold and his cowboys roped wild cattle. They piled salt licks into the pickup and delivered them deeper into the backcountry to attract more mavericks. They fried elk steaks and sent someone to town to buy baking powder for biscuits. They also spent a lot of time spitting and fussing with cans of Copenhagen snuff.

Then Harold's uncle reached the ranch house just about the time his vehicle's tires all went flat. That meant another trip to town to fix four rock-lacerated tires.

That afternoon we all rattled down to the Salt River on the roughest road I've ever traveled. Prickly pear cactuses grew between the ruts.

We passed agave plants whose magnificent towering flower stalks had been ripped off in jagged tears.

"Bears," Harold said.

"What a shame," I said.

He looked at me the way you look at a child when you have a really important lesson to teach but don't know if the child is ready. "I grew up where we respect everything," he said. "I call it 'Apache law.' Us Apaches have great respect for bears. When they've been drinking in a pond, we don't drink there because we respect those bears. What they eat, we respect that, too. They like the sweetness of the agave just like we do."

"I'm sorry I said that."

"In Apache, we don't have words for I'm sorry," he replied mildly.

That night as we bounced for three hours back toward Hilltop, Harold and his cowboys talked softly in Apache.

Once he switched to English. "Scientists are always looking for clues to where the Anasazi went. They should ask us. We know where they went, and why."

"Where?"

He hesitated. "I can't tell you." He switched back to Apache.

Late the next afternoon, Harold announced he was ready to ride. He suggested we climb Springwater Mountain.

We set off through the pines. "This was the old road to Whiteriver for the cavalry, too," he said. "The tribe is talking about improving the road, but I hope they won't because that will bring in too many outsiders."

He trotted along on a white gelding. I rode a horse named Shorty.

The air smelled of dust and freshly digested grass. Except for a few cans and other debris, it might have been 100 years ago. We were all alone with the birds, the trees, and the elk droppings.

We came to a squawberry bush, and Harold pulled off a handful of furry red berries. "In the old days, when we got sick, we'd get all our medicine in the woods," he said. "Now if we have money, we go to a pharmacy. But if we're broke, we come out in the woods."

He handed me some berries. They tasted acidic, like vitamin C.

"They're Apache vitamins," he said. "In the old times, people used to soak them in water and make a drink, like Kool-Aid."

The fuzz on the berries made my nose itch. I sneezed.

"Apaches say when you sneeze, someone is calling your name," he said.

We rounded the side of Springwater Mountain, and a wild turkey gobbler waddled out of the brush. Harold cupped his hands and imitated a turkey hen's call.

The gobbler rushed away. Harold laughed. "I guess I sound like an ugly hen. He's afraid of getting stuck with her."

We reached the summit. To the north, juniper-covered hills sloped down toward Salt River Canyon. To the east, we could look out across more hills toward Point of Pines. Harold gestured to the south beyond the shimmer of San Carlos Lake. "That's Mount Turnbull. All these mountains are sacred, but the old people used to sing about four sacred mountains, Mount Turnbull, Mount Graham, Pinal Mountain. And some mountain in Mexico, Mount San Madre, or something."

"The Sierra Madre?"

He shrugged.

I dismounted and Shorty stepped on my foot. I limped off to watch the last moments of light color the hills.

When I turned back, Harold sat on his horse with his right arm outstretched to the north. He resembled a statue in a park, and I remembered him saying, "I'm against things like dancing in parades or putting up statues of dancers. It takes something sacred and makes it ordinary."

Far in the distance, the landscape rose with the Mogollon Rim. A couple of weeks earlier, I'd gone riding with a young Apache ranger on the Fort Apache Indian Reservation, between McNary and Sunrise. We wandered through picturesque countryside, past evergreens, aspens, and pond-dotted meadows. But that outing gave me no glimpses of another world view the way riding with Harold did.

Harold lowered his arm. "I was praying to the mountain," he said. "Telling it we are here to enjoy the scenery. I was praying for me and my boys. I was praying for you."

I thanked him and remounted.

"In Apache we do not have words for 'thank you,'" he said.

Harold, who belongs to the eagle clan, imitated an eagle call again and again. Then he said, "There's a song goes with this mountain. When people went on the trail through here, they would sing for their loved ones. I'll sing it for you."

With Apacheland spread out below us in the twilight, Harold sat on the motionless horse and sang in Apache. When he finished, he said, "It says that I got to the top of Springwater Mountain, and I'm looking back at old San Carlos. That's where my people are. I left a beautiful hard-working woman back there, and I'm going to miss her. That's why I'm going to have my last look back."

He turned toward the sunset. "In the old days, when Apache scouts were looking for Geronimo, they didn't know if they were going to come back. This is the place where they prayed. For their people. Their children. Their family. One last look back."

He twitched the reins, and we started down the mountainside. "People had feelings then, too," he said.

As he rode, Harold sang more Apache songs. Then he said, "The farthest white people go is the moon. With our prayers and songs, we go a lot farther than that."

It was so dark the ground was a black void beneath us, but the two horses stepped as surefootedly as in daylight.

Harold was little more than the outline of his hat.

"My father is a medicine man," he said. "And my uncles and grandfathers. All my family, for generations. By the old ways, medicine people were chiefs. By the new ways, they elect chiefs. Now it's all politics. I don't want to go into politics because you can't trust politicians. I'd rather be Harold Kenton that people know about as medicine man."

The Milky Way stretched across the tops of the pine trees, milkier and brighter than I'd ever seen.

"My boys say you're pretty brave," he said. "They say, 'That woman is sleeping outside, and we're sleeping in the house.' They say, 'We should be the ones to sleep outside, and she should be in the house.'"

"I don't like mice. I'd be afraid to sleep inside."

He laughed.

I thought about the cowboys and the life they had chosen. For them it means working fifteen-hour days in exchange for an iron cot, greasy food, adventure, and the hope of rounding up enough wild cattle to start small herds of their own. The horses clopped slowly through the darkness. Then Harold's mount struck a rock hard with a hoof, and sparks flew.

"You want to see more sparks?" Harold asked. He kicked the horse and galloped off.

Shorty bolted after him.

I swayed and nearly lost my balance on the runaway horse.

Harold rushed back, and Shorty stopped. "You should have grabbed the saddlehorn."

"Next time I will."

Later a shooting star flew across the Milky Way.

Harold spit. "Spit out," he said.

I spit.

"That's the Apache way. If you spit out when you see a shooting star, that means good luck."

I was thinking about the areas of my life that could use a little luck when Harold asked, "You remember what I was telling you last night?"

"About the Anasazi?"

"I'm going to tell you where they went," he said.

"I'll want to write it down for people to read."

"I know."

For a while, the only sounds came from horseshoes meeting stones.

Finally Harold said, "The way the old people tell it, the ancient people aren't dead. They went somewhere. They were powerful medicine people. They taught us before they left. They are going to come back."

He pointed to the Big Dipper. "That's where our people say the ancient people live. That's why we use the Big Dipper to pray with, like a feather."

I was still thinking about that when we approached the ranch house and heard Harold's uncle singing a medicine song.

The voice stopped, as if he'd been singing to guide us home.

For dinner Harold and I ate leftover elk gravy and biscuits the cowboys had saved. Then I crawled into my tent and fell asleep.

Susan Hazen-Hammond is a photographer, poet, and author of nine nonfiction books including Spiderwoman's Web: Traditional Native American Tales about Woman's Power, *and the award-winning children's book* Thunder Bear and Ko: The Buffalo Nation and Nanbe Pueblo.

★

His only regret, Geronimo often declared in later years, was that he did not die fighting in the Sierra Madres.

That's not quite true. The great Chiricahua Apache warrior, his heart softened by the passing years, had one more haunting regret: that he had caused so much pain to little children.

"Often I would steal up to the homes of white settlers and kill parents," he once admitted to an interviewer quoted by historian David Roberts. "In my hatred I would even take the little ones out of their cradles and toss them in the air. They would like this and would gurgle with glee. But when they came down I would catch them on my sharp hunting knife and kill them. I wake up groaning and very sad at night when I remember the helpless little children."

The atrocities committed by Geronimo and his warriors during their final fifteen months of freedom in 1885–1886 still horrify those who read of them more than a century later.

Sometimes they lanced and beat a terrified victim before stringing him upside down over his wagon and then setting it afire to roast him slowly to death. Often they tortured a husband while his wife was forced to watch.

But these horrors were not much different than those inflicted on the Apaches, beginning with the Spanish in the late sixteenth century when they marched north from Mexico seeking slaves for their silver mines.

—Dean Smith, "Geronimo's Last Raid," *Arizona Highways*

LINDA WATANABE McFERRIN

The Lure of Hoodoos

*Energy vortices or not, this is one
interesting and beautiful place.*

MAYBE IT WAS THE HYPE—A NACREOUS VENEER OF TRANSCEN-
dentalism lacquered over the high desert. Maybe it really was the
call of the vortices, energy points said to exist on the steeples of fire
red rock. I'd like to say it was some mysterious convergence of mystical events that led me to Sedona. Most probably, it was simply the
lure of canyon and mesa, geologic wonders haunted by Indian lore
and legend, where saguaro cactus and sage share space with coyote
and sidewinder.

My friend Samantha, newly pregnant and glad of it, was feeling
the call of the arroyos. Call it a craving. We decided to indulge.

Sedona, a small town in Arizona with a very large mystical reputation, lies north of Scottsdale, a straight shot up Highway 17.

Not even our backgrounds in wide, wild expanses of California
prepared us for the magic of that scrub-strewn terrain. We saw
twelve-foot saguaro cacti that looked like lonesome cowboys heading on home to the ranch. Twilight played coyote trickster with
shadows and light. In the gathering gloom, squat scrub chaparral—
manzanita, mesquite, and shrub live oak—took on the forms of various animals: jackrabbits, prairie dogs, and ringtail cats. The rocks

themselves seemed to come alive, twisting and snaking upward. Then darkness fell like a tomahawk, stars opened up like tiny eyes in the sky, and a full moon rose over the desert.

We hurtled down that rattlesnake of a road, halted on a crescent of gravel and dust, and got out to stretch our legs. After a fast, snappy splattering of rain, the air was humid and cool, the moon a glowing smudge behind a halo of moisture.

On both sides of us, the desert rose in fabulous hoodoos, in snaggle-toothed spires. We thought we heard a wolf howl, an owl hoot. We found ourselves speaking in whispers, like kids at a campfire. A spooky feeling swept over us, and we got back into the car.

It wouldn't start. Not even the comforting whir of the ignition greeted our efforts. Only silence. Was this the Twilight Zone?

Since Samantha could not start the car, I tried. It started right up. We turned nervously to one another, eyes as big as saucers, eyebrows jumping to the tops of our foreheads.

"We're almost there," I said encouragingly.

Samantha just nodded.

We almost passed Sedona. At night this little town is easy to miss, its sprinkling of lights is no match for a big desert sky studded with stars. Even by day, the soft hues and lines of its Southwestern architecture seem lost in the expanse of a land where 300-million-year-old cliffs of limestone, shale, basalt, and sandstone climb to form sheer walls, towers, and elegant minarets.

Our hotel, rather inappropriately named L'Auberge de Sedona, was tucked off the main thoroughfare. Our home for the night was an aerie of an apartment perched on the hillside overlooking a canyon. It was ten o'clock by the time we sat down to eat and midnight by the time we got back to our room. We went out like a couple of well-used candles.

By six the next morning, the sun had already muscled its way into the room. Along with the heat, we were showered in an incredible wraparound sound that seemed to swell mysteriously from the forest below. I couldn't place it. It sounded like cards being shuffled over a PA system. It sounded like a million maracas being shaken at once. But investigation could wait: I substituted the more proximate hiss and splash of my shower.

In our room, a sheaf of newsletters and brochures promised Disneylike adventures, replete with Native American rituals, wildlife encounters, spiritual awakenings, and pink jeeps. We were ready to meet Sedona head-on, but like any good scouts, we first opted to explore our immediate surroundings. We had to walk down the hillside into Oak Creek Canyon and find the source of the sound.

The rattling rose and fell around us on our short descent into the canyon. Fat faces of daisies gazed up at us. June bugs as big as hummingbirds buzzed us. It grew cooler as we closed in on the creek. Irises grew in the small patches of shadow. Oak Creek was so clear we could see flat, gray-green rocks resting like turtles beneath the water on the opposite shore. Ducks cut slow ciphers into the water's glassy surface. I began to feel drowsy.

That's when I met him—my first denizen of the desert. I came face to face with a fat grasshopper with leopard markings and pearl gray eyes at the top of its head. It was clinging to one of the green rushes at the side of the creek. Was this one of those monumental meetings in which creatures from disparate worlds connect spiritually and exchange greetings? It didn't seem frightened.

Suddenly, I was aware of thousands of similarly beadlike eyes. I had not even seen them. They perched on all the rushes around the creek. They peered out from the short grass at my feet. They were the source of the ocean of sound that rolled in great waves through the canyon. It seemed as if some great truth had just been revealed, but I wasn't sure what. I was overwhelmed with the sense of missing some significant point.

I looked around for Samantha. She was sitting on a red rock some distance away, looking over the creek, still as a sandstone statue, already one with the landscape.

My second encounter with a denizen of the desert occurred after breakfast, when our guide arrived. Samantha said I had selected what seemed the most promising tour. Offered in affiliation with a local bookstore, it guaranteed smudge sticks, cornmeal offerings, and prayer-feather rituals. However, for a guide we did not get a

sunburned mercenary or a native mystic. We got Jill, a tiny trans-
plant from Tennessee by way of New York, street-smart, troubled-
scarred, and tough as a prairie chicken.

"Look," Sam said to her, trying to explain our slightly cynical
point of view, "we're not woo-woos."

"Woo-woo?" Jill asked, raising her eyebrow.

"You know, New Agers," Samantha explained.

Actually, I was beginning to have my doubts, after my brief
communion with the grasshopper.

"Yeah," I seconded heartily.

"Well, good," said Jill. "Neither am I. Now that we've got that
out of the way, let's get going."

In Jill's minivan, we set out through a landscape whose beauty has
made it a pilgrimage destination for generations. Jill explained that
the Indians measure time in worlds. The rock that towered around
us accurately recorded these incarnations—ocean five times, fresh-
water lake two times, swamp twice, desert twice—and each incar-
nation had left another layer of personality.

"So, why did you guys choose the Vortex Tour?" Jill asked with
studied carelessness, squinting into the sunlight.

Samantha piped up, "We want to know more about the vortexes."

"Vortices," Jill corrected with a snakelike hiss of the sibilants. I
pictured the warning flick of a rattler's tail. "I prefer 'vortices.' Well,
you picked the right spot. The vortices are power spots, places
where energy collects and swirls. The Bermuda Triangle is a vortex.
There are vortices all over the world. You know about them. They're
where mysterious events occur. People are naturally attracted to
them. We have seen vortices in Sedona. Some are negative, some
are positive.

"Let's start right here. See that rock over there?"

Our eyes followed the apocalyptic pointing of Jill's finger to an
enormous bluff that rose like a callused red giant from the low plane
of the desert.

"That's Apache Leap. It's a powerful negative vortex. I tried to
climb it once." Jill frowned. "I couldn't. Fear gripped me. Do you
know what happened there? The story goes that when General

Crook was rounding up Indians to put them on reservations, the few free remaining Apache got wind of it. The braves, all the men, got on their horses and rode right up to the top of that cliff where it looked as if they had nowhere to go. And then…they leapt over. All the braves in the party plunged to their deaths rather than face white man's captivity. Maybe they stayed free.

"And see that beautiful swath of green stretching beneath the leap? You'd like to say it's a well-tended Indian burial ground, a kind of memorial, right? Wrong. It's a golf course. Yep, a golf course. I guess some people are immune to bad vibes."

Our guide was silent for a while. She seemed deep in rumination. Suddenly she stuck a thin arm out the window again, gesturing toward an immense dome-shaped rock up ahead, to the left of us.

"That over there's Bell Rock," she said. "Remember 1989, the Harmonic Convergence, when all the planets supposedly lined up and big things were supposed to happen? Well, some of the people let on that Bell Rock was a spaceship that was meant to take people away from this planet, which was slated to be destroyed. They even sold tickets. And people bought 'em! But as you can see, old Bell Rock never took off, and I don't think those ticket holders ever got their money back.

One of the most alien places to visit north of Sedona is Meteor Crater. Fifty thousand years ago, a huge nickel and iron meteorite weighing several hundred thousand tons hit the earth and exploded with the force of 20 million tons of TNT. Shock waves devastated everything for miles around on the rocky plain and the impact created a crater 700 feet deep and nearly 4,000 feet across. Astronauts have trained for lunar missions here and extensive scientific research has been conducted by scientists from around the world. Today, you can view the crater from the visitor's center which sits on the ancient impact area like some remote outpost on Mars. Alas, visits to the crater floor are not allowed.

—SO'R and JO'R

"Yeah," she laughed, "it can get pretty weird here, and if you ever want that kind of action, you just go to the Coffee Pot Restaurant in West Sedona. You'll find them there any day of the week, these woo-woos you're talking about, playing flutes and clanging crystals. Heck, these people have to consult a pendulum before they go to the bathroom."

As Jill kept up her gravelly commentary, Samantha and I slammed up and down in the bucking seats of the minivan, which Jill drove with great disregard for stones and potholes. Every so often she'd fling out a botanical note. "See that manzanita. It's a natural fire retardant. When lightning strikes, it puts itself out. The Indians call it the Plant of the Gods. You can use the bark for bronchial problems."

We had turned right, off Highway 179, and were bumping along the back road toward an elegant constellation of spires and towers known as Cathedral Rock.

Jill hit the brakes right before the road ended, jumped from the van, slammed the door shut, and lit a cigarette in a series of quick, well synchronized movements. She fished around in a shabby day pack and, pulling out two bundles of weeds, ignited the tip of each one with her cigarette. The tightly wrapped grass didn't burn, just smoldered, and the air was perfumed with sage.

"Smudge sticks," Jill informed us. "This is Cathedral Rock, your first vortex. Now, I want you to pass the smoke before the different parts of your body and repeat after me:

"I am pure of thought,
I see the truth,
I speak truth,
I am pure of heart,
I walk in peace,
aho."

We repeated the words, waving the sweet-smelling smudge sticks before forehead, eyes, mouth, heart, and feet—the pertinent parts of our bodies.

"Kind of a cleansing," Jill said, grinning. "Now, go." She gave us each a shove in the direction of Cathedral Rock.

The desert was silent and still. We looked back at Jill. She leaned against the minivan, taking long slow pulls on the rest of her cigarette. Midday sun washed over us, warm and soporific. Lizards blinked up at us. Time seemed to stop. Jill had told us that Cathedral Rock was a feminine vortex. A holy place for Indian women, who had come here for centuries to bear children. Shaped like a coronet its several turrets encircled a lower, rocky center. I watched Samantha, my dear friend, in the months before motherhood, as she moved ahead, picking her way past walls of rust-colored stone, a solitary figure climbing up into the high lap of that natural sanctuary.

I could feel it—a kind of gentle tug. Sedona was pulling me into another dimension. It was a wordless dimension of feelings and heightened sensitivity, a sense of inner-connectedness with everything around me. It scared me a little. Perhaps this is a phenomenon similar to what Jill felt on the trail to the summit of Apache Leap.

The terrain I hike through is generally one of physical landmarks, of objective reality. Here, in Sedona, things shifted into a kind of double exposure: the external and internal landscapes seemed to have become superimposed.

I said nothing of this to Samantha. She remained focused, with her own intensity, on an ascent into the rugged saddle of shrub and sandy stone. In fact, we spoke little, if at all, on Cathedral Rock. We climbed about silently, bewitched by our surroundings and the specter of our identities. We descended from those escarpments a quieter and more reverent twosome.

Jill had other adventures in store. At the mouth of Boynton Canyon we stepped carefully into and out of a tangle of wide green leaves and enormous, white funnel-shaped flowers.

"Beautiful, huh?" Jill queried suggestively.

Samantha and I nodded assent.

"Yep," Jill agreed, "very tempting. Datura. You've heard of the deadly nightshade? Well, datura is part of that family. Also called angel's trumpet, jimsonweed. It's an alkaloid hallucinogen. Indians use it. I wouldn't recommend experimenting."

I studied the perfect belled cones, wondering how the hallucinogen was extracted, thinking how easily one could be seduced by these angel white blossoms.

Jill's voice interrupted me.

"Here we are. This is a perfect spot."

She thrust her hand into the battered day pack again and pulled out a small plastic bag.

"Prayer-feather offering," she announced. "Stand on that little pile of rock over there, close your eyes, and hold out your hands."

We did as our guide instructed. Jill turned our hands so that the palms faced upward. She filled them with weightless down.

"Now make a wish," she said breathlessly. "Wish for something you really want and throw the feathers into the air. The wish will come true. This is a sacred ritual."

I thought about wishing, as I generally do, for vast material wealth, but I couldn't bring myself to do it. The moment seemed to dictate something else. I think I wished for something intangible—world peace, love, happiness for all—I honestly can't remember. At the time, whatever it was, it seemed the unequivocal choice. We opened our eyes and stood for a while, in silence, watching the snow-white turkey feathers drift off in the wind. Across the canyon the Enchantment resort sprawled behind its guarded gates. It seemed to be chiseled in rose and ocher from the stone around it, an elaborate and inaccessible four-star cliff dwelling.

We visited other places with Jill. She pointed out the Vortex of Confusion (home of the U.S. Post Office) and a curtain of rock formations—Cockscomb, Chimney Rock, Capitol Butte, Sugar Loaf, Coffee Pot Rock, and Steamboat Rock—that stand north of Sedona like a movie-set backdrop. At Schnedly Hill, an electrical vortex, we made blue corn offerings and squatted for what seemed like hours, our hands on the earth, struggling to sense an energetic surge. If we felt anything it was the numbness in our legs spreading upward with an old, familiar tingle.

"Feel anything?" Jill asked.

"No," we shook our heads dumbly.

Jill shrugged. "Oh, well, not everyone does."

The vortex tour took four hours. We returned to L'Auberge de

Sedona under a soft blue sky in which angelic puffs of cotton-white cloud floated.

"Too bad," Jill said. "This is monsoon season. We haven't had enough rain this year."

I puzzled over Sedona, cynical and chastened in turns, still trying to figure out what the place was all about. It's difficult to be arrogant in that towering landscape, difficult to shelter under the puny umbrella of self, that entity full of doubt, cynicism, and fear, and not be edified by the broader context. It's hard to ignore the big picture. That awareness is, in its way, a miracle.

What humans make of their miracles is another matter. In Sedona, as in so many places, the spiritual, inspirational, and miraculous fall prey to capitalism. Everyone's trying to make a buck. Yet there always have been hawkers at pilgrimage sites. They cater to our need to bring back tokens, a long-lasting memento of the ineffable. To stand in the center of honest wonder and its glitzy overlay of hype seems to be an experience of great value. It is highly educational to embrace both sides of a paradox.

We paid Jill and said good-bye in the parking lot of the resort. Money changed hands. The sky opened up, and it started to rain.

"Monsoon," Jill announced, winking at us from the window of the minivan.

"Call me next time you're in Sedona. I'll give you a midnight Medicine Wheel Tour. No charge."

Linda Watanabe McFerrin has been traveling since she was two and writing about it since she was six. Her travel stories have appeared in numerous publications and she is the author of two poetry collections, Chisel, Rice, Paper, Stone *and* The Impossibility of Redemption Is Something We Hadn't Figured On. *Editor of the fourth edition of* Best Places Northern California, *McFerrin is a winner of the Katherine Anne Porter Prize for Fiction and author of a novel,* Namako: Sea Cucumber, *and a short story collection,* The Hand of Buddha.

TONY HILLERMAN

A Museum Etched
in Stone

*Canyon de Chelly leaves its mark
on a modern author.*

DOWN THROUGH THE YEARS, I HAVE DEVELOPED MY OWN RITUAL for visiting the vast stone labyrinth called Canyon de Chelly. I drive north from the Navajo town of Window Rock, then follow the road that snakes along the canyon's main branch. I stop at overlooks that allow spectacular aerial views of the 800-year-old ruins below.

Seen from the north rim, the canyon is awe inspiring. From this height, which is like standing on top of a sixty-story building, even the larger ruins seem trivialized by the vastness. The fields, horses, and hogans of the Navajo who now live along the stream on the canyon floor are diminished to toy-box size.

The atmosphere is far different down on the canyon floor, which is accessible to the public only on tours led by Navajo guides and park rangers or by making the long climb down the trail to the White House Ruin. The cliffs close in around you, excluding the outside world as thoroughly as if you were standing on the bottom of a giant stone bottle. If you stay late, you can watch darkness creep up the sandstone walls as the sun sinks. Stay later, and you can watch the opposite effect—pale yellow moonlight moving down the cliffs.

The effect is even more dramatic if you risk the climb out on a moonless night, when the canyon floor is lit only by stars. With no man-made lights to diminish the effect and no haze to dilute it, starlight at this altitude is dazzling. In the narrow slot of sky visible above the rim, a billion stars shine.

On the map mounted on the wall above my word processor, Canyon de Chelly (pronounced de SHAY) resembles the track a bird might leave in the mud. The heel mark is the canyon mouth. The toes form its three main branches: Canyon de Chelly itself in the center, cutting twenty-five miles eastward into the Defiance Plateau; Canyon del Muerto (Massacre Canyon), extending twenty miles to the northeast; and Monument Canyon, angling southeastward.

On that map Canyon de Chelly seems relatively insignificant, a medium-size gorge (by Rocky Mountain standards) sharing the territory with the immensity of the Grand Canyon. Unlike the view from the north rim, de Chelly does not make much of an impression when you drive to its mouth, near the town of Chinle. While its flat, sandy bottom is almost 300 yards wide, the cliffs

Navajo mythology is bathed in stardust. Crosses depicting stars occur not only on ceremonial paraphernalia, but in sacred sand paintings as well. Anyone who gazes upon an open sky in the Southwest finds the constellations imprinted on his eyelids for nights to come.

It is known among the Navajo that each constellation represents a law which the people must obey. When the Diné stop obeying the laws which are written in the sky, the Navajo tribe will come to an end.

Celestial wisdom finds its roots in story:

> …First Woman, after all the stars were placed in the sky, said, "Now all the laws our people will need are printed in the sky where everyone can see them…. The commands written in the stars must be obeyed forever."

—Terry Tempest Williams, *Pieces of White Shell: A Journey to Navajoland* walling it in at this point rise only about thirty feet. In terms of geology or hydrology, it seems to be just another of those washes that drain snowmelt and summer rains from the Chuska Mountains.

But in terms of history and the human spirit, Canyon de Chelly is a unique outdoor museum chronicling a progression of cultures over the last 3,000 years. And then there is the beauty of its sheer sandstone walls. The shapes and colors of those stratified layers tell the story of seas advancing and retreating 230 million years ago, of sand and gravel and sediment piling up in layers hundreds of feet deep, of streams slicing through the layers, of weathering and erosion widening the channels into a labyrinth of canyons.

Many of the canyon cliffs are formed of smooth sandstone. In the flat light of a midsummer noon, their colors range from pale pink to the faintest tan. But as afternoon turns to dusk and shadows form, the walls take on sculptured shapes. The pink deepens into a rich salmon. The manganese oxide streaking the cliffs, dark brown at noon, develops undertones of black and red. In places, the cliffs suggest the canvas of a cosmic abstractionist whose palette had every color except blue.

No one knows when hunter-gatherers first wandered into this desert canyon, but we do know what lured them here: a permanent source of water. Even in the driest of years, these nomads knew they could find springs seeping cold, clear water by walking upcanyon. In fact, the name de Chelly comes from the Navajo word for "where the water comes out of the rock," an apt description for the canyon mouth, where Chinle Wash is as wide as three football fields.

This water first supported year-round inhabitants just before the birth of Christ—a culture that scholars call the Basketmakers. Only a few families lived here, 200 people at most. They wove baskets, grew corn and squash in the same fields that Navajo farm today, and kept their surplus in storage cysts scooped out of the sandstone beneath overhanging cliffs. In these cysts, still visible at Mummy Cave in Canyon del Muerto, they also buried their dead. Soon, as their numbers grew, the Basketmakers began building large stone granaries above ground.

Over the next nine centuries, these canyon-bottom dwellers

learned to make pottery and hunt with the bow and arrow. As the population continued to grow, they moved into stone-walled, apartment-style cliff houses. We call these pueblo dwellers the Anasazi, part of the same culture that flourished at Mesa Verde and Chaco Canyon and throughout the Colorado Plateau.

By the thirteenth century, 800 or so Anasazi inhabited the canyon. They raised dogs and turkeys, wove cotton textiles, and made fine pottery decorated with intricate designs. They had a political hierarchy and a complex religion that may have been influenced by cultures from as far away as Central America.

In 1264 the Anasazi cut the last timber for their cliff dwellings at Canyon de Chelly; this timber became a roof beam in the three-story stone

> One of the most extraordinary hidden treasures of the Southwest is Grand Falls on the Little Colorado River. Located on the Navajo Reservation northeast of Flagstaff, Grand Falls, a series of lava steps, higher than Niagara Falls was formed roughly 100,000 years ago. In the spring, snowmelt and rain can create an awesome spectacle as a torrent of muddy water plunges 185 feet to the bottom of the Little Colorado River Canyon.
>
> —Sean O'Reilly, "Notes from the Southwest"

structure know as the Tower, which perches high on a sandstone shelf on the east cliff of Canyon del Muerto, next to Mummy Cave. The first time I saw the Tower was late one afternoon, when the slanting sunlight illuminated the top of the cliff above it. Seen from the premature twilight of the canyon depth, the walls of the ruin seemed to glow. Absolute silence. My imagination began to stir.

Had the Tower been built as a fortress? I wondered. Were the Anasazi or their predecessors seeking refuge from hostile nomads? We know that several mummified bodies found inside the Tower had died violently. Had there been combat, then, in this peaceful place?

As I leaned against the cool cliff, I let my thoughts travel back in time. In my minds eye, I imagined invaders scrambling up that steep slope under the walls to slaughter exhausted defenders. I could see the last Anasazi families hurrying away, carrying only a few baskets and pots and ceremonial objects. They may have migrated to the east, settling the Hopi villages and developing the Pueblo Indian cultures of the Rio Grande Valley and western New Mexico.

Whatever the cause, civilization ended between the great pink cliffs. Silence descended on the canyon, disturbed only by the wind and the occasional visitor.

Canyon de Chelly had no full-time residents again until about 1750, when Navajo being pushed westward by Ute and Comanche tribes found refuge in the canyon and began farming land aban-doned five centuries before. Today about 450 Navajo still plant corn and tend goats and sheep on the canyon bottom during the sum-mer, then move out to their winter homes on the plateau or in nearby Chinle when the snow comes. Frigid air sinks to the canyon floor, and the winter sun, low on the southern horizon, doesn't reach in with its heat. But if you enjoy lonely silence, as I do, win-ter afternoons are a good time to come to Canyon de Chelly.

Reminders of man's efforts to survive in this harsh land surround you at Standing Cow Ruin, one of the largest ruins in the 84,000-acre national monument. Here the Anasazi built sixty stone-walled rooms for living and storage, as well as three round underground kivas for ceremonies. The cliffs for hundreds of yards up and down the canyon are a gallery of pictographs recording more than a thou-sand years of art and graffiti, from hand prints and abstractions left by the Basketmakers to nineteenth-century Navajo renderings of their deadly encounters with Mexican and American soldiers. Within a mile you can puzzle over concentric circles, stylized humanoids with looped arms and birdlike feet, figures holding hands, humans with horns, and a life-size Navajo drawing of a standing cow that gives the ruin its name.

Up the cliff, pale against the dark red sandstone, is one of the West's most remarkable pictographs. A troop of Mexican dragoons march in a line across the stone; they wear broad-brimmed hats, carry muskets, and ride stick-legged horses toward their terrible victory. Dispatched in 1804 to help New Mexico militiamen fight the Navajo, the Mexicans drove Navajo braves and their families deep into Canyon del Muerto, where they took refuge in a cliffside cave 600 feet above the canyon floor. I doubt if a veteran of ground combat in any war can walk up the canyon's sandy floor without respecting the courage of those troops or the brutality of their campaign. Riding into this canyon must have been like riding into the jaws of death.

The Mexicans slaughtered the Navajo by deflecting musket balls off the overhanging roof. The cave roof and walls still bear the pockmarks of hundreds of bullets, and the floor is littered with bones, many of them of children. That bloody incident gave both this branch of the canyon and Massacre Cave their names.

After Canyon de Chelly became United States territory, whites pushed into Navajo lands. In 1863 the territorial governor decided to apply a "final solution," believing that gold could be found in the Chuskas and points west if the Navajo were eliminated. He sent an expedition led by Colonel Kit Carson to harass the Navajo and kill or capture as many as possible. When winter came, Carson's troops rode through deep snow into Canyon de Chelly and rounded up hundreds of Navajo. More troops returned the following summer; they burned Navajo hogans, chopped down 5,000 peach trees, and captured Barboncito, one of the most respected headmen. More than 8,000 captives were herded eastward onto the dismal Bosque Redondo reservation in New Mexico.

Canyon de Chelly lay silent for four heartbreaking years, until General William Tecumseh Sherman freed the Navajo, and Barboncito brought his people home to the "very heart of our country." Since that spring of 1868, Canyon de Chelly has enjoyed unbroken peace.

To traditional Navajo, the canyon represents much more than a historic battleground. It is one of the holiest places in the tribe's mythology. It was here that the mythological Holy People taught the Navajo how to live, and only here can their medicine people conduct the ceremonies that restore harmony to mind and spirit.

★

I must confess that I have a weakness for empty places. Even in the busy summer season—when Navajo guides are driving tourists around, and farmers are working their cornfields, and herders are tending their flocks under the silvery leaves of the olive trees—it's easy enough to find silence and solitude in this huge stone labyrinth. But if you share my taste for isolation, late autumn and early spring are ideal times to visit. I like to follow the self-guided trail from the south rim to the White House Ruin, take off my shoes and socks, and splash through the shallow water to the cottonwoods, under the cliff dwelling, once home to several Anasazi families. It's a quiet place. The 600-foot sandstone cliffs soaring toward the open sky make the ruin seem small as a dollhouse.

Sitting in the shade here many years ago and gazing up at those stone houses, just as their builders did almost a thousand years ago, I thought I heard the trill of a flute drifting from upcanyon. A flute like that of Kokopelli, the humpbacked figure drawn on these cliffs by Anasazi artists. But no, it was the tinkling bells of a Navajo's goats, blended into a tenor-like warble by the echoing cliffs. That day I decided to devote my writings to the Navajo and their sacred land.

Up and down the stream, painted on the dark, sooty stains of desert varnish that streak the canyon walls, are pictographs—the work of Basketmaker, Anasazi, and Navajo. I wander among the cliffs, finding abstractions, snakes, birds, men with the feet of birds, the humpbacked Kokopelli playing his flute, a frog, a large man with arms raised in supplication, a mountain goat impaled by a lance.

I think of these as messages left for me that I have forgotten how to read. The cliffs remind me of how little space I occupy; the pictographs, of how little time.

A resident of Albuquerque, New Mexico, and the author of many books, Tony Hillerman is best know for mystery novels involving the Navajo Tribal Police. He was elected Grand Master of the Mystery Writers of America in 1990. He has won the French Grand Prix de Littérature Policière and the Special Friend of the Dineh Award of the Navajo tribe.

✶

A short list of some of the most dramatic Indian ruins in the Southwest:

- Chaco Culture National Historical Park, New Mexico
- Canyon de Chelly National Monument, Arizona
- Montezuma Castle National Monument, Arizona
- Casa Grande National Monument, Arizona
- Gila Cliff Dwellings National Monument, New Mexico
- Navajo National Monument, Arizona
- Tonto National Monument, Arizona
- Tuzigoot National Monument, Arizona
- Walnut Canyon National Monument, Arizona

—SO'R and JO'R

JOHN ANNERINO

Running Wild

An adventurer seeks the "running power"
of the Apaches.

I'M RUNNING ALONE THROUGH THE GALIURO MOUNTAINS. IT'S A cool, clear day in March; a brisk wind rustles out of the north. My legs feel strong, and I feel confident I can run fifty miles across the mountain island in a day. That's only half the distance the Apaches reportedly ran between sunup and sunset through these parts; then, that's what's lured me to this isolated tract of southeastern Arizona to begin with—the idea of running, as I now am, carrying little more than a knife, flint and steel, some rations.

I suck wind in, I blow air out: *hih-huh, hih-huh, hih-huh, hih-huh.* My lungs heave in and out, my legs charge toward the power I hunger for, "running power." Apaches called it *galke ʔho ʔndi*. Keith Basso described it in *Western Apache Raiding & Warfare*: "A man who has this power can run long distances, and even on the shortest day could run from Fort Grant to Fort Apache and get there in mid-afternoon."

An 1881 military map from the Court Martial Case Files, on record at the National Archives, shows this Indian trail: by way of the crow, it's 80 miles from the north end of the Galiuro Mountains to the foot of the White Mountains; throw in the endless twists and turns of the rugged topography in between and you're looking at

100 miles. In a day. A hundred miles in a day! What was it like for the Apache to run that? No one knows for certain. Native Americans have a great oral tradition of recording events and tribal history, so one can only speculate on what they thought about, or what it actually felt like to run 100 miles wearing little more than a pair of leather moccasins, or straw sandals, and a traditional breech cloth. The one known case documenting such a run concerns the remarkable escape of two Apache women circa 1865. Shanghaied by government troops, the women broke out of a military garrison in Tucson and ran more than 170 miles back to their village near Goodwin Springs, surviving on roasted mescal hearts along the way. But the single, most telling piece of evidence from the account in Basso's book came at the end of that extraordinary run when one of the women was later recognized by one of her original captors. According to Basso's principal informant, David Longstreet added, "He wanted to know how she got home. She told him her legs were like horses!"

That's how my legs still felt 10 miles into the Galiuros, which some early travelers named the Sierra del Arivaya for the creek they followed north between the Galiuro and Pinaleño Mountains. Averaging 250 miles of running a month since Granite Mountain, I had few worries, other than fatigue, about trying to bite off half the distance the Apache historically ran in a day. Four miles later, however, my legs are seized with cramps, as if they've been painfully trussed in the same kind of air splint I wore after my fall. I walk peg leg-like for a few minutes and guzzle a liter of water from one of the two bota bags I'm wearing crisscrossed across my chest, Pancho Villa style. I cinch down my camera to my survival belt and start running again, trying to shake out the rigid cramps with a flick at each step, as if I'm practicing a military drill.

But the trail I'm running up, stiff-legged, is covered with fallen trees called blowdown, and to make any progress at all I have to crawl under or climb over them. The gymnastic moves, however, combined with the abrupt ascent, exhaust me by the time I finally reach the East Divide 17 miles out. My thighs are screaming and my eyelids are starting to droop. I am totally spent. I can't go any farther. I should turn back, it's all downhill. But I can't; I've been dropped off on the southern end of one of the most remote and seldom-visited wilderness areas in the Southwest.

Sitting alone atop the Galiuros, halfway between hell and gone, I can see Eagle Pass between the Santa Teresa and Pinaleño Mountains; the Spaniards used that pass when they called the Galiuros the Sierra de San Calistro. But I quickly lose that train of thought because I feel weak, unnaturally so. I must have a low-grade infection. My face feels flushed and the recovery I'm patiently waiting for never materializes. I look at my maps; I have no options. The shortest distance to any kind of help is to my rendezvous point at Power's Garden, 16 miles north. Somehow I have to make it there by nightfall. I'm not carrying any kind of sleeping gear and it's too cold to spend the night in the open. Sick or not, somehow I have to run it; I'm too lightly clad to move any slower.

> The mountains of southeastern Arizona are not the stuff of posters and coffee-table books. They are rather the stuff of wary beauty and abiding love, a beauty that lies as much in the contrast of rock and leaf as in splendid views, a love that lies less in easy responses than in intimate acquaintance, doggedly pursued.
>
> —Janice Emily Bowers, *Fear Falls Away and Other Essays from Hard and Rocky Places*

I stand up, stretch my legs, and start running due north along the highline spine of the Galiuro Mountains, an unforgivingly rugged, 76,317-acre wilderness area. In terms of natural direction finding, I visualize this 7,000-foot mountain range in my mind's eye as a capital H lying on its backside. I am running along the lower right leg of that H, and somehow I have to reach Power's Garden, situated in a deep cleft of a canyon between the two upper arms of the H. But the slippery, narrow path I'm following is heavily overgrown with manzanita bushes, which shove me back and forth across the ridgeline, like an unruly mob. Consequently, it takes all my concentration to maintain a run.

Feeling weaker by the yard, I'm not sure how much longer I can maintain this awkward, simian lurching, so I try daydreaming about the climb I'm going to attempt in the middle of the Grand Canyon two months from now. But the suggestion doesn't take. A degenerative fatigue and malaise overcome me, and I repeatedly fall like a drunken sailor as I continue staggering toward Bassett Peak.

When I reach what looks like a dull mirage of that peak, dots are swirling in front of my eyes and I feel like heaving. I stick my fingers in my mouth and try to throw up in hopes of ridding myself of the debilitating bug that's apparently infected me. But I only gag and spit out a vile, bitter-tasting phlegm. I want to turn back, but there is no place to turn back to. I want there to be an easy way out of here, but I can't fly as the redtail hawks now do, soaring lazily overhead. I no longer *want* the "running power," I *need* it! But Apaches didn't come by that knowledge easily, and for a non-Indian, I now realize, it's out of my reach. I want to cry.

And I wonder if mountain man James Ohio Pattie cried when he descended from the crest of the Galiuro Mountains somewhere near here while traversing the range between March 31 and April 2, 1824. Wrote Pattie: "On the 31st, we reached the top of the mountain, and fed upon the last meat of our beavers. We met with no traces of game…. On the morning of the first of April, we commenced descending the mountain, from the side of which we could discern a plain before us, which, however, it required two severe days to reach…we had nothing to eat or drink. In descending from the icy mountains, we were surprised to find how warm it was on the plains. On reaching them, I killed an antelope, of which we drank the warm blood; and however revolting the recital may be, to us it was refreshing, tasting like fresh milk."

There are no antelope in sight to quench my thirst, even if I'd carried a gun to kill one for survival rations. I'd given up hunting and guns not long after my Grandpa died, and since then I'd resolved only to carry a knife while traveling alone in the wilderness. I am low on food, but I am too sick to hold anything down anyway. My bota bags are both dry, and my lips are cracked and bleeding. I keep running, through dirt, ice, and snow; my lungs heave in and out:

hih-huh, hih-huh, hih-huh, hih-huh. A whirling blur of synaptic images shrouds me for hours on end in deep snow and vicious brush. Tiny acacia thorns tear at me like the claws of a thousand scrawny alley cats, and they always win, shredding my arms and legs with painfully long, blood-streaked scratches. My movement is more atavistic than conscious. I'm getting colder. I keep running. I've got to find the sign. I'm now drooling.

By the time I reach the weather-blasted trail marker sticking out of the brush like a sawed-off street sign, I'm reduced to a whimpering little boy who strayed too far from home. What looks like huge block letters proves that, despite the fear and doubt I had traveling blindly through the brush, my dead reckoning was right: RATTLESNAKE CREEK. There it is! It's my ticket back from oblivion.

I think.

And I start mumbling with joy as I gallop off the west side of an unnamed peak called BM 7,099 confident that I know the way back home. I am nothing more than a runner now; I no longer have a personal identity as I once knew it. I am merely movement from one physical clue to the next. And each time I sniff out a blaze mark on a tree, an old piece of trail, a small pile of rocks, I cry out, relieved that I'm actually tying this incipient track together through the feline jungle of upper Rattlesnake Creek.

I follow the serpentine path back and forth into the underbrush until it deadends in the catclaw. WHEOOWW!!! I backtrack, always running, but they're all deadends now. I throw up, but I am too cold and anxious to stop and clean the foul slime off my shirt. So down I go, hopping from one boulder to the next, moving not as the runner I once knew, but more like an infantile animal trying to make sense of the tenuous footing along the sharp rocks and narrow walls of the creek. This is treacherous ground, even if I wasn't sick. One slip and it'll be a bloody and agonizing crawl out of here to God knows where. I can't think about the consequences, though, or the mere thought of breaking a leg or reinjuring my stiff ankle will distract me long enough to turn my sublimated fears into reality. All I can do now is move, instinctively. Running.

Gravity and declivity control my running speed, until I am going faster and faster; the painful jarring shudders through my legs as if somebody is whipping them against the ground. WHAP! WHAP! WHAP! But I can't stop. A furious series of steep drops unreels before me and I continue leaping like a wild man until I suddenly realize I'm making seven-foot jumps back and forth across a creek, and it's running with water. I stop, frequently, and gulp the untreated water from my cupped hands, but never for more than a few moments at a time. Running is everything now.

The setting sun is blanketing Rattlesnake Canyon with a cold shadow just as I reach the Power's Mine road, and my running becomes a race with the edge of the shadow wall. If I can somehow stay ahead of it before it reaches Power's Garden, everything will be all right, but if that dark veil eclipses my arrival, well, I'm scared. It's not even a thought process, only a reaction to the tenuous threshold between day and night.

It's twilight when I finally reach Power's Garden, which I'd been promising myself was the end of this run. "Chris!" I scream. No answer. "Chris!…Chris!" Still no answer. Frenzied, I start racing around the old line shack, but it's bolted shut. Signs warn to stay the hell out. I try to busy my mind with synaptic images of this historic homestead. 1918, a tragic shootout, the largest manhunt in the history of Arizona…but I can't take my mind off Chris; I imagine the worst. Where is she?

I'd first met Chris in the Valley of the Sun a year earlier. Her reputation as a photographer preceded her, and we frequently talked by phone. Our friendship grew and we decided to join forces, move back to Prescott, and split living expenses.

The cheapest, most respectable place we could find was a small studio apartment next to a funeral home. We pow-wowed over the workspace, and it was agreed that I could use the kitchen table throughout the summer to bang out my novel of love, violence, and native pathways called *White Coyote…Running*, while Chris remodeled the small bathroom into a darkroom where she turned out masterful prints.

Frequent visits to Chris's darkroom revealed the depth of her ability to capture the essence of people in her portraits. Hanging, dripping wet, from a spiderweb of thin steel wires were black-and-white images of people from a world I hadn't known before: an eight-year-old girl carrying her month-old sister through the streets of Antigua, Guatemala; a Mao tribeswoman trading opium on the Burmese border of northern Thailand; El Zarco, a Chicano sculptor, firing a Zuñiga-influenced bronze in Tepoztlán, Mexico. These were the exotic locales Chris had ventured to, and from those travels she brought back soul-stirring images that demonstrated her willingness to expose a part of herself in order to make a picture that needed no explanation. My own photographic efforts seemed like footnotes by comparison. Little did I know at the time that my intense exposure to Chris's work would leave a lasting imprint on me that would soon change the course of my own future, from that of a camara-starved actor laboring on the novel he only dreamed of starring in, to an aspiring photojournalist who, like Chris, wanted to capture the people, places and events that shape our lives and the world in which we live.

Chris also had studied a difficult form of Buddhist meditation called *vipassana*, or "mindfulness," while in Chiang Mai, Thailand, a few years earlier; part of the practice required Chris to walk for hours on end across a teak-wood floor of a small, empty room called a *gutee*, meditating solely about the acts of walking and breathing and their individual components. So I assumed Chris was far more adept at living and working within the constraints of a suffocatingly small studio apartment while I grew restless with the prolonged inactivity writing demanded. In fact, the more I worked alongside Chris the more I came to realize that the dog work of writing bore a strong resemblance to the long, punishing sessions of homework I sometimes faced at detention after school. Photography took you outside that stultifying room to discover places and people, to see the world and life. Comparing the two, I knew a change was in the air for me.

But before I made the leap from writing to photography, I frequently broke out of my cell and roamed the mountains of Prescott looking for new and exciting places to run the daily 10 miles I tried to maintain. That was the magic number, 10. I don't know where it came from, but I decided one night while running on the Salt River Indian Reservation that if you could run 10 miles a day there wasn't anything you couldn't do. But running 10 miles a day in the high mountains of Prescott was a whole different ball game, and that made for daily running adventures that ultimately led to my attempting Granite Mountain at about the time I burned my first shoeboxful of rejection slips.

Once I survived that wild 12 mile run, as clumsy and as ignorant as I'd been, I quickly embarked on a string of other runs in hopes of building on the knowledge of running wild I was learning, both through the trial and error of running through a barrage of canyons, mountains, and desert, and through ethnographic accounts and bits and pieces of historical fact I'd ferreted out during painstaking, often fruitless, hours of research at local libraries. One gem I'd discovered was about the Apaches, who used a "running power"...

But that's why I was now in way over my head.

I break down again and again as I run and stumble along the boulder-strewn canyon bottom, but I'm too exhausted and dehydrated to cry. Tears no longer form, and my legs are too painful to move by conscious thought; they are controlled by something beyond me now. That something is fear. Darkness completely engulfs me as I continue thrashing down the floodswept black gash of Rattlesnake Canyon, and I'm frightened beyond anything I've ever imagined.

The sound of rushing water screams at me. Tree limbs hit me like night sticks. Brush tears at me. Logs trip me. Rocks stop me, just long enough to let me know that something other than conscious thought is controlling my movement, as if I'm now outside myself watching someone else struggle through the oil-black, thigh-deep torrent. I feel weird and unworldly, as if I haven't been here before; but I *have* been here before, with a friend on a 250 mile trek from the Chincahua Mountains to Aravaipa Canyon. The water's cold, I know it is, but it doesn't feel that way, only wet. The only thought I have now is that somehow my eyes are still open and that my body—not me—is still running. And it won't, can't stop!

The wind is gusting across Power's Hill, and I am shivering violently with cold, wet chills when I finally crawl out of Rattlesnake Canyon and head across the black plain to Aravaipa Creek. I have to stop and start a fire, now, or I'm going to die. I hastily gather black shapes of wood, but my hands tremble as my stiff fingers strip damp bark away from the dry tinder beneath; without it, there will be no fire tonight. I pile it, shaking uncontrollably, the tufts of tinder, the incrementally larger pieces of kindling, into a small tepee sheltered from the wind by my body, which had grown rigid with cramps; squatting there, I'm becoming a cold, knotted ball of blood, muscle, and bone. I struggle desperately to stay coherent long enough to ignite the fire.

One strike. Another. Nothing. The wind is howling around me and my body continues to shake uncontrollably. I take in a full deep breath, then exhale in an attempt to control my spastic shivering; it doesn't help. I strike the knife along the flint again. Nothing. I strike it again and again, scraping the razor-sharp steel down the length of the flint, showering the ground with a celebration of dying sparks. Nothing. I try again and again. Finally a single spark takes hold of the dry yucca fiber, and still shaking in fits and stammers, I add small bits of kindling to that tiny, miraculous flame, afraid I'll snuff it out by adding too much fuel too quickly. Piece by piece, I slowly pile on more and more wood, as if I'm stoking a furnace, until the eruption of flames singes my face and eyebrows and my body slowly begins to warm. When it does, I know I'm going to survive, and that Chris, mindfully pacing somewhere out there in the middle of the night next to her car, has been unable to ford Aravaipa Creek, which is swollen with the same runoff that boiled down Rattlesnake Canyon. Dreaming the fire, I no longer have any idea what "running power" is.

Author and photojournalist John Annerino has photographed and written nine books, including the critically acclaimed border saga Dead in Their Tracks: Crossing America's Desert Borderlands*, and a photo/art book on American cowboys and cowgirls,* Roughstock: The Toughest Events in Rodeo. *This story was excerpted from* Running Wild: Through the Grand Canyon on the Ancient Path.

✷

Two college students were exploring the hills near the Whetstone Mountains in 1971 outside of Benton, Arizona, when they suddenly caught a whiff of guano coming from a fissure in the rocks. They knew that the possibility of a cave system existed as the area had considerable quantities of limestone which makes for prime caving. They squirmed through the crack and found themselves in a modest cave which had a small round hole at the back. Air was blowing through the hole and the smell of guano was very strong. They enlarged the hole and had found themselves in a virgin cave that opened onto other equally large caverns. After they had gotten over their initial excitement at discovering a brand new cave, they suddenly realized that they were the only people on the face of the earth who knew where it was. From that point on, Randy Tufts and Gary Tenen pledged themselves to secrecy and took a stewardship role in developing the caverns that they initially called Xanadu. In 1999, and more than twenty-five years after their original discovery, the Kartchner Cavern State Park opened to the general public.

—SO'R and JO'R

CRAIG CHILDS

Seeking Father
Kino's *Tinajas*

Knowing where to find a water hole can mean
the difference between life and death.

MY INTEREST IN FATHER KINO CAME FROM A PROJECT I PER-
formed for the U.S. Fish and Wildlife Service while working on a
master's thesis in Desert Studies. For thirty-seven days, I walked
through the Cabeza Prieta Wildlife Refuge, onto cathedral desert
peaks made of white-quartz granite, looking for water holes. Those
holes, called *tinajas*, are rare and well-hidden among canyons and
pinnacles. Natural cisterns, they sometimes hold thousands of gallons of rainwater.

My assignment called for me to map these *tinajas*, to venture
into the cracks of the Cabeza Prieta with a global positioning
device, marking the latitude and longitude of each water source,
recording the volume of water and then the array of invertebrates
living there.

The first map of *tinajas* I found, and one of the most useful,
was the elegantly drawn work of Father Eusebio Francisco Kino, a
seventeenth-century Jesuit missionary-explorer. It was rendered to
paper in 1701, and nearly 300 years later I carried a copy of it
with my gear, unfolding it across the sands as I rested in the shade
of ironwood trees. The side borders of the map were divided into
strikingly accurate scales of latitude. Kino's handwriting was clean,

each work given mindful strokes; his serifs not too bold, yet not obscured.

In this particular area, he marked and named La Tinaja (the jar), Agua Escondida (hidden water), and Aguaje de la Luna (watering place of the moon).

I drew my fingers over those places, those great swaths of land stitched together by nothing but water holes and the tracks of Father Kino as he sought one *tinaja* and then the next.

The desert is a place to carry only what you need and no more. Across the vast Sonoran expanse, Father Kino brought few items. He was not a minimalist. He was, rather, an essentialist. He carried the basic gear of survival: a wool blanket, canteens, and devices for fire starting. His black robe he kept folded in a leather saddlebag, reserved for formal encounters. Items for trading, such as rosary beads and metal knife blades, also went into the saddlebags. There were devotional necessities, including a chalice, a gourd of wine, and bread and water for Mass, which was performed on the desert floor each morning. A crucifix, probably made of brass and inlaid with a wooden corpus, hung around his neck.

Belongings of most interest to this story were his telescope — small enough to be kept handy—his field notes, and his astrolabe for studying the stars. He would withdraw the astrolabe in the evening, measuring with it the angle between the horizon and certain celestial bodies. Then he wrote the measurements in his notes, adding coordinates day after day across the desert.

During the sunlight hours, he would dismount his horse on the smooth, endless *bajadas*, and with his telescope scan the distant mountain ranges, which looked like the masts of tall ships just past the horizon. His knowledge of the landscape of what is now southwestern Arizona and northwestern Mexico grew much each day.

When, in 1678, Kino was first sent to this place, a little-known region called Pimeria Alta, he had no desire to be there. He had studied cartography, mathematics, and cosmology with the hope of serving in the Orient. Jesuit mathematicians were said to be of much use in the Chinese court.

During his scholarly studies, he made his geographic interest known through letters to the Father General. When his assignment came, it was to be either the Philippines or New Spain, what is now known as Mexico. He drew lots with another padre, and did not draw the Philippines.

Disappointed, he pressed for an assignment change, sending entreating letters to the Duchess of Aveiro y Arcos, a patroness of Jesuit missions in the Orient. Even after arriving in Mexico, he sought to join a missionary entourage bound for the East, but his pleas were fruitless.

At the age of thirty-six, Kino, a scholar who had studied under premier Renaissance cosmographers, arrived in a rugged desert that had yet to be mapped.

As I searched for *tinajas* among boulders and deep canyons, I contemplated Kino's own odyssey. I read his notes, which first surfaced early this century when a researcher acquired them from a Mexico City library. From them, I retraced his steps through the Cabeza Prieta, southeast of Yuma.

His routes there parallel a pathway now known as El Camino del Diablo, "the devil's highway," strewn with countless stories of death, and with graves scattered among mountain ranges.

In this land, I studied Kino's record, making computations on how long it took him to get from Aguaje de la Luna to Agua Escondida, what time of the day he took a siesta, and how many more hours he spent in motion. I read of his arrival at Aguaje de la Luna before it was named, how in the light of the full moon he climbed through sharpened rocks until stumbling across this massive *tinaja*.

During his twenty-four years in this country, Kino made more than fifty *entradas*, journeys of between 100 and 1,000 miles. On each *entrada*, he kept prudent notes and ritually employed his astrolabe to place the land onto a map. Hidden in his notes lurks a peculiar fascination with this desert. I take a risk in saying this, but I came to believe that his personal mission here was not the conversion of the indigenous people but to understand a place he had, originally, never wanted to see. His last thoughts before sleep under the powdering of desert stars may have been not of heaven but of the extent of the dry and embittered Pimeria Alta.

Kino brought to Pimeria Alta a yearning to know, a thirst that his teacher, the famous cosmologist Athanasius Kircher, had undoubtedly helped along. Instead of continuing his scholarly and esoteric work in the Chinese court, Kino faced the distressing but visually enchanting landscape of the Sonoran Desert.

Instead of rebelling against it, he was swallowed by it. He learned how to manage livestock during drought and how to find water for himself. His humble, pleading letters to the Duchess of Aveiro y Arcos ceased.

No other skyline is as raw and laid bare as this. Kino must have seen here each of the elements that Kircher had so diligently tried to express. The fires of Earth, the shimmering air above, and the sweet, rare peace of water.

Kino was the first to proclaim California not an island but a seamless part of North America. Usually this type of mapping was done from ships that followed coastlines. Kino did it from the ground, traveling across the desert and inquiring of those he converted. His curiosity grew markedly from month to month, as he sought ways to show that California was an uninterrupted segment of this desert.

Kino's legendary generosity played a key role in his quest. He commonly offered gifts to the Indians, sometimes even his personal belongings. He often gave livestock along with instructions on how to care for the creatures. In return for his gifts, a group of Yuman Indians gave him some blue shells. Kino admired the gifts, writing that they were "curious and beautiful blue shells, which, so far as I know, are found only in the opposite, or western coast of California." The shells set him to thinking about a passage to that far coast, and he wrote that "shortly, by Divine Grace, we shall try to find it out and see it with all exactness."

Later the Cocomaricopa Indians offered Kino a holy cross laced with a string of twenty blue shells, the same kind of shells he'd received from the Yumans. So Kino gathered members of nearby tribes, inquiring about the origin of the shells and the extent of the land. He conducted talks late into the night. In those long discussions, Kino informed the people about Christianity, as was his duty, but he seemed to concentrate more on interests geographic.

He wrote, "I made further and further inquiries as to whence came the blue shells, and all asserted that there were none in the nearest sea of California, but that they come from other lands more remote."

His search for those other lands more remote took him across the Cabeza Prieta numerous times until he had proved that a person could walk to California. The crossings required a specialized knowledge of *tinajas*, so Kino traveled under the tutelage of indigenous guides. As he was led to the various *tinajas*, he marked them on his map. They would become the lifeline for people traveling between what is now Mexico and California.

After Kino, though, this lifeline became less known. His map went unused. Hundreds upon hundreds of people perished trying to cross to the California gold fields. The lack of water led to those delirious deaths, but water was there all along. La Tinaja and Agua Escondida were often full to their edges while people died in the desert beyond.

From reading Kino's words, I came to know him as a patient and deliberate man. Each day he celebrated Mass. His calibration of the astrolabe required diligence and a steady hand. He studied the horizon many times a day with his telescope, reading the distant mountain ranges. Kino did not rush to cross Cabeza Prieta because his questions could not be answered quickly, but only with judicious observation.

Upon reaching a *tinaja* I believe Kino had located, I steadied my hand on the tape measure, thinking back some 300 years to when the Jesuit arrived there. I slowed my breathing and measured the smooth disk of water, water so pleasing that days could be spent just staring at it.

The *tinaja* measured slightly more than fifteen feet across at the widest point. I imagined Kino's eyes, his posture, his thirst to understand this land. From my pack I retrieved my global positioning device, turned it on, and waited for it to gather signals from satellites that passed against the stars. The display gave coordinates: North 32° 18'51.2" West 113° 48'.

I recorded this in my notes, then out of my palm drank water from the *tinaja* that had once kept Kino alive.

Craig Childs is a former river guide, natural history field instructor, and writer who lives near Crawford, Colorado. This trek was part of his master's thesis on the natural history of water in American deserts. He cautions would-be visitors to the harsh Cabeza Prieta that water holes are difficult to locate.

*

Chimayo, which is just outside of Taos, is one of the most unusual pilgrimage sites in the United States. Here a cross was found near the Santa Cruz River in the early 1800s when light was seen by a farmer emerging from the ground. The miracles attributed to the dirt of this sacred ground have made El Santuario de Chimayo a holy place that is visited by those seeking cures from around the world. Such places attract all manner of characters. Eighty-year-old Fr. Roca restored the site forty years ago and still keeps secret the exact location of the source of the sacred dirt that is brought to a room inside the Santuario for the public to bring home. His chief assistant is a woman from California who was once a volunteer in the Israeli army.

—Sean O'Reilly, "Notes from the Southwest"

PART THREE

GOING YOUR OWN WAY

MARIANA GOSNELL

Where the Wind
Takes You

Flying across America in her single engine Luscombe Silvaire,
she sees the Southwest from a different vantage point.

PAST CLARKE AIRPORT AT GALLUP, NEW MEXICO LAY ALL SORTS
of Western wonders: craters, canyons, hot springs, stone arches,
painted deserts, lakes that had once been canyons, salt flats that were
sometimes lakes. I couldn't make up my mind where to go next.
Three briefers had been on duty at once when I got to Gallup, and
I asked them for ideas. One said Monument Valley. Another said
Canyon de Chelly. The third insisted on the Grand Canyon. After
Guthrie got there I asked his advice too. Almost in anger, he said
he couldn't think of anyplace worth seeing in the lower forty-
eight, then relented. Lake Powell, he admitted, was "spectacular."
So in the morning I decided to try all four places, fly a large
inverted U starting with Canyon de Chelly and ending with the
Grand Canyon. Starting, however, involved figuring out where
Canyon de Chelly was. The chart showed only a series of broken
blue lines ("intermittent streams") about where I thought it should
be. Guthrie was gone by the time I got up (having left some grape-
fruit juice in the refrigerator for me—still looking out for travelers) so I asked the briefer who came on duty after him. "You see
that chimney?" he asked, leading me outside and pointing toward
a range of mountains, one of which was higher than the others.

"Well, aim to the left of it and you'll be here"—he touched one of the blue lines, no different from the other blue lines so far as I could see and miles on the chart from the words "prominent canyon." "*That's* Canyon de Chelly."

I did indeed find a crevice to the left of the chimney and followed it westward, hoping the briefer was right (there were times when you'd like confirming signboards aloft). Narrow and high-walled at first, it gradually opened up, as if reluctantly yielding its ancient secrets, the walls growing lower, moving apart, until the whole thing emptied out into the valley of Chinle. However, it didn't yield many of its secrets to me. Even throttled back I flew down it so fast I couldn't spot as I'd wanted to any of the apartment-style pueblos carved into the rock walls by the old cliff dwellers. Out of consideration for the sightseers below, I didn't allow myself a second run, but I felt unfulfilled by the first. By Jeep, I figured, the run beginning to end would have taken a day, on foot as much as three days. By plane it took under twenty minutes. When I found myself at the end of the canyon, I felt as if I'd gobbled a gourmet meal in the time it took to shake out the napkin.

In compensation, Chinle was a lovely valley, of wide, green meadows with cascading pale-orange cliffs on the side away from Chelly and a dry wash running up the middle. I turned and flew north over the wash, toward Monument Valley. A few cows were standing here and there on the grass, as well as in the wash, and a few abandoned cars were standing on the grass too, like cows, except being metal they caught the sun as I passed and gave off tiny bursts of light. Where I first started following the wash, it was almost flush with the fields around it, but gradually it sank in relation to them until it had walls on either side maybe twenty-five feet high. In places niches had been gouged out of the walls by erosion, and in several of the niches I could see something green—sagebrush?—growing part of the way up, which gave them the look from the air of little outdoor amphitheaters, with stage scenery already in place for sylvan dramas.

After sixty miles, a highway slashed across the wash, and on the other side of it was, I believed (again I wouldn't have minded a floating signboard), the southernmost section of Monument Valley. From there I flew pretty much free-form, to a monument I liked the shape of, then around and around and sometimes over it, watching the rock contours bend and bulge and contract as I flew by, peering out at spires and into the recesses between spires, then picking another monument and flying the miles of empty scrubland to it, circling it. On one long passage between monuments I flew over a Navajo hogan, a six-sided, metal-roofed dwelling with two white geese attacking the dirt beside it, and tried to imagine what it would be like to live daily with these monuments, as if they were ordinary. Some of those I'd been circumnavigating were charming, gay even—crooked chimneypots, coneheads in capes too long for them, chubby thumbs— but most were dignified, imposing, keepers of secrets too. I imagined they could serve a local resident as mountains, icons, sculpture, and the architecture of the neighborhood all at once. What a skyline

As I cruised around northeastern Arizona, I repeatedly had the sensation that I was traveling along an old sea floor. The landscape would seem to be thirsting for the water that had once been everywhere, the canyons would seem to plunge to murky depths; the mesas and monuments to be remnant shallows. Even the vegetation contributed to the illusion: sinuous wands of ocotillo wavered like seaweed, cacti bristled like sea urchins encrusted on the rock. Ship rocks—the ancient volcanic necks eroded in Gibraltar-like slants that crop up here and there on the Colorado Plateau—seemed to belong to a fleet sailing a ghost sea.
—Alex Shoumatoff, *Legends of the American Desert: Sojourns in the Greater Southwest*

they produced! Years ago I got a postcard from young friends who visited Monument Valley shortly before one of them died, and on the back of the card they had copied lines from the well-known White Corn By Navajo creation-myth poem: "Beauty before us, with it we wander/Beauty above us, with it we wander/Beauty all around us, with it we wander/On the beautiful trail are we, with it we wander." Beauty was the ordinary, everyday thing here, and when it came time for me to go down I wasn't ready to forget it. I landed at Oljato, an airport on the western side of the valley, just over the state line in Utah, with the idea of canceling my flight plan, getting more fuel, and taking off again, wandering again in the valley, Beauty below me.

Oljato was a Navajo trading post with a "composition" airstrip beside it (whatever the composition was, it was a pale, sickly green color). Between the strip and the post ran a fence of thin wire strung between small wooden poles, too low and too weak, it seemed to me, to stop anything from wandering onto the runway except maybe an exhausted sheep. I stepped over the fence—there was no gate—and walked up a path to the front door of the post, a one-story, mud-brown building. Inside was a modest-sized room painted a slightly darker green than the runway. It had shelves running from the floor to the ceiling on two sides, and on the shelves, arranged neatly but according to no scheme I could figure out, were among other things, bolts of electric-blue and electric-pink cloth, horse saddles, plastic bracelets, metal lunch boxes, a bed pillow, cowboy boots, umbrellas, potholders, Jockey shorts, paste-on tattoos, hand saws, aprons, Frisbees, sequins, nylon blankets, tweezers, suede shirts, penny candy, chiffon scarves, and canned and packaged food.

At the back a Navajo woman was standing behind a counter. There was nobody else in the room. I noticed a radio on a shelf near the counter and assumed it was the Unicom; I also assumed it was turned off because I didn't hear any of the faint static fuzz, like breathing, a radio of that type puts out when it's set to receive. Why have a Unicom, I thought grumpily, if you kept if turned off? I told the woman I needed fuel for my plane. "Mr. Smith isn't here," she said, as if that settled it. Mr. Smith? "He's got the key to the pumps." Uh-oh. Before I left Clarke, a briefer had told me, "If you go to Monument Valley it'll be a one-way trip, since you can't go anywhere else on your tanks, not without refueling. There's only one place to refuel up there and that's Oljato, but don't worry,

Oljato's always got fuel." Uh-huh. I pictured Mr. Smith splayed under some beach umbrella, or hunched beside the bed of an ailing mother, the key to the pumps deep in his pocket, and I ran through my options. Taking off with the little fuel remaining in my tanks and hoping for a sixty-mph tailwind all the way to Lake Powell; draining fuel from somebody else's tanks to fill mine (the Luscombe was the only plane on the strip); using automobile gas and risking a fouled plug or vapor lock over rocky terrain; kicking myself for not phoning ahead. Then I heard the woman say, in answer to a question I must have asked, "Tonight, Mr. Smith will be back tonight."

So I waited on fuel, instead of weather this time, but I didn't much mind because I had never been to a trading post and was curious. When I went out to tie down my plane I noticed a handwritten sign on one of the locked fuel pumps. "OLJATO HAS AN IDEAL CLIMATE," it went. "NEVER TOO HOT AND NEVER TOO COLD. NEVER TOO HOT IN WINTER, NEVER TOO COLD IN SUMMER." Oh that Mr. Smith must be a sketch!

It was too hot to wait by the strip, so I went back to the post, and by then several customers had come in, a Navajo woman with a baby and two young Navajo men. She sat on one end of a short bench, a bit tentatively, as if she might be chased off at any minute, although it was the only place in the room to sit. I soon caught on that the post didn't exactly encourage hanging out, in the tradition of general stores, which trading posts certainly were. I bought things for lunch—baloney, potato chips, and a large, round, soft, prepackaged loaf of unsliced white bread, rather like a communal hamburger bun—then sat at the other end of the bench from the woman with the baby and made sandwiches for myself by tearing off chunks of the bread, pulling the chunks apart, and stuffing the openings with baloney and potato chips. As more people came in I began to feel self-conscious, eating in front of them all, the potato chips snapping. The mood in the room was constrained, almost formal; the talk—what talk there was, all of it in Navajo—brief and carried on in low tones. There weren't any hearty greetings or long-winded exchanges, in the tradition of general stores, although I guessed most of the customers had driven a fair distance to get there. The post was quiet even with people in it, *awkwardly* quiet from my perspective. There I sat, right in the middle of traffic, almost underfoot, sometimes making the only sound in the room, smashing the potato chips with my teeth, masticating publicly.

Lunch over, I leaned back against a display case and watched customers come and go. A bell above the door would ring and the screen door would open and somebody would enter (twice it was a woman with silver-and-turquoise jewelry in her dark hair pulled back in a bun, a gathered three-tiered, ankle-length skirt—in one case the skirt was purple, the other aqua—and white sneakers), approach the counter, say something softly to the woman behind it, then wait, usually without saying anything more. Even teenagers in jeans and t-shirts didn't do anything more rambunctious than that. One white family came in, looking like Appalachian poor, the girls pale and skinny with peaked faces and patched clothes, the father picking up his mail and buying antifreeze (for which climate? I wondered). They didn't say much either.

One Navajo man particularly intrigued me. He was about forty and powerfully built. His cheeks, forehead, and chin had the strong, sharp planes of the old Indian portraits. His hair was pulled back into a ponytail bound top to bottom with strands of white string and pulled up to form a loop on the back of his head. The same white string had been wound around his high-crowned black hat, as a hatband. He spoke to the clerk in Navajo, and I stood up, feigning a stretch, so I could see what it was that he had ordered, what an obviously authentic Native American would choose to buy, probably for lunch. She took one thing out of a refrigerator, one thing out of a case, one thing off a shelf, and set them on the counter. There for me to see and marvel at were a six-pack of 7-Up, a can of Spam, and a loaf of Tip Top bread. I sat down. What had I expected? Wolf jerky? Dehydrated bear paw?

I was suffering from a case of Indian awe. It had started probably when I was a kid back in Ohio and read about the special powers of Indians, how they could smell weather on the wind, talk to muskrats, take the pain of sharp sticks through the collarbone, etc., etc.; amplified by adult guilt about what my kind had done to theirs; and complicated by my current tendency to interpret solemnity as spiritual strength. The gravity of these Navajos made me shy, as if they could see through me, knew I was flying around just for fun, or for some vague enlightenment that they had already attained. I realized I wanted to impress them or at least not look stupid to them. At one point I got up and looked into a miniature display case on top of the larger case I'd been leaning against, to take an unfeigned stretch and pass the time, and I found several pieces of "Indian" jewelry inside with machine-stamped designs and plastic "turquoise." Who bought it? I wondered. Was it the jewelry equivalent of Spam and did the Navajos buy it? One item was clearly handmade, though, and looked old. I lifted it out so I could get a better look at it. It consisted of a dozen or so embossed silver rectangles, each rectangle about the size of a large postage stamp, with a leather cord strung through them, to form a belt. I wrapped the belt around my waist and maneuvered myself in front of a mirror on the countertop so I could see how I looked in it. I heard a strange sound: laughter! A soft giggling from all the women in the room—an older woman, two teenage girls, and the clerk—all trying not to giggle but unable to stop. What, I wondered, was so funny about a belt? About *me* in a belt? Was this a *man's* belt? A belt for brides? Babies? The *dead*?

One of the girls looked at me shyly and tapped her temple. I didn't understand. "For the head," she whispered. Ohh, I said, "a *head*band!" More giggling. She pointed higher on her head. Oh, "a *hat*band!" I said and laughed too. Then, although I had been thinking of buying the belt, when it was a belt, I laid it back in the case and closed the door on it, not wanting to appear any more stupid to them than I already had, stupid tourist.

Shortly after that an old woman came into the post and walked straight up to the bench instead of the counter and gestured for me to come outside with her. She climbed into a truck where another woman was already sitting and began pulling from a large plastic bag pairs of crossed sticks with yarns of different colors wound around them in a diamond pattern: Ojos de Dios. The things were all about two feet long, and one by one she held them up for me to see, her movements saying what she evidently couldn't in English, "This one?" "Do you want to buy this one?" In my turn I told her, using my hands a lot, that I had flown an airplane in—see, that one over there, the only one—and I didn't have room for anything so large—crowded cockpit, no room, sorry, sorry, sorry. I *was* sorry. As I watched her put the Ojos de Dios back in the plastic bag, one by one, I felt, again, unable to do the right thing.

Sometime in mid-afternoon I discovered another room in the post, one behind the store, a combination "museum" of old Navajo artifacts (tomahawks, squaw dresses, medicine-man kits) and display area for new Navajo crafts, rugs and baskets mostly, for sale. A sofa in the middle had a tall stack of rugs on one half so someone could sit on the other half and go through the stack and pick out a rug to buy. I headed right for that other half, made myself as inconspicuous as possible behind the stack of rugs, and dozed off. Now and then I would wake up to see, tacked up along the dark, wooden beams of the ceiling and walls, dozens of old Indian baskets, all of them round and shallow like plates, with red, brown, and black fibers forming designs, of birds, swastikas, and mazes, against pale grounds. Some of the designs were complicated and some were simple, but all had one thing in common: a break, sometimes no more than a single strand of grass, in the finished pattern. No border on the plates were ever closed, no silhouette remained intact. Beaks were always open, circles broken. "So the spirit can get out," the woman behind the counter said when I asked her on her way through to the bathroom. For a couple of hours I half-sat, half-lay on half of the sofa, content knowing there was always a ray of light coming through somewhere, a door left ajar, a straw to breathe through....

Thus the afternoon ticked away, punctuated with sounds from other parts of the post: soft voices in the main store, the doorbell tinkling, muffled noises from trucks pulling up in front. At one point the sounds grew louder and went on longer and I deduced that Mr. Smith had something to do with it. I went into the main room and saw a lanky, round-shouldered man of a certain age wearing a bemused expression, as you'd expect of someone who'd put up a sign like the one at the pumps. I told him I'd been waiting for fuel and he went right out and gave me some, but when I mentioned that I was getting it so I could go flying around the valley as soon as he finished giving it to me, he didn't encourage me. "I'd think about it," he said. "The air's pretty choppy." I decided he should know, but not flying around the valley left me with a lot of time to fill before bedtime, and no place to fill it except around the empty strip. The trading post closed at five o'clock, and it was almost five by then. I began bombarding Mr. Smith with questions about flying in Monument Valley, so after a while, unable to get away from me but wanting to get out of the sun, he asked me inside to answer them. He lived with his wife in rooms back of the store, and while she busied herself across the living room, he and I sat on rocking chairs near the door and talked about flying. He didn't introduce her but he did mention her; it was really *her* trading post, he said.

Years ago, he recounted, he had been a cowboy, helping the federal government reduce stock on public lands. One day he stopped by the trading post; it was the same day that the owner's second daughter was home from school. Three weeks later he and she were married and he became what he is now, "the husband of an Indian trader." (Bemused look.) "We really were *traders* back then," he said. "The Indians would give us wool, sheep, blankets, and cattle, and we'd give those to the wholesale house, then the wholesale house would give us groceries and we'd give those to the Indians. It was uranium that started the cash flow. Now we don't buy lambs or wool anymore, we don't build or repair wagons the way we used to, and the Indians usually pay by check, from welfare or the new coal mine on Black Mesa, but otherwise, outside of a few tourists, things aren't much different than they were at the beginning. If an Indian wants something notarized or a check cashed or car parts or somebody to write a letter for him, he still comes here."

The flying got started during World War II, and largely because of it. The reservation didn't have any paved roads then, and the Navajos used horses and wagons to get around. "We used horses and wagons too," said Mr. Smith, "except we had a bobtail truck for picking up groceries in the city once a month. Even in the truck we had to drive daylight-to-dark to go 150 miles; the road was mud and wagon ruts all the way. During the war there wasn't much fuel even for trucks, so a guy over in Farmington got the bright idea of flying around the reservation. He figured a small plane could do on 10 gallons of gas what a car could do on 200. He bought a T-craft [Taylorcraft] and flew it around to different trading posts to pick up food orders [there weren't any phones then]. If he couldn't land near a post, the Indians would clear a space for him with mules. *That* started the flying in the valley."

As for Mr. Smith, he started flying after the war, in a Tri-Pacer. "Even the big airports didn't have paved runways in those days and *nobody* had towers, so we pilots would look out for each other," he said. We'd call Unicom and say, 'Has the dust settled from the DC-3s yet?' and if somebody said no we'd circle ten miles out and then come in. Those days were heaven, just horses and airplanes, hardly any trucks.

"Then came the uranium, and there were Supercubs all over the valley, prospecting. Fighter pilots with thousands of hours were up in little bitty Cubs using scintillators. Every trading post had its own strip then. Ten or twelve planes were based here all the time, and we had a trailer park beside our runway with thirteen trailers in it. Five years later the uranium market fell flat and all the planes left. Then the government paved the roads in the reservation and that cut out the excuse for flying. A car needed as much fuel as an airplane but a car could carry a ton. Instead of it taking ten hours to get to town by truck, it took about three. By then some of the posts had already moved out to the highways to take care of the suckers from the city, and they didn't build any new strips. They didn't need to; it didn't pay to fly anymore. Even I went everywhere by car, except for emergencies, like hospital runs. I never flew for fun; I still don't. When you get over 150 horsepower [he owned a 230-hp Cessna 182] you don't fly for fun." I must have had an expression of pity on my face because he added quickly, "Well, I could go back to flying putt-putts, but when you've been married to someone that long [he'd had the 182 for ten years] you don't get divorced easily!"

Speaking of marriage, I asked Mr. Smith if he and his wife got the articles in the museum by trade (medicine-man kits for bread or baloney?). "I don't know," he said. "My wife collected those things. I didn't pay much attention. As far as I'm concerned, if you can't eat it, shoot it, fly, or ride it, it has no purpose in life. What good is it?" There was, however, one item he did get himself, and he couldn't eat, shoot, fly it, or ride it. He could, but he didn't, wear it. It was the wristwatch that Paul Mantz, one of the greatest stunt pilots in the history of filmmaking, was wearing when he died. Mantz had been in Arizona working on *Flight of the Phoenix*, a movie about a group of men who crash in the Sahara and save themselves by rebuilding, under the direction of a German "engineer" who turns out to be a toymaker, their wrecked twin-engine plane as a single-engine one. The single-engine "Phoenix" was jerry-built in fact as well as fiction, and at the time Mantz was to fly the contraption over the desert the temperature was eighty-five degrees. The director insisted on a third take, and during it the Phoenix split in half and Mantz went down with one half. He died instantly. His son sold the wristwatch, one of three Mantz always wore simultaneously whenever he flew cross-country air races, to Mr. Smith. It wasn't damaged in the crash and worked perfectly but Mr. Smith wouldn't even put it on. "I'm too Navajo," he said, "to wear a dead man's watch."

Yes, I thought, too Navajo. For despite the droll sign at the pumps and his look of bemusement and the fact that he invited me to talk when I made it hard for him not to, there was a reserve about him, a social distance unusual at little airports. Nothing about the trading post or the airport got too friendly. Even with Mr. Smith I felt like an outsider, a bit *de trop*, also unusual at little airports. But then Oljato wasn't primarily an airport; it was a trading post with an airstrip next to it.

It was still light out when I started making up my bed by the runway, and I found another hand-lettered sign taped to the pumps. BEWARE OF RATTLESNAKES, it said. This one probably wasn't a joke. All I could do to beware, though, was drag my sleeping bag closer to the runway and farther from the bushes. I sat on top of the bag and ate the last of the baloney, then lay down and looked at the sky.

From a passing truck somewhere I heard a sheep bleating; probably on its way to market, dead soon. The sky darkened and the stars came out. Some of them were shooting stars; it was the season of the Perseid shower. I lay awake and watched the stars for a while. The tip of one wing intruded on my view of them but I didn't mind. I like having the wingtip there, a dense black tongue against the more watery black of the sky, an anchor among the heaving stars.

After the sheep's cry I didn't hear anything for a long time. Lightning flashed somewhere to the east but so far off the sky just shook around the edges, without sound. Then a dog barked. Before long another dog barked. Then a third dog, and a fourth. Soon the sound of dogs barking came from many directions and distances, in many keys and states of arousal, so many dogs that I thought they might be in packs. One dog was so keyed up that he responded to the smallest grunt, the faintest moan of any other dog with a bark of his own. Then followed a long period of quiet, and sometime in the middle of the night the barking began again. I opened my eyes and looked up. The Milky Way was lined up perfectly with my plane, and my body. We were all on the same axis. Finally I felt right with the world in Oljato. Before dawn I woke again and washed with water from my Thermos, then did a line check, repacked my baggage, and sat on the strip and ate the last of the big bun. As I settled into the cockpit and was about to taxi out of my spot—at the very instant that I pushed the throttle forward—the sun broke over the hill in front of me and white light shattered, exploded on the sharp point of the stone. It was now day and I took off.

Mr. Smith's phone had been out of order—okay by him, he'd had it only two years anyway—so I couldn't file a flight plan before taking off. Nobody else knew where I was, even what state I was in, and nobody back home would think to go looking for me until at least a week had passed without their getting a phone call. So I'd be going solo on this leg, truly solo. Quickly I became all too aware of my solo status. I planned to fly back through the valley again, aiming north so I could intercept the San Juan River well upstream, then turn and follow the river west all the way to Lake Powell, then follow the lake (really a flooded canyon, long, thin and vine-like) to the airstrip at the far end, where I'd land, I sincerely hoped.

At the point where I picked the San Juan up, near the town of Mexican Hat, it flowed through a very deep, steep, and narrow gorge, yet it was the rock the gorge was cut from that made my breath come faster when I saw it. The surface of the rock all around was never flat, never smooth. Always it was either scored, pitted, chiseled, corrugated, or spiked. In places it had been cut into rectangles as regular as sidewalk squares but containing surfaces that were insanely irregular. Rocks lay on top of rocks down there, stuck up through other rocks, split from rocks to form steps of rock. What bushes there were looked small, round, and hard as rocks. I didn't see any place within gliding distance of my plane where I could put it down and survive, period. I might as well have been on Saturn, I figured, for all the good Earth would do me in case of trouble.

As I flew along I became preternaturally conscious of

Lake Powell is disturbingly beautiful. There is something surreal about huge quantities of water and a nearly 2,000-mile coastline in the middle of the desert. Perhaps the haunting quality of Lake Powell is due to the drowned presence of Glen Canyon, which was filled by the rising of water behind the massive Glen Canyon Dam in the early 1960s. This resurgence of large bodies of water would not, however, surprise a student of history and geology. At one point, prehistoric oceans and lakes covered much of the Southwest. Why is it that Arizona has the largest percentage of private boat owners in the United States? Could it be that the land and the people are all collectively sensing the presence of water like some long-vanished and vast phantom limb?

— Sean O'Reilly, "Notes from the Southwest"

---

my bones—hollow and crushable! My brain—squash on the rock! My insignificant size—I was like prey, my only chance in life to be as alert as prey. I opened my eyes wide. I took out my earplugs. I made no sudden moves. Slowly, not calling any attention, I picked up my camera, focused it—wanting a photo of this cold, Saturnian landscape—and pressed the shutter. The lens went black! I stiffened; if the camera failed, why not the airplane? Without realizing I was doing it at first, I ran my fingertips back and forth over the fabric of the ledge above my panel (black, to soften sun glare). In appeasement: "Nice plane, nice plane."

Weeks, hours went by as I kept on going down the river, scared but not expecting any favors. Then I became aware that something below was changing. At one point the waters of the river clearly ended and those of the lake began. The river had been a brownish color but the lake was a deep forest-green, with a band of white mineral-stained rock just above water level on either side, separating the green of the water from the rose of the canyon walls. Although the lake didn't appear to be much wider than the river had been, and the rocks on either side of it weren't much flatter, somehow with the change in colors everything seemed more...sympathetic. Inlets began appearing in the steep canyon walls, and there was a modest, almost cozy look to them. Halfway down one of the inlets I caught sight of a couple of small white boats, bobbing at anchor, and felt immediate relief at seeing this unexpected sign of humanity—lighthearted, carefree, frivolous humanity!

But as I kept on going down the lake, and as more small white boats made their appearances in more cozy inlets, and as the surface of the rock on either side developed an occasional smooth patch, I wasn't so sure. Then I saw, worming its way down the middle of Lake Powell, coming from out of nowhere it seemed, trailing a tiny white rickrack of spray...a water-skier. A *water-skier*? I was appalled. Too frivolous! I felt like some hermit who had just emerged from months of meditation and been forced to sit and watch a sitcom. There I'd been, suspended in ether by the thread of a single functioning camshaft, alone over one of the harshest, most unconsoling landscapes in the world, my thoughts reduced to core subjects, living, dying, luck, the unforgiving quality of stone, the perishability of the human frame, the lie of my personal mastery, what would my family think?, etc., etc., while on the water only a few miles away there was this wriggling water-skier!

Soon another water-skier swished into view, then another. Peeved at the sight of them, I began to curse the confusion in me, the way I sought isolation (had in fact delighted in the condition of being out of reach, without a flight plan), the invigorating effects of (reasonable amounts of) danger, the perspective that being in austere circumstances provides, the opportunity to forget so completely the daily gerbil wheel, etc., yet the nervousness I felt sometimes if I got these things; the need when I was at risk to be reminded of other's people's existence, then when signs of their existence presented themselves, the resentment at the intrusion and the yearning all over again for the separateness, the uncertainty, even the fear I left behind. "I can't take total freedom," I said to myself when frightened. "I must have it," I said when reassured. There they were again, those two old birds, just in a different set of feathers: dread and desire.

For many years Mariana Gosnell reported on medicine and science for Newsweek *magazine. She took a leave from her job for a three-month adventure, flying solo across America in her single-engine tailwheel airplane. She is the author of a record of that trip,* Zero Three Bravo: Solo Across America in a Small Plane, *from which this story was excerpted. She was born and grew up in Columbus, Ohio, and graduated from Ohio Wesleyan University.*

✳

There are wonderful, pine-forested towns such as Prescott in the Arizona high country where the lack of underbrush makes the forests look almost as if they have been vacuumed clean. Much further to the northeast and close to the border of New Mexico is the fishing village of Greer and the laid-back town of Show Low. These are great places for visitors and recreational amenities such as fine dining, fishing, horseback riding, snowmobile racing, and skiing remind one again and again that the Southwest is a land of constant surprises.

—Brenda Davis, "Driving Across the Southwest"

In Cahoots with Coyote

Come and howl with the woman.

RUMOR HAS IT, GEORGIA O'KEEFFE WAS WALKING IN THE DESERT; her long, black skirt swept the sand. She could smell bones. With palette and paintbrush in hand, she walked west to find them.

It was high noon, hot, but O'Keeffe would not be deterred. She walked down arroyos and up steep slopes; her instincts were her guide. Ravens cavorted above her, following this black-clothed creature through the maze of juniper and sage.

Suddenly, O'Keeffe stopped. She saw bones. She also saw Coyote and hid behind a piñon.

Coyote's yellow eyes burned like flames as he danced around the cow carcass with a femur in each hand. His lasso made of barbed wire had brought the bovine down. Maggots, beetles, and buzzards had miraculously cleaned the bones. The skull glistened. Coyote had succeeded once again. He had stripped the desert of another sacred cow.

Georgia stepped forward. Coyote stopped dancing. They struck a deal. She would agree not to expose him as the scoundrel he was, keeping his desert secrets safe, if he promised to save bones for her—bleached bones. Stones—smooth black stones would also do. And so, for the price of secrecy, anonymity, and just plain fun—

O'Keeffe and Coyote became friends. Good friends. Through the years, he brought her bones and stones and Georgia O'Keeffe kept her word. She never painted Coyote. Instead, she embodied him.

Eliot Porter knew O'Keeffe as Trickster. It is a well-known story. I heard it from the photographer himself at a dinner party in Salt Lake City.

Porter told of traveling with Georgia into Glen Canyon, how much she loved the slickrock walls, and the hours she spent scouring the edges of the riverbed in search of stones.

"She was obsessed," he said, "very particular in what stones she would keep. They had to speak to her."

He paused. Grinned.

"But I was the one that found the perfectly black, perfectly round, perfectly smooth stone. I showed it to Georgia. She was furious that it was in my hands instead of hers. This stone not only spoke to her, it cried out and echoed off redrock walls!"

Porter smiled deviously.

"I didn't give it to her. I kept it for myself, saying it would be a gift for my wife, Aline.

"A few months later," Porter continued, "we invited Georgia to our home in Tesuque for Thanksgiving dinner. Aline and I knew how much Georgia loved that stone. We also knew her well enough to suspect she had not forgotten about it. And so we conducted an experiment. We set the black stone on our coffee table. O'Keeffe entered the room. Her eyes caught the stone. We disappeared into the kitchen to prepare the food, and when we returned, the stone was gone. Georgia said nothing. I said nothing. Neither did Aline. The next time I saw my black smooth stone, it was in a photograph in *Life* magazine taken by John Loengard, in the palm of O'Keeffe's hand."

Georgia O'Keeffe had the ability to trick the public, as well as her friends. She seduced critics with her flowers, arousing sexual suspicion:

Well—I made you take time to look at what I saw and when you took time to really notice my flower you hung all your

own associations with flowers on my flower and you write
about my flower as if I think and see what you think and see
of the flower—and I don't.

She transformed desert landscapes into emotional ones, using
color and form to startle the senses. Scale belonged to the landscape
of the imagination. When asked by friends if these places really
existed, O'Keeffe responded with her usual candor, "I simply paint
what I see."

What O'Keeffe saw was what O'Keeffe felt—in her own bones.
Her brush strokes remind us again and again, nothing is as it appears:
roads that seem to stand in the air like charmed snakes; a pelvis bone
that becomes a gateway to the sky; another that is rendered like an
angel; and "music translated into something for the eye."

O'Keeffe's eye caught other nuances besides the artistic. She was
a woman painter among men. Although she resisted the call of gender separation and in many ways embodied an androgynous soul,
she was not without political savvy and humor on the subject:

When I arrived at Lake George I painted a horse's skull—
then another horse's skull. After that came a cow's skull on
blue. In my Amarillo days cows had been so much a part of
the country I couldn't think without them. As I was working
I thought of the city men I had been seeing in the East. They
talked so often of writing the Great American Novel—the
Great American Play—the Great American Poetry. I am not
sure that they aspired to the Great American Painting.
Cézanne was so much in the air that I think the Great
American Painting didn't even seem a possible dream.

    I knew cattle country—I was quite excited over our
own country and I knew that at the time almost any one of
those great minds would have been living in Europe if it had
been possible for them. They didn't even want to live in New
York—how was the Great American Thing going to happen?
So as I painted along on my cow's skull on blue I thought to
myself, "I'll make it an American painting. They will not

think it great with the red stripes down the sides—-Red, White and Blue—but they will notice it."

Georgia O'Keeffe had things to do in her own country and she knew it. She would bring the wanderlust men home, even to her beloved Southwest, by tricking them once again, into seeing the world her way, through bold color and the integrity of organic form. O'Keeffe's clarity would become the American art scene's confusion. The art of perception is deception—a lesson Coyote knows well.

Perhaps the beginning of O'Keeffe's communion with Coyote began in the Texas Panhandle. The year was 1916, the place Palo Duro Canyon. O'Keeffe saw this cut in the earth as "a burning, seething cauldron, almost like a blast furnace full of dramatic light and color."

Her pilgrimages to the canyon were frequent, often with her sister, Claudia. "Saturdays, right after breakfast we often drove the twenty miles to the Palo Duro Canyon. It was colorful—like a small Grand Canyon, but most of it only a mile wide. It was a place where few people went.... It was quiet down in the canyon. We saw the wind and snow blow across the slit in the plains as if the slit didn't exist."

She goes on to say:

The only paths were narrow, winding cow paths. There were sharp, high edges between long, soft earth banks so steep that you couldn't see the bottom. They made the canyon seem very deep. We took different paths from the edge so that we could climb down in new places. We sometimes had to go down together holding to a horizontal stick to keep one another from falling. It was usually very dry, and it was a lone place. We never met anyone there. Often as we were leaving, we would see a long line of cattle like black lace against the sunset sky.

Painting No. 21, *Palo Duro Canyon* (1916), celebrates an earth on fire, an artist's soul response to the dance of heat waves in the desert and the embrace one feels when standing at the bottom of a canyon with steep slopes of scree rising upward to touch a cobalt sky. It is as though O'Keeffe is standing with all her passion inside a red-hot circle with everything around her in motion.

And it is not without fear. O'Keeffe writes, "I'm frightened all the time...scared to death. But I've never let it stop me. Never!"

Once, after descending into a side canyon to look closely at the striations in the rock that resembled the multicolored petticoats of Spanish dancers, Georgia could contain herself no longer. She howled. Her companions, worried sick that she might have fallen, called to her to inquire about her safety. She was fine. Her response, "I can't help it—it's all so beautiful!"

I believe Coyote howled back.

O'Keeffe's watercolor *Canyon with Crows* (1917) creates a heart-felt wash of "her spiritual home," a country that elicits participation. The two crows (I believe they are ravens) flying above the green, blue, and magenta canyon are enjoying the same perspective of the desert below as the artist did while painting. O'Keeffe is the raven, uplifted and free from the urban life she left behind.

I had forgotten about Georgia O'Keeffe's roots in Palo Duro Canyon. I was traveling to Amarillo, Texas, for the first time in June 1988, to speak to a group of Mormons about the spirituality of nature. A woman in charge of the conference asked if I had any special needs.

"Just one," I replied. "We need to be outside."

What had originally been conceived as an indoor seminar was transformed into a camping trip. One hundred Mormons and I descended into Palo Duro Canyon in a rainstorm.

The country was familiar to me. It was more than reminiscent of my homeland. Certainly, the canyons of southern Utah are sisters to Palo Duro, but it was something else, a déjà vu, of sorts.

Cows hung on the red hillside between junipers and mesquite. I saw three new birds—a scaled quail, a golden-fronted woodpecker, and wild turkeys. Other birds were old friends: roadrunner, turkey vulture, scissor-tailed flycatcher, and rock wren. Burrowing owls stood their ground as mockingbirds threw their voices down-canyon, imitating all the others. It was a feathered landscape.

The Lighthouse, Spanish Dancers, and Sad Monkey Train were all landmarks of place. The bentonite hills were banded in ocher and mauve. Strange caves within the fickle rock looked like dark eyes in the desert, tears streaming from the rain.

We crossed three washes with a foot of water flowing through. Markers indicated that five feet was not unusual. Flash floods were frequent.

Mesquite had been brought in for a campfire. Food was being prepared. The rain stopped. The land dried quickly. A group of us sat on a hillside and watched the sun sink into the plains—a sun, large, round, and orange in a lavender sky.

At dusk, I knelt in the brown clay, dried and cracked, and rubbed it between my hands—a healing balm. Desert music of mourning doves and crickets began. Two ravens flew above the canyon. I looked up and suddenly remembered O'Keeffe. This was her country. Her watercolor *Canyon with Crows* came back to me. It was an animated canvas. I wondered if Georgia had knelt where I was, rubbing the same clay over her hands and arms as I was, some seventy years ago?

It was time for the fireside.

I stood in front of the burning mesquite with chalked arms and my *Book of Mormon* in hand. If I quoted a scripture first, whatever followed would be legitimate. This was important. The Priesthood leaders, men, had inquired about my status in the Church. When I replied, "Naturalist," they were not comforted.

I opened my scriptures and spoke of the earth, the desert, how nature mirrors our own. I began to read from the Doctrine and Covenants, section eighty-eight, verse forty-four—"And the Lord spoke…" when all at once, a pack of coyotes behind the rocks burst forth in a chorus of howls.

God's dogs.

I was so overcome with delight at the perfectness of this moment, I forgot all religious protocol and joined them. Throwing back my head, I howled too—and invited the congregation to do likewise—which they did. Mormons and coyotes, united together in a desert howl-lelujah chorus!

I said, "Amen." Silence was resumed and the fireside ended.

That night, we slept under stars. I overheard a conversation between two women.

"Did you think that was a little weird tonight?"

"I don't know," the other replied, "howling with the coyotes just seemed like the natural thing to do."

With her first book, Refuge: An Unnatural History of Family and
Place, *Terry Tempest Williams won an immediate reputation as an eloquent
and impassioned naturalist-writer in the traditions of John Muir, Rachel
Carson, and Wallace Stegner. Her books since then have included* Pieces
of White Shell, Coyote's Canyon, Leap, *and* An Unspoken Hunger,
*from which this story was excerpted. She lives in Salt Lake City with her
husband, Brooke.*

★

In Southern Utah, between the Vermilion Cliffs and the Buckskin Mountains, lies Paria Valley, in the past a remote setting for many Westerns. Even to those of us accustomed to the geological wonders of the Southwest, Paria is nothing less than spectacular. And this landscape, unlike its depiction in the movies, is not a backdrop but a formidable presence, immediately enfolding the visitor in its heat and silence.

We set up our tent at the foot of one of Paria's multicolored bentonite hills, close to the spreading paws of what looks like a gigantic sphinx with its head blown off, a battlement of broken, red rock left behind.

Beyond our primitive campsite lies an old movie set, with a dirt street leading between a saloon and hotel on one side, and a bank and jail on the other. Wind and sun have removed the lettering from these simple, wooden structures, while there is further evidence of erosion—the hitching post for horses is now far too high above the ground.

As the writer Edward Abbey has pointed out, Paria is the home of two ghost towns, one real and one false. The real one is the ruins of a Mormon settlement several miles up the valley. Abandoned in 1890, only a few sandstone houses have survived.

—Richard von Sturmer, "Sagebrush Lizards"

BARBARA AND JON BECKWITH

★ ★ ★

Detectives of the Desert

Tracking down Indian rock art is an art in itself.

OUR JEEP LURCHES OFF HIGHWAY I-70 BETWEEN MILEPOSTS 122 and 123 west of Green River, Utah. At the head of a rutted road, we are stopped by a gate meant to keep in cows. Slipping the steel pole from a wire loop, we shove open the makeshift barrier, drive through, and rehook the gate. After a half-mile of sand and ruts, we repeat the ritual. Jolting along, we scan the sandstone cliffs to the west for a glimmer of multicolored designs or of white figures pecked on red stone.

We are in a corner of southeastern Utah known as the Sinbad area, where no one seems to live. We are not rounding up cows. We are not running from the law. We may be lost, but if so, we don't know it yet. We've traveled from Boston, Massachusetts, to find Indian rock art. Not to collect, steal, or even touch, but to gaze at, alone, in the wilderness.

The panels we're searching for in Sinbad have haunted us since we first saw them in a book on ancient Southwestern art. Elongated figures in priestlike robes, stalklike heads with goggle eyes, snakes with protruding tongues floating like halos over each figure. On either side, drooping figures with a single horn—or is it a feather?— protruding from the top. The experts can't agree.

Our passion for finding ancient Indian rock art began five years earlier when we got our first glimpse on a hike into Grand Gulch Canyon, west of Monticello, Utah. Our goal had been exercise; instead we spent our time staring at walls. Our first sight of panels of the centuries-old pictographs, images painted on rock, and petroglyphs, figures pecked into rock, stunned us. Some were crude cartoonlike figures of animals, humans and symbols. Others were six-foot tall, twenty-foot wide, multicolored scenes. Many were whimsical, but others seemed solemn and even menacing.

Whoever had created these images had done so hundreds or even thousands of years ago. They date back, archeologists surmise, to as early as 6,000 B.C. Their origin and meaning eludes scholars. It is this mystery that both delights and frustrates us.

But more important a challenge than understanding the art is simply finding it. When we first set out to see the Indian rock art of the Southwest, we had no idea of the roadblocks we would encounter. It had all seemed so easy. After all, we could park by the entrance road to Canyonlands National Park and peer at petroglyph-covered Newspaper Rock along with dozens of other tourists. We could easily locate other rock etchings along the highway, announced by official markers.

But the real gems, it soon became clear, are hidden in anonymous canyons or among remote desert cliffs. Some are inside fenced-in private ranches or located on Native American land, where trespassing is not appreciated. Others are protected by willow-choked canyons, or by rattlesnakes jealous of their territory. Certain images along the Southwest's rivers can be reached only by raft, while others were drowned when hundreds of miles of canyons were flooded to create Lake Powell and other reservoirs.

The official custodians of the rock art—government rangers and museum personnel—don't make our task easier. To keep the best sites safe from vandals and to preserve them for anthropological study before opening them to public scrutiny and possible destruction, most rangers simply don't acknowledge they exist. They've resorted to a protective conspiracy of silence.

As a result, pilgrims like ourselves must turn into detectives if we want to see the best ancient art that decorates hidden canyons and cliff faces. Our first attempts at sleuthing, took us only so far. We looked at maps and archeological books—one of the best collections on ancient rock art is at Harvard's Peabody Museum—and planned more trips to the West. Our scholarly books unfortunately never gave the precise location of the sites. But even though the directions were not explicit, we assumed that they would get us there.

Now, as we bounce along, bucking Sinbad sand, we hold a naive faith that we'll find the images we seek. Weaving deeper into the wilderness, we feel like the ancients may have in pre-white man's times, following instructions our elders have kept deliberately mysterious. The caption under our book's illustration of the Sinbad panel reads only: "on the south side of cliffs at Head of Sinbad." Unfortunately, the Sinbad area, we now see, encompasses hundreds of acres of buttes, canyons, and cliffs.

We spot some sandstone walls that we think might hold our rock art. But our jeep can't leave the rutted track without sinking in sand. We get out and hike. The earth is hot, the brush scrabbly, the ground's surface is caked soil over sand. At the base of the cliff, we spot a few small vague red shapes. These are not the striking images we'd come to see. We hunt around the nearby cliffs, then give up and drive back through our gauntlet of cattle gates. We've failed for now, but we will not be defeated.

Assuming that the officials at an Indian Museum in northern Utah do know where the Sinbad site is, we go there and ask for help. The staff person we speak to is clearly checking us out. We chatter on about the panels we've come from Massachusetts to find, and how our book's descriptions of locations have gotten us nowhere. Finally, satisfied that our goal is not to pockmark a precious panel with bullet holes, she reaches underneath the counter and pulls out a set of directions to the Sinbad site. The papers are marked CONFIDENTIAL. By this time, we're 100 miles north of Sinbad, so we tuck the precious instructions away like an amulet, to bring with us on a future trip.

*

The museum official's worry about bullet holes is real. We'd seen 5,000-year-old petroglyphs riddled by rifle shots. Off the highway near Moab, we'd seen the pale remains of a multicolored pictograph, one of the most unusual of the Southwest's wall paintings. In the middle of the night, unknown vandals had taken a scouring pad to the ancient figures that had been there for thousands of years. We realized that rock art accessible to cars and four-wheel drives is in real danger.

What would prompt a person to destroy a painting that may be as much as 8,000 years old? The Moab pictograph, we were told, may have been defaced by a Native American who believed in—and was afraid of—its power. But most vandalism is a result of pure ego or willful destruction. Teenagers seek immortality by scratching their initials on a panel. Souvenir collectors trace a panel on paper or outline a figure in white chalk to enhance their photographs. They do not know that such rubbing destroys the very artwork they admire.

> If these artifacts are lifted from their birthplace they cease to speak. Like a piece of coral broken from its reef, they lose their color, becoming pale and brittle. Somehow we need to acquaint ourselves with the art of letting go, for to own a piece of the past is to destroy it.
>
> But it's a difficult thing to do. I know because I have pocketed a piece of pottery. In the context of all the desert's loveliness it became numinous: I had to possess it. Somewhere deep inside me I hoped this potshard might become a talisman, an amulet. I was wrong. What once glistened in those pastel sands collected dust on my dressing table. Its loss of dignity haunted me.
>
> —Terry Tempest Williams,
> *Pieces of White Shell: A Journey to Navajoland*

That's why museum personnel and park rangers, usually irrepressible sources of information, stay mum when we ask for the location of a prized piece of ancient art. At Capitol Reef National Park headquarters, we ask for directions to panels we'd seen in books but had no way to find. A pregnant pause. "I'm sorry, but I can't tell you that." In Escalante near the southern edge of the state we ask a woman at the local tourist information stand. She says she's never heard of pictographs. At Salt Lake City's Anthropology Museum we press the Director for the location of the Stansbury Island site on the Great Salt Lake. We are met with a curt refusal. Clearly, the official custodians of this art will not guide us on our quest. We realize we will have to be resourceful. We'll have to use more than experts, maps, and books.

In the end we found a way. We located our rock art by making friends.

Getting to know people was the key to finding the striking petroglyphs in the Behind-the-Rocks area near Moab, Utah. The image of the site's Kokopelli — a dramatic line of marching humpbacked men — glowed in our imaginations like an image of the Northern Lights. We wanted to see it for ourselves.

We had tried once before to find these panels and failed. We had entered Behind-the-Rocks by a path mentioned in a hiking book. The path soon meandered, split in two, then led to bare rock and disappeared. We found ourselves in a vast area without a hint where to look. After an hour or so in the blazing heat, never having seen the reality behind our vision, we turned back. Even though we had walked through some of the most beautiful canyonland in the Southwest, our yearning to face that line of mythical Kokopelli remained undimmed.

The next year, we went straight to a Moab artist we had formed a friendship with by mail. She tracks down rock art on solitary winter hikes, and sketches them for batik t-shirts and wall hangings. We had found an enthusiast who trusted us enough to share her favorite sites. She directed us to a trail that would take us to the marching Kokopellis.

Still, it took some scrambling along canyon wall ledges to find the panels, since her directions were from memory ("a half hour after the rocky pass...."). When we saw the Kokopelli panel, we burst out laughing with delight. Two dozen hump-backed figures marched in a row, each with a featherlike protuberance emanating from its head, flutes in their mouths, and bold protruding penises.

The Kokopelli are odd figures, thought by Hopi Indians and archaeologists to be wandering merchants. Myth says that they roamed the countryside trading seed for shells and taking the opportunity to impregnate women—an ancient version of the "traveling salesman." The humpback is thought, in fact, to represent their pack of merchandise. Over the line of marching men, square letters spell R. PULLIAM, the remains of nineteenth-century graffiti.

You'd expect such ancient figures to be found in the dark of a Lascaux-like cave, or buried in the depths of a pyramid. But they are here in the open air, protected only by a rock overhang and Utah's bone-dry air.

On our next journey, this time to northern Arizona, one person helped us find what we sought, while others kept us from it. We were entranced by the ornately drawn figures dotting cliff faces somewhere in an area called the Arizona Strip. We had seen photographs of the panel in *Arizona Highways*, whose caption identified the panel simply as "The Labyrinth."

With this single clue to go on, we tried to pinpoint the site through telephone calls before leaving home. Conversations with Arizona National Park and Bureau of Land Management rangers failed to elicit any information. Stonewalled again, we would have to rely on our ingenuity once we got there.

Asking every Arizonan we met, we eventually succeeded. At the John Wesley Powell Museum in the town of Page, we met a local man who'd surveyed the area's canyons by airplane to gather information for topographical maps. He liked to joke about rock art, calling one panel "tire tracks" and another "Egyptians." But he knew his turf. He told us that "The Labyrinth" was probably in a canyon near Fredonia. We left his company with exact instructions for getting there, directions we promised not to repeat.

Excited by our fresh lead, we headed west to an area not far from the Grand Canyon. After four miles of careening along a muddy road in our rented four-wheel drive, we backpacked two miles into the canyon so we could spend the next day sitting and staring at any images we could find. By now, we had faith that we were on the right track.

Rock art is hard to spot from a distance. Because petroglyphs are pecked in shiny black basalt or dark mineral-varnished cliffs, they are hard to see, especially when the sun is overhead. Pictographs, often painted a rich red-brown, blend from a distance with the red sandstone cliffs. We stayed close to likely looking cliffs so we wouldn't miss anything.

Suddenly we met a live roadblock. Passing by thick brush a mile down the trail, we recognized the telltale buzz of a rattler. The sound alone kept us on the far side of the trail for a while. A second rattler, this time coiled at the base of a cliff we were trying to explore, let us know we'd invaded his territory. We backed off slowly, and he did too. That cliff remained unexplored. But we didn't let rattlers stop us altogether. We had come too far. We kept on walking, scanning the walls for art and the ground for snakes.

In the afternoon, a harsh wind picked up, coating our bodies with red dust and forcing us to set up camp. To get out of the wind, we climbed up to an overhang. We were surrounded by images we would not have spotted from afar. There, under the lee of the cliff, was the panel we'd been searching for.

We had never seen such figures before: huge, squarish, and blood-red. Some of their bodies were half buried by sand and stone at the base of the cliff. Each mask-like head was hung with V-shaped pendants: four white strands and four red against a backdrop of faded ochre. On some figures, there remained only a ghost of the head. Each torso was patterned with rich red squares. At one place, where a slab of cliff face had fallen to the ground, one figure was cut in half at the waist. We stood there with our wind-whipped hair, sand-coated clothes and hennaed hands, like pilgrims standing before icons.

Luck, ingenuity, and people came together for us on our last rock art sleuthing expedition to New Mexico. Our books showed us photographs of impressive petroglyphs in the northern part of the state, but, as usual, gave no particulars about exact locations. One series of rocks engraved with petroglyphs was described only as being "north of Espanola," an area encompassing hundreds of square miles. We drove to the library at Santa Fe's Indian Museum for clues.

When our inquiries hit a dead end, we hung around, trying politely to pry information from the librarian who professed to know nothing about rock art sites. Then a denim-clad man who had been standing by the book stacks, listening to our conversation, told us he could help. He turned out to be one of the leading experts on Indian rock art of the Southwest. We felt like prospectors hitting pay dirt.

The low-key but gregarious man was a gold mine of information. He listened to our saga of fruitless pursuit of New Mexico's best rock art. Somehow, he could see we were "good guys" and directed us to a number of sites we would never have found on our own. His precise directions took us directly to our "north of Espanola" petroglyphs. After clambering over cactus-studded terrain, we located the remote hillside strewn with black boulders, many of them decorated with petroglyphs. Whoever carved these images chose the basalt rocks for their dark patina. By scraping away the surface, the rock artists had chiseled out figures of people, animals, and designs. One figure has a large round circle in the place of body, a smaller circle at its center, and swirls of flame-like designs radiating from the larger circle. A pregnant woman? A man with a shield? An image of the sun? The possibilities abound.

At the base of one rock, a Kokopelli strides along with his trademark hump, flute, and erect penis. On the side of another rock, a figure spears an animal of some sort—a rare hunting scene. We felt like privileged beings in that field of petroglyphs, alone in an outdoor museum of the finest art.

We can't pretend that we've solved every problem confronting the hunters of rock art. When we asked our Santa Fe Museum friend where to find the set of fierce-looking, sharp-toothed and horned human heads in the Galisteo Basin, south of Santa Fe, he warned us, "Don't mess with cowboys." Gun-toting ranchers and cowboys had been known, he said, to run curious tourists off their land, where many of the rare petroglyphs are found. We passed up that treasure.

We met another obstacle in Bluff, Utah, population 250, where we planned to hike down a particular wash to the San Juan River. Somewhere along the cliffs, we expected to spot the large human figures with ornate headdresses of ray-like lines above the heads.

The night before our expedition, we met a Native American guide at a local restaurant. When we asked him about the area's petroglyphs, he coldly informed us that this was land owned by his people and trespassing was not allowed. Two "young hot-heads," he told us, had just gone to prison for shooting at hikers as they made their way up the wash. We left Bluff the next morning. His story sounded too close to a Tony Hillerman murder mystery for comfort.

Our rock art quest is not over. We will go back again this year to follow leads we've not yet explored. We'll carry our "CONFIDENTIAL" instructions for finding the art at Sinbad. We are still waiting for the ultimate experience, like that of Terry Alderman, a photographer we met in Kanab, Utah. Alderman spends his days wandering up the hundreds of canyons in the area, and photographing the art he finds there.

Once, he discovered a giant pictograph of a human-like figure with a mysterious shape and striking colors in a canyon he had never before explored. He went to the Bureau of Land Management office to tell them about it. The rangers there seemed strangely hostile. Finally, they took him into an inner office and said, "Yes, we know about the canyon. But we wish you didn't." Archaeologists had not yet recorded the canyon's treasures and they worried that if Terry spread the word, the site would eventually be vandalized. The rangers left him with a plea: "Please don't tell anyone else."

They needn't worry. For Alderman, the discovery itself excited him—the fact that he saw a panel that maybe only a few other people had ever seen.

Alderman did not share the location of his "find" with us. We're sad for ourselves, but glad for the sake of the art itself. And we won't share locations of the art we saw aside from vague hints like "North of Espanola." We love this art too much. We're part of the conspiracy now.

Barbara and Jon Beckwith are Easterners who love Southwest canyonlands.
Barbara Beckwith is a freelance writer and National Writers Union activist.
Jon Beckwith is a professor of microbiology at Harvard Medical School. They
are both Southern Utah wilderness activists.

★

During my days alone Jeeping, hiking, and camping in a pair of canyons outside Canyonlands National Park, I thought long and hard about all this. I walked through a wilderness the equal of anything in Arches or Canyonlands, and crossed paths with but a single other party. The trail register in the first canyon recorded only twenty-seven visitors during the whole month of September; in the second, only fourteen.

As long as I could have days like this in southeastern Utah, it was unlikely that I would regard the growth of Moab as a tragedy or believe the backcountry was being overrun. All that was needed was some homework and a willingness to hike to find the Edens in the outback that few others knew about.

On my last night in Moab, camping on a shelf above a dry streambed, I engaged in a brief and halfhearted internal debate, then gathered dead juniper and piñon sticks. According to the official regulations governing the parcel of federal land upon which I had laid my sleeping bag, campfires were not allowed. "Tough shit," I said to the bureaucrats in my head, desk-bound ghosts in Moab and Monticello.

Of the small fire I sat beside for three peaceful hours, as Cygnus and Lyra wheeled overhead, not a trace remained when I left in the morning. My foray had made an infinitesimal dent in the stock of dead branches decomposing on the shelf behind me. My fire was built neither for warmth—it was a mild night—nor for cooking.

I built a fire because that was what my ancestors had done in the Neolithic. The flame was to stare into, to muse upon, ignited to pry open the senses. The wilderness was there to be touched.

—David Roberts, "Whose Wilderness Is It?"

Men's Journal

JAMES CROTTY AND
MICHAEL LANE

* * *

Planet Nevada

Two guys called the Monks enjoy a slice of life in Nevada.

THE OLD WEST STOOD BY THE SIDE OF THE ROAD BLOWING THE same dust mites, a thousand years old. Packs of desert dogs picked meat off the lean bones of water-parched rodents and fresh road kill. Bombing ranges and dry lake beds made moon-crater landscapes as far as the eye could see.

It's a bomb and water state. Lots of one and little of the other.

Driving south on 95 past Twenty Mile Beach the Monks passed The Desert Doll House, a point of interest for horny men and traveling monks. Jim got a passing fancy, dreaming of buxom Russ Meyer babes, preening and purring in the desert heat.

"Mike, let's check out this brothel thing."

"And you guilt-trip me for gambling?"

"I mean, out of curiosity, you know, don't you think we should see one?"

Mike was distracted, his eyes glued to the roadside.

"Well, I'll be damned. Hawthorn Army Ammunition Depot. There must be thousands of bunkers there."

As far as the eye could see, concrete, low-to-the-ground, oversized ammunition bunkers marched for miles across the valley.

"What's in there?" asked Mike.

"One of the world's largest arsenals of high explosives," said Jim, resident factoid machine.

"Should we go in?"

"I'm game."

The Monks had gotten all curious about explosives since the pyrotechnic high jinks of Burning Man the previous summer. Besides, both Monks had a secret dread of the military, and yearned to expose its secret stash any time they could.

So Mike and Jim put on their Joe Tourist hats and dare-to-be-dangerous gut-sucking smirks and pulled up the road to the first guarded gate.

"I'll do the talking," Jim stated firmly.

"I can talk too."

"Just let me talk," said Jim.

"I'm driving. They'll be talking to me."

"You can never pull it off!"

"Bullshit, Jim, what are you going to say that I can't say?"

"Just watch!"

Jim rolled up his sleeves.

A guard sat at his station reading a paper and picking his teeth. He was holstered and packing, in full dress and glazed from the heat. He jumped up when he saw the car approaching and stood defiant by the gate.

The wimpy Ford Escort slowly rolled to a stop. Jim leaned across Mike and yelled out the window, "I suspect you're not going to let us in."

"That's right!" said the guard.

"You ever have any big demonstrations up here?"

"Don't know about that."

"Guess we should be going?"

"That's right!" said the guard.

Mike turned the car around and headed back out to the highway, fuming all the while.

"I could have said that!"

"Don't worry, we'll find another ammunition depot."

Mike drove on toward Tonopah, past the Monte Cristo Range,

across more lonely highway and through the Air Force Gunnery Range. Around sunset Jim took over the wheel and near Mercury decided to visit the fabled Nevada Test Site, where they blast all the nuclear weapons. Years ago folks in Vegas used to watch these tests from casino rooftops.

The signs said no trespassing. Jim did the talking as Mike crossed his arms. Up at the gate was another stolid, militaristic Bill Bennett-style security guard.

Jim leaned out the window, "I suspect you're not going to let us in."

"That's right!"

"You ever have any big demonstrations up here?"

"Don't know about that."

"Guess we should be going?"

"That's right!" said the guard.

Jim swung the car around and headed back for the road.

Mike sat smirking, "O.K. State Debate Champion, I thought you were going to get us in."

"Well, sometimes you can work it right, you know, like cajole them and get a tour of the whole area, and then they'll show you where the earth has imploded. Just have to find the right guard. I heard they have these signs that warn you if an area is still radiated. It's like fenced off and you can't go near it. But then they have all of the area right outside the fence that's still safe. I don't understand how radiation just suddenly stops at the fence."

"Guess we'll never know," Mike said clucking.

The Monks headed south to Pahrump because Jim still had brothels on his mind. They were in Nye County, the last legal county for prostitution before entering Vegas.

It wasn't like Jim was horny for a prostitute, the ever-curious Gemini just wanted to, like, you know, "check it out," or so he said. Mike had a solid suspicion that if there were any golden-haired goddesses, Jim would be slapping down twenties till they piled to the sky.

Jim pulled up a long dirt road. A big sign said, "Chicken Ranch." There were fire station lights rotating in the night, their red bulbs blinking as they turned. The Monks and their "insurance replacement car" pulled beyond the first ramshackle brothel with its boarded up doors and white picket fence. Further down the road was the only open brothel, with an Oriental motif, next to a bar.

Mike parked the car so he could snooze, while Jim walked into the bar past two friendly, surprisingly respectable guys hanging on the rails.

"Do you know where I can get some food?" Jim asked.

"Well, let me see, I think they're serving food at that motorcycle gathering down the way," answered one of the men, looking up from his paper.

"Great, I'll get to that." Jim paused. "So, ah, which way to the..."

The men motioned Jim outside to a gate, from where he was buzzed into the brothel, a place known as Sherrie's Ranch.

A sixty-year-old woman (must have been Sherrie), with hair pulled back and wearing tight, black, crotch-hugging slacks, and exuding a brass tacks rancher's wife vibe, came up and said in a deep guttural matter-of-fact voice, "I want you to sit on the couch, don't move, and the ladies will come out. You'll get to look at the ladies, no touching. You'll pick the one you want and you'll go back to their room and discuss the price of what you want with her. Then you'll do it and leave."

"All right, cool."

Jim promptly sat down on the couch like a good submissive, doing as he'd been told.

Sherrie rang a buzzer, looked sternly at Jim, then made a phone call to the back. Jim waited on the couch for five minutes, very still. The room was doctor's office plain, with no hint of the sleaze that lay beyond the particle board walls. The matron was talking with another lady who worked there. They were going on about one of the girls who was so homesick she wanted to leave.

Suddenly twelve women strutted out single file like they were in a police lineup. In fact, from the looks of them, most probably *had* been in a police lineup.

Jim was in shock. He pulled forward on the couch, eyes alert, breathing short quick breaths, hyper awake, expecting Amazon beauties to come slithering through.

Instead, the room was filled with flat-out whores, posing and posturing before him a scant eight feet away. There were all sorts of "ladies": coquettish Asians, skanky white trash, friendly Latinas, beat-to-hell blacks, women with really big boobs, women with really big boob jobs, blondes with poofed up hair, scrawny thin waifs, six-foot transsexuals, really vampish and trampish girls wearing buckets of makeup, high heels, topless, unsmiling, looking like major drugs were a steady diet; in other words, just a mess of decrepit humanity.

Jim just sat with his eyes wide open and a look of total confusion on his face. It was quiet. The women stood in a row facing the couch; all eyes were on Jim. As they awaited the monk's decision, they shifted their weight from leg to leg, adjusting negligees, brushing back hair, hands on hips, clicking nails, chewing gum.

Nothing was said.

Jim sat speechless, lost in a vortex of thought.

"This was IT?! This is what people drive fifty miles out in the desert for?!"

After a few minutes, Jim finally blurted out, "I'm so sorry, but I don't think I'm interested in anyone."

The Zuni also have a strong berdache tradition. A berdache is a biological male with reduced genitals who dresses like a woman, acts like a woman, does work and hangs out with the women, and is sexually available to unmarried young men, is a sex teacher and a condoned extra outlet for married men. The Spaniards called the berdaches *putos*, male whores, or *sodomitas*, not understanding their spiritual importance. The Zuni berdaches are revered as both male and female. Some have fathered children. They elect the role after having a sacred vision on the threshold of adulthood or are appointed by the community. The beloved berdache, Wéwha, who died in 1956, was taken to Washington, where he was received by Grover Cleveland and became a good friend of the Speaker of the House and his wife.

—Alex Shoumatoff, *Legends of the American Desert: Sojourns in the Greater Southwest*

And within a split second, a dark-haired Italian-American with perky silicone breasts and an upturned smirk said in a gnarly, nasal voice, "Well, at least he's honest." Then, without fanfare, they all turned and marched back to their rooms, murmuring among themselves.

Feeling sorry for the lot of them, Jim left the place with his head down and went back to the car where Mike and our resident feline, Her Holiness The Great Dolly Lama, waited in the dusty night air.

"Any luck?" Mike asked.

Jim looked shell-shocked.

"What a horrible life," Jim answered pensively.

The Monks quietly drove back down the road past the desperate trailers, where "the ladies" lived. The red lights of the brothel flashed in the rear view mirror, and the building where they went to "work" slowly faded into the distance.

"Let's eat, I'm starved," said Mike finally.

Jim sat quietly a moment longer, then stated softly, "Someone in the bar mentioned a gathering of motorcycle enthusiasts up the road who are serving food."

The Monks stopped at a bar a few miles down the road where dozens of Harleys were parked outside a dusty bar with a big sign that read, THE TRIBE/SHORT BRANCH MOTORCYCLE RALLY.

Looked promising. Anything looks promising when one is famished. But only a few steps after leaving their "insurance replacement" car, the Monks realized, *"These were not weekend, suburban, motorcycle enthusiasts. This was a gathering of hard-core Hell's Angels!"*

Next to the bar was a truck selling tattoos. A line of drunk-on-their-ass bikers were getting tats and shouting obscenities. More were gathered in the bar. The Monks parked and went in, pushing through the mob. Inside, the crowds were noisy, with everyone milling around holding beers. The air was thick with sweat-soaked leather. The smell of piss pervaded the room.

Back outside was a long buffet table. The bikers were loading up on vittles, eating in front of a stage. The Monks quietly found a plate, piled on the chicken and coleslaw and moved to a corner to nervously eat. No one seemed to notice.

Then things started getting rowdy. Bikers started yelling back and forth, tossing bottles at the floor. It seemed like the motorcycle enthusiasts were wanting some entertainment. They were either on the verge of a riot or just having a good time. It wasn't clear.

Finally one of the bikers in the back yelled, "Get the bitch and make her sing!"

Everyone loudly agreed—"Yeah, get the bitch, get the bitch!!"—tossing more bottles, cackling all the while.

"Yeah, get the bitch, and make her sing!" another biker howled, a little late to the joke.

Glass was clinking, and most of the enthusiasts seemed happy just yukking it up about the "bitch," until a hairy bear of a man, with a long greasy ponytail, a belly rolling like surf over his piss-soaked jeans, with menacing tattoos covering his rock hard arms, got up off his drunken derriere and went into the bar to "get the bitch."

A few minutes later out came a surprisingly smart, tall and *sober* woman, who gracefully walked past the crowd, her face a picture of demure Southern beauty. The so-called "bitch," who was more like a diva, got up on the stage, adjusted the mike, gave a little cue to her backup quartet, and immediately launched into a song the biker enthusiasts dearly loved.

"Keep your motor runnin'
Head out on the highway!
Looking for adventure….
In whatever comes my way!
Born to be…wiiiiillllllld!!!!!"

There was a total uproar. Bottles started flying through the air, bikers pushed and shoved over tables, stomped their feet, kicked on the walls, slam danced, screamed, yelled and went totally ballistic outside on the desert floor.

The "bitch" had the bikers in her hands, and wouldn't let go.

"Born to be…wiiiiieeeeellllllld!!!!!"

The Monks stood off to the side—Jim looking extra dweeby in white pen-stained shorts, wire-rim glasses and a black I'VE BEEN MONKED t-shirt, Mike looking like the grandfather of freaks. Both Monks were so totally conspicuous and out of place that the meanest biker in the bunch finally noticed the two intruders and looked Mike and Jim over with this glazed "who the fuck are you faggots?" stare that sent The Monks packing for good. They snuck out the back door past the tattoo truck and into their dorky Ford Escort, the "insurance replacement car," leaving a dusty plume in its wake. In the rear view mirror The Monks could see the Hells Angels dancing wildly in the night, like primordial cavemen, egged on by the beautiful tall siren singing their national anthem.

"Jesus Mike, we could have been killed!"

"Get *the Bitch* and make her sing!? Could you believe that?"

"Born to be...wiiiiieeeeel-llllld!!!!!" wailed the diva.

The Monks headed for Pahrump in a hurry. However, within a few miles Mike was stuck behind a long line of Chevy and Chrysler family

---

Elvis Presley was heading toward Hollywood, driving his van somewhere outside Flagstaff with his hairdresser-guru Larry Geller riding shot-gun and the knuckle-grumbling crowd from Graceland sitting in back, when he saw the face of Joseph Stalin in the clouds above and watched it turn, by long billows, into the face of Jesus.

Presley pulled the van over to the side of the road and grabbed Geller for a run through the tilted desert, yelling, "I thought to myself, why Stalin?" When the cloud image changed to Jesus, Presley told Geller, "He smiled at me and every fiber of my being felt it. For the first time in my life God and Christ are a living reality."

Geller remembered Presley saying "Oh, God, Oh, God," over and over, "then he paused and added a peculiar aside—'Can you imagine what the fans would think if they saw me like this?'"

—Edvins Beitiks, "Clear Vision of Elvis' Final Days," *San Francisco Examiner* cars, moving at less than ten mph. It was nearly midnight. And here in the middle of the desert on the outskirts of a small town were hundreds of motorhomes parked by the side of the road with tables set up selling donuts and coffee.

"Now what the hell is this?" Jim looked bug-eyed out the window. Cars were inching along at a snail's pace. It took twenty minutes just to drive through the small town of Pahrump.

"What's this all about?" Jim finally yelled out the window.

"It's The Baker-to-Vegas Challenge Cup Relay Race," answered a friendly female table-side vendor with a butch hairdo.

"What's that?"

"Cops from all over the country come here with their local teams for a yearly relay race. It goes for two days and nights, all weekend long."

"What's with all the motor homes?"

"We're their backup. We just follow them around with donuts and coffee." And sure enough, just a few cars up, Jim could see a solitary runner, in his running shorts and number on back, followed closely behind by a guide car.

The Monks wrinkled their brows and let out a collective sigh. Stranded in a midnight traffic jam in the middle of the desert with practically every damn cop in the country jogging past brothels, nuclear test sites, rioting Hell's Angels, munitions dumps and vendors selling donuts on the side of the road?

"Hello, hello, is anyone home? Nevada. Come in, come in. Nevada, can you read me?"

Michael Lane and James Crotty (The Monks) are the authors of The Mad Monks' Guide to California *and* The Mad Monks' Guide to New York City, *and are the motive force behind the alternative travel web site,* Monk.com. *Email them at* Monk@Monk.com.

Encounter at Ghost Ranch

*A red hill doesn't touch everyone's heart as it touches
mine and I suppose there is no reason why
it should.* —*Georgia O'Keeffe*

RIDING THE BUS NORTH FROM SANTA FE ALONG HIGHWAY 84, THE
fierce land beyond the window threatened to burst the glass
through which I looked. The brilliant red hills and black mesas, the
mountain silhouette of Pedernal, the twisted trunks of old piñon
trees above the Chama River—all were there just as I remembered
them from the painting of Georgia O'Keeffe. I'd come to Ghost
Ranch, New Mexico, for a seminar on mountain and desert spirituality. It was my first trip there, and I arrived with a bag full of
mountain slides, notes on the desert fathers, and a longing for landscape. Most of all I'd come for healing, seeking respite from a
mother dying of cancer, needing to let the poetry of William Butler
Yeats and Robert Bly work its way into changes begun in my life.
I came to the desert to find peace, to seek a safe place, to read deep
consolation off steep canyon walls.

That was what I came for, but that wasn't what the desert had to
teach me. One seldom learns what he thinks he most needs to be
taught. I began on the first day of the seminar talking about "spirituality," a word that frankly makes a lot of people apprehensive. Too
often it brings to mind a *contemptus mundi* tradition, smelling of
snake-oil remedies, overly preoccupied with escape, speaking of the

next world in its persistent flight from this one. Many of us at Ghost Ranch that week were looking for just such an escape, half-broken people coming to the desert to be put back together again. But as the Rev. Tom Marshfield learned in John Updike's novel, *A Month of Sundays*, the desert rarely functions as a resort.

Spirituality and the desert are alike in that regard. They share a common ambiguity, a certain difficulty of access. Their "meanings" can't be summarized in neat Cartesian categories. Their answers are painful. Barry Lopez points to the opaque way in which the desert refuses to open itself to glib analysis. "You can't get at it this way," he urges. "You must come with no intentions of discovery. You must overhear things, as though you'd come into a small and desolate town and paused by an open window." As the early desert is marked invariably by confusion and loss. Something will always seem amiss.

I sensed that keenly during my first few days at Ghost Ranch. The group was going well. The food was good. The place was beginning to grow on us all with a deep mystery. But something still was missing. We'd not yet encountered the desert's wildness. It posed no danger to us. The structures of our world had not yet been threatened.

I kept thinking of three wild people who, had they been there, would have perceived the same landscape so differently from the rest of us. We were in need of a John Muir, that crazy fool who would tie himself to the top of a Douglas fir tree, riding out a fierce storm in the High Sierras as the tree whipped back and forth some thirty degrees in the wind. We needed Georgia O'Keeffe, that wonderfully irreverent saint who would have thrown up at the idea of some sappy teacher talking about the desert in a limp-wristed church camp where people were afraid of firsthand experience. And I knew what Ed Abbey would have thought of the whole thing. That wild and irascible writer of the American Southwest would have growled that the desert is "nothing but a goddamned place to die"—a place where all your easy answers fall to pieces, where you yourself may end up as nothing more than buzzard meat.

These were the people we needed there in the desert, these wild, almost blasphemous people, whose fierce honesty makes them the finest teachers of all. It strikes me as odd that sometimes the most "irreverent" people are the ones most in touch with the holy. These are the wild men and women of whom Robert Bly and Clarissa Pinkola Estés speak. They're a desert product, nurtured by a desolate and God-forsaken terrain. In keeping with the meaning of the Hebrew word for wilderness, *midbar*, they are "the cut-off ones," those "driven out" from society's mainstream. Like Elijah and John the Baptist, they thrive on the edges of culture, threatening its structures, speaking the language of fiery serpents and Lilith, the night hag (Deut. 8:15; Isa. 34:14). They know inherently that "it is in the wildness that justice comes to live" (Isa.32:16).

Edward Abbey came up in a conversation at lunch on Wednesday of that week. I was eating with John Fife, a Presbyterian minister from Tucson, Arizona who has been an important figure in the sanctuary movement over the last decade or more, seeking justice for Central American refugees. He's a gentle man, but more honest than some people can take. I asked if he'd ever met Abbey. He smiled widely and spoke of a letter he'd gotten some years before (at the time of his trial), one that wasn't signed and that read something like this:

> I'm just a cowpoke who's read a little about what you've been doing. I don't especially agree with you. [Abbey favored closing the U.S.-Mexican border to immigration.] But I had my bedroll out on the desert the other night, looking out at the stars. And it struck me that there's probably room enough here for anybody who wants to come. So if those government bastards come for you someday, knocking on the front door, and you can get out the back door before they kick your ass, I'd be glad to offer you a place to stay.

There was only a telephone number at the bottom of the page. No name.

Out of curiosity, John Fife called the number and learned it was Abbey. They became friends. A couple of years later, Fife invited him on a float trip down the Green River in Utah through Desolation Canyon. John told him that he would come with what he was as a theologian and Abbey could come with all his sharp edges and they'd argue their way back and forth down the river. Abbey liked the idea and they planned to go, but death intervened. Edward Abbey died on March 14, 1989.

John Fife went to see him in the hospital before his death. Abbey asked him, "What the hell are you doing here? You didn't come to preach to me, did you?" "No," John answered, "I've got too much respect for you to do that. I just wanted to see you." There was something about Ed Abbey's crotchetiness and fierce indifference to unimportant things that inevitably drew people to him.

That story haunted me as I went hiking alone in the desert that afternoon. Thinking of Abbey, I determined to meet the landscape on its own terms, without expectations, submitting at last to its sublime disregard for all my petty concerns. Abandonment, after all, is what the desert teaches best. As Abbey would say, the central spiritual lesson to remember about the desert is that "it doesn't give a shit." Its capacity to ignore is immense. Yet in that very indifference, one discovers an enormous freedom.

Gary Snyder says "the wilderness can be a ferocious teacher, rapidly stripping down the inexperienced or the careless. It is easy to make the mistakes that will bring one to an extremity." Being brought to the end of oneself is the terrifying (and enthralling) possibility that the desert enjoins. Here it is that we enter an interior wilderness more fearful and promising than anything charted on terrestrial maps. The wildest, most dangerous trails are always the ones within.

With the sun still shining, I took the path into a box canyon several miles behind Ghost Ranch. Thunderstorms had been coming up every afternoon and people were reluctant to venture far. Yet I desperately needed the time alone, getting away far enough to approach the border of that interior landscape I'd neglected so long. It was a beautiful afternoon. A slight breeze rustled leaves on the cottonwood trees. The smell of sage was sharpened by recent rains. I followed a small creek into the canyon, noticing deer tracks along

its bank. Later in the week, tracks of a mountain lion were seen
along that same trail. It was a fine place for a lion to trap deer, up a
narrow canyon with no escape.

By the time I'd followed the creek to the canyon's end, the cliffs
had risen to a hundred feet on either side. The rock had chipped
away from the edge at the top, leaving an overhang all the way
around. There was no way out. Tripping over talus fragments fallen
from above, I heard a loud and sustained echo, filling the place
with sound. It was a compelling place, a strange end to which I'd
somehow been invited. Certain places are like that, says Wendell
Berry. They offer a sense of meeting, if one can only learn to wait
and be patient.

In the center of the space at the end of the canyon lay a large,
flat rock. Nearby, a trickle of water seeped out from under the
canyon wall, feeding the creek I'd been following. I lay on the rock
for a long while, waiting for nothing in particular—watching cliff
swallows sweep over the canyon rim above, noticing a hummingbird in the fir tree nearby, being aware of gradually gathering clouds.
I'd brought along a pipe and tobacco but had forgotten matches. Yet
the tobacco seemed a good gift in itself. Impulsively I threw a pinch
of it in each of the four directions, so as to sanctify the place and
honor its spirit. At the time the action seemed perfectly natural, not
at all an effort to mimic native practice. In its origins, I suspect, ritual is not learned; it is earth-taught.

As I lay in silence, dark, churning clouds began to fill the space
of sky framed by the canyon rim above. Then came the first loud
crash of thunder, and I knew I was about to be caught by a cloud-
burst in the middle of the desert. As the initial drops of rain fell, I
scrambled up a nearby ledge, looking for shelter, finding the small
opening of a cave going into the canyon wall. It wasn't large. I
looked carefully to make sure it was empty, then crawled in just as
the heavy rains let loose. Soon they were followed by hail the size
of quarters—bouncing everywhere, ricocheting off the rocks, dancing in the fierce thunder and lightning. There I lay, under the
mountain, looking wide-eyed at this glorious apocalypse, scribbling
away in the yellow pad I use for a journal.

Soon sheets of water begin to pour over the top of the canyon rim, loosening the dirt and rocks high above. Then the sound of falling boulders echoed through the canyon like shotgun blasts, crashing right before me onto the path I'd followed an hour or so before. I heard the sound of other rocks falling further down the ravine. Torrents of water flowed wildly in every direction. What was it that had followed me into the remoteness of that box canyon, having stalked me to the very end, hiding now in the cleft of the rock? What had I been suckered into all along in coming to Ghost Ranch?

I learned later that there were Indian petroglyphs scratched on the inside of the cave where I lay. I never saw them, but I knew from the place itself that they must have been pictures of death. There was no doubt that this was a dying place, a place where things necessarily came to an end. That's often the way of the desert. The pictures there in the cave would be ones of a deer stalked by a young brave or a mountain lion. They would tell stories I

Carlsbad Caverns National Park in New Mexico lies in the Chihuahuan Desert in the shadow of the Guadalupe Mountains. The caverns are like a vast temple to Mother Earth. The only thing missing are statues to a god. The Caverns, up to 1,000 feet below a Fortress of Solitude escarpment with enough acreage underground to house a town, seems to be in the middle of nowhere because it is. Big Bend National Park in Texas sits 200 miles to the south and Roswell, New Mexico is 160 miles north. One can either walk 750 feet down the trail of the Natural Entrance Route or take the elevator. Personally, I love the elevator. There is nothing quite like dropping 750 feet into another world. My kids and I walked around slack-jawed at the enormous stalactites and Jabba-the-Hut formations that seem to erupt out of the ground in the 14-acre, 1-mile loop that makes up the Big Room tour.

—Sean O'Reilly, "Notes from the Southwest"

didn't want to remember. Pictures of a thirteen-year-old boy whose father had been suddenly and violently killed. A boy who all of his life would see the lost father. Pictures of that same boy, now in his forties, sitting beside a mother and waiting for her long and painful death to end. A boy whose parents had both died (or were dying) at times in his life when he was struggling most to be born. I knew the pictures. But I hadn't known the grieving that had to go with them.

The day before this trip into the canyon, I'd been given a session of shiatsu massage by a woman in our group who was a healer. Shiatsu is a Japanese form of deep massage, based on the idea that painful (and joyous) memories are often retained in particular parts of the body. The human body is seen to offer a microgeography of past traumas in an individual's experience. Through the process of deep massage, as one feels his life breath virtually forced out of him, there can be an accompanying release of forgotten pain.

I had experienced this the previous afternoon as the healing woman reached a point in my left hip, pushing a finger deep into my side. It was a place that hurt intensely. But it also released an incredible sobbing that came from some place deeper within me than I knew existed. I had no image of what this grieving was about. At the time, I could only think of the Fisher King in the Grail legend who was also wounded in the thigh. And Jacob…who limped away at dawn from his wrestling with the angel, the hollow of his thigh now out of joint. All men, I suspect, are wounded in the thigh—at that place where they give life, where they are most vulnerable, where they've failed and been failed by others.

It's only now, as I tell the story, that I realize how the thunder and the cave and the grieving over my father's death (and my mother's dying) were all tied together with something that had been carried in my left side, maybe for years. The healing woman had said the effects of shiatsu might continue for a day or more, that it was not uncommon for people to be deeply touched in the spirit as a result of the fierce and hard touch experienced in their bodies.

When the rain passed and the rock slides ended, I crawled out of the cave. The winds quickly carried the storm clouds away, and before long the sun was out again, shining on a world made perfectly new. Water droplets on every leaf and rock were lit by the sun. The air was clear as crystal, cleansed by the rain. Silence had returned.

Then gradually, a trickle of water began to flow over the rim at the canyon's end, cascading a hundred feet down the sunlit brilliance onto the rock where I'd lain before. It grew in strength, becoming a massive waterfall of light-tan waters, fed by arroyos from high above, bringing the runoff of rain from surrounding mesas. These waters of life poured down into the place of death. I stood there watching. Then slowly I walked through the falling water, being soaked in its sand-filled wetness, as a loud, resounding laughter erupted spontaneously from deep inside. This fierce, good laughter came from the same dark place from where the sobbing had come the day before. It echoed down the canyon, summoning everything to life.

What was this place? Everywhere I walked, life burst out of the ground before and behind me. The desert after a hard rain is incredibly alive. Falling water courses over the rocks and fills arroyos. One can practically feel the trees and sagebrush gorging themselves with it. I began to walk back down the canyon, following the creek that was now quickly rising, coming to a place I'd passed on the way in, where a side canyon joined the one I'd been walking. The place where the two canyons came together was filled with vegetation, sparkling now with life.

Dark red waters flowed down from the side canyon to join the light-tan waters from the upper creek, flowing side by side, then merging together in some great mystery. The new waters entering the creek were a deep, chocolate red, the runoff of multicolored mesas from above. They formed a menstrual flow, these dark waters, as if the land were cleansing itself of its life-giving blood. Viscous and thick, they poured especially heavy from between two large boulders. I climbed over to the place, cupped my hands, and let the waters fall over my head, rolling down my hair and onto my shoulders. Here, at the place of the joining of the two waters, everything came together.

Up at the end of the box canyon I'd been struck by the masculine power of the place. There the Sky Father had let loose his energy, with a wild display of thunder and lightning. It had been the place of Zeus, of Thor, Yahweh, the Thunderbird. A place of fierceness and death. But this was a different place. Here, the waters from above came down to join the waters from below, and all became whole. This was the place of the Earth Mother, life-giving, connecting, sinking deep roots into the anchoredness of the land. It was the place of Demeter, the Old Spider Woman, Mother Guadelupe. A place of birth and nurture.

This place answered the questions posed by the earlier place. How would I live again on the far side of the experience of death, surviving the loss of the father and the mother, discovering a new wildness and rootedness? The answer came in being baptized, first with water and then with blood. Only as I came to terms with the loss of one, could I deal with the loss of the other. Only then could I be set free to live as the person I'd longed all my life to become.

I had always sought that deep masculine energy of the wildman, who lives his life without being tentative and fearful, who (like Joseph Campbell's hero) loves and risks much for the sake of truth. In my dreams, he often sits by the front window of a village taverna, drinking a glass of raki and arm-wrestling one of the young Greek fishermen at the tables, laughing loudly. I watch him at a distance, wishing profoundly that his abandonment were mine. He wanders over, almost drunk now, and leans against the chair where I sit at the corner table, writing on a yellow pad. Always writing on a yellow pad!

"To hell with your fine words, my friend," he says with a smile and an arm on my shoulder. "Come, I buy you some raki and deliver you from the dangers of your pen." I smell the sea in his beard. He is Zorba, Neptune, Odysseus, the Fisher King, this man. In my dream, I laugh back. I toss my papers under the table, and with tears running down my face, say, "Yes, father, I've waited for you a long time. Sit and drink. Teach me...to dance!"

What comes first in a man's midlife experience may be this baptism in the wild waters of the father, the wildman. Only then can he reaffirm also the mother, being baptized with blood, accepting the feminine energy of the Pacha Mama, the Earth Mother. She is the one who knows her power to create and give birth, to put down roots, to weave the fabric of life into a mystery of interconnectedness. This is a baptism that makes possible a new intimacy. Wholeness will always be found at the middle place, where the two waters join to become one.

In the joy of that afternoon sun, I walked on back down the canyon toward home, stopping to take off my clothes (it just seemed the right thing to do). Walking naked through the land, I turned in slow circles, drinking in the red and orange grandeur of the rocky cliffs around me, all newly washed by rain. In those few moments, I moved through the canyon landscape as one of its details, knowing the land had taught me something I could not name.

Belden C. Lane is Professor of Theological Studies and American Studies at Saint Louis University and the author of Landscapes of the Sacred: Geography and Narrative in American Spirituality *and* The Solace of Fierce Landscapes: Exploring Desert and Mountain Spirituality, *from which this story was excerpted. He lives in St. Louis.*

✳

Mysteries and ambiguities abound in the desert and one such mystery is to be found in Santa Fe. In 1873, the Sisters of Loretto had finished building a school called the Loretto Academy of Our Lady of Light but they still needed a chapel. French and Italian masons were hired but when the job was complete, a dreadful mistake was discerned. There was no room to artfully connect the choir loft and the chapel with a normal set of stairs due to the exceptional height of the loft. Many carpenters were summoned to try their hand at executing a tight design in minimal space. All attempts failed, with the last expert saying that such a job could not be done. The Sisters prayed to St. Joseph for help. On the last day of their novena, a gray-haired man came up to the convent with a donkey and a tool chest. He asked if he might help. He had only a hammer, a saw and a T-square. He took six to eight months to build the stairs and then mysteriously departed without accepting payment for his work. The winding staircase that he left is a masterpiece. It makes two 360-degree turns with no supporting pole. The entire weight is supported by the base and that is where the mystery lies. According to architects and engineers who have examined the stairs, they should have crashed to the floor the moment anyone stepped on them. According to a timber expert, formerly with the U.S. Navy Research and Development Laboratory in China Lake, the wood used in the stairs does not conform to any know species of wood in the Southwest. Angel in disguise or unknown genius? Visit the stairs and decide for yourself.

—Sean O'Reilly, "Notes from the Southwest"

JAMES C. WORK

✦ ✦ ✦

Bridge over the Wind

The life of stone can teach the human heart.

THE TWO-MILE WALK TO LANDSCAPE ARCH IS BEST TAKEN AT sunset. At that time of day, the shadows will be growing long and the heat will still be intense. The sun will be directly in your face as you go up, and the trail will be dark and hard to follow as you come down again. But it is the best time to go, because it is in those closing hours of daylight that the desert can make an acute observer out of you.

You are going to feel overheated and thirsty even before leaving the trailhead and starting up the trail. You will feel the skin of your face shrinking and roasting under that horizontal solar broiler; the sensation makes me think of those barbequed chicken carcasses that turn on spits in supermarket delicatessens. This feeling that your face is turning into a crispy entrée is good: it makes you attentive to the trail. It is the desert's way of getting your attention. Before venturing into the narrow sandstone alley at the very beginning of the trail, you will probably take careful notice of where you are and how far you will be going and in what direction you intend to go. Back at home, when I walk out of my house, I habitually pat my pocket to see if I have my keys. At Arches, I shake my canteen to see that it's full and take a bearing on my surroundings.

The narrow alley I mentioned is a redstone passageway, easy to confuse with a hundred others. The floor is sand, and the walls curve gracefully inward, overhead. There are a few clusters of sage and cactus and juniper, huddled close to the base of the wall.

When you walk in the city, you see so many things in motion that you tend to see none of them. In the desert, there are very few things that move, and so you tend to notice them. It might be a little windspout whirling over the horizon, or a lizard darting up a nearby rock. Along the Landscape Arch Trail, you will notice more birds, not because there are more of them here than elsewhere, but because they are more constantly in motion than anything else in the area. Many of them are daytime foragers, but at sunset the desert launches her best fliers. The nighthawk, a little sweptwing gray falcon with white wingstrips, makes its "*keeee — aaaahee*" cry each time it goes into a steep banking maneuver and accelerates after an airborne bug. The wings are thin, sharply bent backward in the middle of the leading edge, sharply pointed at the tip, built for effortless sustained soaring and for breathless downward dives.

The other flier is a true night fighter, getting an early start before the dim dusk turns to black. When you spot the first one of these, you will think that it is a shadow in your eye. You might see it as an optical illusion, a tiny bug flying close to your face. It sometimes makes a small, faraway noise and it is shaped almost like a housefly or a moth. Then you see more of them. Here they come, flying down the alleyway in bandit formation, pulling up as they reach you, going into a tight fast turn. Each one turns as if it had a wingtip thumbtacked to the sky. Then they dip into a free fall and then easily rise again to the top of the alley wall. Wings like sails, like sport parachutes, only chunky and leathery. The nighthawk may justifiably exult in its gracefulness, in the sheer aesthetic of narrowwing flight, but the bat seems more interested in being quick and effective than in being beautiful. It is quiet Death in motion—and flies as if it knows it.

The sun setting behind the slickrock shapes will burn images into your awareness. At your feet, long shadows are flat carbon copies of the stone forms that loom ahead. The horizon beyond the rocks looks like goblin silhouettes cut out of hot thin tin, backlit by an eerie orange sky. The extraterrestrial light of evening is blue-orange and orange-black. Dead juniper trees along the trail hold their desiccated branches away from their twisted trunks as if in agony. You hurry around a corner to get away from them. You come up a slight hill between sand dune and rock, and the sun hits you full in the face; this time it is as bright as a carbon-arc spotlight. It seems as if the sun has exploded at the instant of sunset.

And now you are wading in knee-deep shadows and you begin to wonder whether the sidewinders and rattlers are coming out to lie on the warm trail; you wonder if the scorpions and the tarantulas saw the sunset from their shaded dens and are now on their way out for the evening hunting. After all, the bats are already out. Do you watch the sky for bats, or the trail for the slower-moving hunters? Actually, you look for a familiar formation so that you can get your bearings, but suddenly a sunset trick of the shadows makes that formation look unfamiliar. Your mind—the rational one— knows that it is the same stone monolith as before, but some other mind of yours can simultaneously believe just the opposite.

You will also distrust your senses when you come over that final rise in the sand and see Landscape Arch there before you. You must have strayed onto the trail to another arch: this soaring sliver of curved stone, this pink thin rainbow arched over the debris-choked canyon, is probably called Delicate Arch, or Fragile Arch. But it is Landscape Arch, which is a way of saying that names matter very little.

Almost 300 feet from base to base, this is the longest known natural arch in the world. To imagine how thin it is, and how graceful, start with a picture of two tall Egyptian obelisks, standing 300 feet apart. No, first you have to imagine 300 feet. Think of the largest football stadium you can remember. The football field there is 300 feet long, so this arch would reach from one set of end bleachers into the other end. It would soar above the grandstand.

Now imagine those Egyptian obelisks again. Imagine what they would look like if they began to melt in the desert sun, curving toward each other until the thin tips meet. The bases have slumped but are still square at the bottom. Stand here and imagine yourself climbing up there on the arch—it is 100 feet up there—and the thought will make you dizzy.

I find myself almost hypnotized as I stand at the base of one of the legs. I am inside the arch, leaning back against the warm flat face of the arch rock, and the rock stretches upward from my heels, along my spine, and curves over my head; it continues the same curve, up and over and up and over and on and on to the center of the span, and it grows narrower and narrower as it curves, and narrower and narrower still, still flat-surfaced and still soaring, and becomes an optical illusion.

The problem I have is that I cannot make my mind register the fact that the rock tapers toward the span's center. It is something like looking down a long railroad track and not being able to believe that the two parallel tracks do not converge out there in the distance. This illusion is just the reverse of that: the long span of rock does *not* taper, says my head, and therefore the slim center of this reach of stone is the *same* dimension as this block against which I am leaning, and *therefore* the structure is so long that the base of the other leg must be perched on the nether edge of eternity.

Call it vertigo, or tell me it is only a phenomenon of failing light. The mind can do odd things with perspective. Falling down through the thin sky in your disabled airplane, watching your altimeter unwind at a rate of fifty-eight feet per second, it is possible to have the sensation that the earth is moving away from you at the same speed and you will never reach it. I was in a mystery house once, where the rooms look plumb and square and everything looks level—until the guide drops a ball and it rolls quickly *up* the floor and out the door—or until you turn the tap at a sink and the water runs out sideways. I have seen it, can explain it, and know it is an illusion. Maybe my mind sees an extra dimension sometimes, or is short on one dimension. Whichever the case, I am content to let others see that Landscape Arch actually tapers toward the center, if they will be content to let me see it touching down at the margin of eternity. What *we* see doesn't matter: the stone knows where it touches earth and where it touches sky, and what its name is.

I said that "Landscape Arch" seems like a pretty tame name for this ossified red rainbow. Over a year after being there, I dug into my old copy of Skeat's *Etymological Dictionary* and found out that the name is less of a misnomer than I thought. "Arch," according to Skeat, has Latin origins that have nothing to do with curving bridgelike structures. In Latin the word *arcum* means bow-shaped and gives us the word "arc," which people confused with *arca*. The latter refers to a box or coffer, an "ark" used to carry things in, like the ark of the covenant. "Landscape" comes from two Middle Dutch words. *Land* means "region" or "area": the *−scap* part means "condition" and is a collective suffix. So, if we put the words together, we have an ark which safeguards the condition of the collective region. And that's true.

Like everything else in the desert slickrock country, Landscape Arch has ancient origins and is in the ages-slow process of metamorphosing into other forms. All the material that has fallen away from it has become sand again and may become sandstone again, given time. Like everything else out here, the aging effect is very visible in the rock because there is no overgrowth to hide it. Like everything else in the arch and canyon region, it has taken a form that seems to have no natural function. If it is a bridge, it is a bridge over the wind. Will any humans be there to hear it when the arch's end comes, or will the arch be alone again in the thunder of its final collapse?

It amuses me to hear some arch-watchers speak about "falling" and "collapsing" and to read the ranger-written signs that use the words "erosion" and "decay." This is the short view of things. The arches are not eroding—merely reforming. There are more arches waiting to take the place of the fallen ones, unborn and buried in the sandstone mesas. The sand of former arches is going down the Colorado River right now, into the sea to be pressed into stone again and thence once more into arches. The rain washes tiny grains away from cracked blocks that mark the place where an arch used to span a gorge; those grains are the arch being taken to the seabed to become arches again on some other side of eternity. I suppose it reassures us, we who have such short spans ourselves, to smugly tell one another that even the rocks are in a state of "decay."

James C. Work is a professor of English at Colorado State University where he designed and taught the university's first class in nature writing. He has also spent five summers as an in-the-field wilderness writing instructor with Colorado College's Wilderness Experience program. He is editor of Prose and Poetry of the American West, Shane: The Critical Edition, *and a collection of short stories,* Gunfight! *He is the author of several books, including* Ride West to Dawn *and* Following Where the River Begins— *winner of a Charles Redd Award in Western Studies—from which this story was excerpted.*

★

Nobody even knows how many arches are in Arches National Park because nature is continually making new ones. Sixty years ago the park's superintendent reported he had seen 47 arches. A few years later his successor upped the total to 81. In 1984 a Brigham Young University geographer undertook a meticulous count and he soon reported a total of 450.

What's the right number? On the trail, it scarcely matters. What does matter is that, inch by inch, we are immersed into a mind-boggling natural wonder where wind and rain and snow have combined to erode holes in soft Entrada sandstone, a rock that's held together by unevenly distributed calcium deposits that act as a geological glue. The uneven distribution is crucial. Where the calcium isn't, holes emerge—and the results are, for instance, the stunning Double Arch, with its dual openings. The larger hole is 163 feet; the smaller is 60 feet. Hike there—and this is an easy 0.4 mile trail—and you are enveloped by the shadows of the giant arch. "It's like a cathedral," an awed woman hiker gasped as she stepped inside the arches.

—Robert McGarvey, "Feets, Don't Fail Me Now!"

$\star \overset{\star}{} \star$

In the Superstitions

Gold fever strikes anew along the Peralta Trail.

"As the story goes," I say, "the Peralta family came up from Mexico in the 1840s and discovered a fortune in gold in these mountains. But the Apache supposedly killed them and sealed the mine entrance. Ever since, gold seekers have been searching for it. Personally, I have strong reason to believe that the mine never existed."

That's what I tell my hiking companion (a transplanted New Yorker) as we strike out on the Peralta Trail, heading north into the overpowering desolation of Arizona's Superstition Mountains. Our destination is Fremont Saddle, a 2.3-mile walk, and a close-up view of the awesome spire of Weavers Needle.

The desert trail is well-defined, crossing and recrossing a boulder-strewn wash, angling always upward.

Now the trail follows along the canyon wall—steeper, weaving its way through the fields of house-size boulders. "Sometime in the 1870s," I tell my friend, "an old Dutchman named Jacob Waltz, or Walz, started paying for his supplies with raw gold. The story spread that he had located the old Peralta mine in the Superstitions, or a brand new mine, depending on who was telling the story."

"Ah," comments my companion, "and thus the legend of the Lost Dutchman Mine."

"Right," I reply, "but I'm a skeptic. I don't believe the Lost Dutchman Mine ever existed either." We stop to drink from our water bottles.

"Then there was poor Adolf Ruth," I say. "Like hundreds of others, he came into possession of the only accurate map to the Lost Dutchman Mine. He quit his job and, in 1931, came into these mountains alone. Months later they discovered him in two places. His skull with bullet holes was found in one place, and the rest of his body in another. All of his belongings were intact, except..."

"The map was missing," my friend interjects. We stop for a breather.

"Some estimate," I say, "that more than a hundred hardy gold seekers have died in these mountains. And thousands of others have spent their savings looking for the Dutchman's mine."

"I took a geology course in college," my companion tells me. "Lava rock is the very last place you would ever expect to find gold."

I smile. My friend is correct. "That's why I'm a nonbeliever."

"Well," says my friend, "we can forget about those silly tales and concentrate on the scenery."

After a moderately strenuous two-hour climb, we top out at Fremont Saddle. And there before us is the immense spire of Weavers Needle, approximately 1,300 feet high from base to top. Legends state that the needle is the key to locating the lost mine and incredible amounts of gold.

We sit and rest, drinking in the brooding, overpowering majesty of the vast and empty wilderness that surrounds us.

And though I am convinced there is no gold in the Superstitions, I feel a sudden rush of excitement. For a certain period when I was a kid, I became swept up by tales of lost Superstition gold. I devoured every book I could find on the subject and floated off frequently on fantasy expeditions.

Since our arrival at the saddle, a small cloud has been blocking the sun. As I sit, the cloud moves away, and harsh sunlight causes the towering needle to cast a sharp and lengthy shadow across the tossed landscape.

A storage cabinet of my mind suddenly swings open, and a diagram from one of those childhood books leapt out. The hair stands up on the back of my neck. Nearly word for word, I can see the caption beneath a diagram. It's all coming back. Something like, "When the sun reaches the proper position in the sky…" What was the rest of it? "The needle will cast a long shadow into a dark crevasse on a distant canyon wall."

Holy cow. That is exactly what the needle is doing! It's a deep crevasse. An almost hidden crevasse. Oh brother! I'm remembering the rest of it. "The dark crevasse is the location of the lost mine." That's what it said. And I'm looking right at it.

I stand up suddenly. "We need to head back," I say.

"Head back?" replies my friend. "Why head back?"

"Burros," I say.

"Burros?"

"I need to get back to town and price a couple of burros."

"Why don't we go over there and sit in the shade," suggests my friend. "That sun is hot."

"A pick, and shovel, too," I tell him.

"Rest for a few minutes…relax."

My friend is splashing water on a handkerchief. "Put this against your forehead."

"And dynamite…we'll need lots of dynamite!"

He's looking at me strangely. He doesn't seem to understand.

William Hafford passed away in 1992.

✳

Three great collapsed volcanoes (calderas) have merged to form today's Superstition Mountains. Some geologists map as many as five overlapping calderas here. Largest is the Superstition Caldera, which poured out ash about 25 million years ago, collapsing on itself while still erupting….

Jacob Walz and Jacob Wiser disappeared into this volcanic maze in 1871. Walz finally returned to Florence with a sackful of gold nuggets, but without Wiser, whom he had evidently killed. Walz was German, but his mine became "the Dutchman's" because on the frontier all Germans were "Dutchmen." Walz eluded (or killed) every pursuing prospector during the six years he worked the mine, bringing out gold for his sprees in Phoenix and Tucson, then disappearing into the Superstitions again.

Finally, he retired. He settled down as a chicken farmer in Phoenix, acquired a girlfriend named Julie Thomas, and in 1891 survived a flood just long enough to dictate directions to the mine to Julia and another friend.

But they could not find the mine. And neither has anyone else. And so it is the Lost Dutchman Mine.... The Superstitions keep safe their treasure. The Apaches still know things no one else knows. The Arizona interior remains elusive.

—Stephen Trimble, *Arizona: The Land and the People*
edited by Tom Miller

TIMOTHY EGAN

The Place That Always Was

Acoma, New Mexico is a place you won't easily forget.

YOU STAND AT THE LIP OF A CINNAMON-COLORED LEDGE, FOUR-and-a-half centuries after the same ground rattled with Francisco Vásquez de Coronado's column, and see nothing that could lure an army up the spine of the continent. From five miles out, you can see homes, terraced and weathered, facing south. It bears some resemblance to the pictures in yellowed books, pictures that go back 100 years or more, labeling this view, these homes, as the ruins of Acoma. Some maps, sadly misled, contain the same caption. You rub your eyes at the spot where Spanish hearts sank and see a place pulsing with life. The ruins are alive. Nothing extraordinary appears to be going on, just the routine of a day. You are close enough to see that the pueblo is made of beige New Mexican mud, not gold, and so you can hear with minimal effort the sigh of the conquistadors, the empty wind blowing their Latin banners, which proclaimed Plus Ultra—More Beyond.

The way to counter the Western malaise of drift and rootlessness, says the poet Gary Snyder, is to find your place, dig in, and defend it. And so here is Acoma, possibly the oldest continuously inhabited city in the United States, living by the poet's dictum. The Sky City is nearly 7,000 feet above sea level, burnished today by the low-angled sunlight of the late winter. It is built on the crown of a sandstone butte that soars from a table 400 feet below. In the usual tellings of the national story, Acoma is an asterisk. It deserves better, if for no other reason than because people have lived atop the same wind-scoured rock for perhaps 1,000 years or more, and from that perch fought the first battle over religious freedom in what is now the United States.

The story of America usually starts in the East, with Pilgrims in New England and tobacco farmers in Virginia, finally making its way toward the sunset for barely a generation's worth of gunfighting and gold-digging, using a clock's tick of history, roughly 1849 to 1890, to define the West. The well-worn narrative, not unlike many modern Western politicians, is heavily influenced by the movement and slaughter of domestic cattle and grubstaking for off-colored rocks—a pitiful excuse for a history. The Spanish drove a herd of cattle across the Rio Grande 350 years before the streets of Laredo were knee-deep in cow shit. But nobody comes West today in search of ancient steak bones. They come to see why a place like Acoma is still standing.

Acoma is where one nation's motto of More Beyond met another's End of the Line. Plymouth Rock pilgrims were yet to be born, nor had the first draft of the Jamestown narrative been sketched when a dust cloud carrying bearded men on horses arrived at the foot of Acoma in 1540. Loaded for gold and costumed for war, the Spanish were chasing an 800-year-old rumor: the gilded cities of Nuevo Mexico. Three hundred soldiers, trailed by Franciscan friars, long-conquered Aztecs, and brass cannons on wheels, had traveled north by foot and hoof more than 1,000 miles, living largely on a diet of anticipation. They would gaze into the Grand Canyon, drink snowmelt from two-mile-high peaks rising from the whiskered face of the Sonoran Desert, chase bison on the Great Plains, and plod through city after city of people who knew how to live a reasonable life in a land without reliable rain. The vistas stretched to earthly infinity under a sky that made people feel insignificant. The Spanish understood north from south and east from west, but what they found most troubling were the two other dimensions of the Acoman compass—up and down, the directions in eternity.

The first residents of Acoma, descendants of the Anasazi, had also wandered, abandoning their 100-unit apartments on the Colorado Plateau. They buttoned up the carefully masoned homes, walked away from the maze of funnels and diversions used to channel water onto farm fields, and headed south. Over the years, they strayed down one withered wash or another, shouting into the sandstone walls, waiting for the echo that would tell them they had arrived at their long-prophesied new home. West of the Rio Grande, within view of the white-haired summit of an 11,000-foot-high mountain, the shouts were returned. The echo epic was over. Here, atop the rock, on the flat, thin-soiled, unwatered high point, they founded Acoma, a Keresan word meaning the Place That Always Was. More Beyond? No, Señor Coronado. This is it.

You feel like a stranger here, not unwelcome, but uncertain. From the road heading west out of Albuquerque, you see nothing to entice you on a detour to the Sky City. There is a casino near the exit. The real payoff is ahead, down a winding road through modest homes, past a few vacant-eyed mules rubbing against barbed-wire fences, to the ledge that looks out to the initial views of Acoma. No pictures are allowed, even from afar, without permission. The Acomans want to control what they can of their image, their story. You think what a corporate cowboy publicist could do with this material, angling for subsidies in the name of tradition.

Down in the valley, closer to the pedestal of Acoma, is a flat plain sliced by an ancient road. At Christmastime it is lined with candles, a luminaria, all lights leading to the top. Now, at road's end, you either move up by foot or out by car. As in Coronado's day, an escort to the pueblo in the sky is required. You ascend.

In 1540, Coronado's men followed the same route, crawling up the rock, guided by handholds in the stone worn by the fingers of many generations. Pushed by the fading promise of Plus Ultra, the conquistadors scaled the flank with swords clanking at their sides. "The ascent was so difficult that we repented climbing to the top,"

Captain Hernando de Alvarado wrote. They would come to repent many things in the Land of Disenchantment.

The people who live at Acoma say their ancestors first came to the rock about 800 A.D., though most archaeologists date the point of habitation at about 1150. The more compelling fact is that they never left.

"From the beginning of time we have been told there was such a place," says Mary Tenorio, an Acoma native, who lives down below on the flat land. "So this is as far as we can ever go."

You mention the bones found on a bank in the Columbia River not long ago, the remains of a man about five feet, nine inches tall, a man who by the reading of radiocarbon datings lived 9,000 years ago. You don't want to argue with Mary Tenorio, an artist, standing with you in the blood-slowing wind of a winter day, at the base of the Place That Always Was. The facial bones of the Columbia River man do not match the features of any other native people in the Americas. He appears to be of northern European stock, the anthropologists say. A white guy. You are not disputing the prophecy of Acoma, but simply wondering why some people stayed around and some did not, whether some people followed prophetic destinies and some did not. Maybe the Anglos from the Columbia Plateau simply died out before they could find a Place That Always Was. Maybe that will be the problem Phoenix will face.

Five hundred years ago, the entire Rio Grande pueblo community was more densely populated, in places, than it is today. The inhabitants lived in tight little communities, entirely surrounded, they believed then as now, by envy. There were about 60,000 people in the broad valley at the time of Coronado's arrival.

Along the ledge today, you can hear long-ago voices in Spanish and Keresan, dimming the fires of Coronado's imagination. You can imagine the look the conquistador gave his scout, as he checked his map, his eyesight. What the hell is this?

"The greatest stronghold ever seen in the world," one of Coronado's men wrote.

The curse of Coronado was what had come before him, the big

shadow of expectations. He was thirty years old, an aristocrat, full of himself as only someone chosen for greatness by church and state can be. In the parlance of modern politics, he did worse than expected. His chief guides were pathological prevaricators. His financial supporters, the Spanish Crown and noblemen who had sold their homes to bankroll the next great treasure hunt, expected a tenfold return and enough adventure stories on which to dine into their dying years.

Barely twenty years earlier, Hernando Cortés had landed on the coast of Mexico and marched a path to the peak of Spanish glory. So confident was Cortés of Plus Ultra that his men burned their boats near Vera Cruz. Inland, after hacking through the Mexican rain forest and stumbling upon a golden valley, they found Tenochtitlán, the Aztec capital. With its floating gardens, canals, and massive pyramids, it was as grand as any city of sixteenth-century Europe, but also much larger—with a population of nearly a quarter million. Jewels were cheap, gold ubiquitous, food plentiful. The Aztec pact with the sun gods required a mere human heart— freshly cut and live—a day. Without this daily sacrifice, the sun would fall out of the sky forever.

Through dealmaking with native factions, superior weaponry, and the silent front flank of disease, Cortés gradually broke the Aztecs. Spain had its gravy train of gold to fortify its armies for another century of European wars.

"We have a strange disease of the heart," Cortés told the Aztec emperor Montezuma, "for which gold is the only cure."

So what to make of Acoma, all mud walls and squawking turkeys, the people plain and squat, the ordinary lives of ordinary people a joke compared with Tenochtitlán? This Nuevo Mexico high country was supposed to be the heart of the Seven Cities of Cibola. The conquistadors went to bed every night on tales of the cities, said to have been founded by seven bishops who had fled the Moorish occupation of Spain hundreds of years before. And more recently, there had been all these encouraging reports, the advance word. After a disastrous landing in Florida, a little knot of lost Spaniards and a Moorish slave had straggled west across the conti-

nent, over eight years, through Texas and New Mexico, finally arriving in Mexico City, the headquarters of New Spain. They built a
bonfire of lies, leaping details of the Seven Cities of Cibola, places
where doors were trimmed in turquoise and stairways lined in
gold. Somewhere in Nuevo Mexico. Somewhere in the Rio
Grande Valley. Somewhere in El Norte. You had to squint, at first,
but it was there. Once the Pueblo people saw how hungry the
Spanish were for nuggets of Cibola information, they too started
spreading rumors—basically as a way to send them on to the next
village. Just over the rise, Señor Coronado.

Coronado traveled 4,000 miles in all. He was a truly atrocious
guest, arriving at one Pueblo village or another to consume most of
their winter food supplies, trash their homes, mock their religion,
and paw at their women. He burned at least 100 warriors at the
stake, piñon smoke never smelled so bitter. The Zuni pueblo of
Hawikuh was described by one of the conquistadors as "a little
crowded village that looks as if it had been all crumpled together."
And Hawikuh was a Cibola highlight, one of the places where the
streets were supposed to be cobbled in gold.

In truth, the villages were no better or worse than the basic western farm town of modern America. Each had anywhere from 400
to 2,000 people. They kept domesticated birds and raised corn,
squash, and beans in irrigated fields. The food wasn't bad. "They
make the best tortillas that I have seen anywhere," wrote Pedro de
Castañeda, the first journalist of the West, who went along with
Coronado, keeping a chronicle. Hired as a propagandist, he became
disenchanted, ultimately siding with the natives. The Indians were
good masons, good potters, and good clothiers, making colored
outfits from the cotton they grew. They had never seen a horse. As
for precious metals, the closest thing they had was turquoise, but
certainly nothing to set a conquistador's pulse racing.

The first encounter between Europeans and natives in the West
was violent. A battle with the Zunis knocked Coronado unconscious and made him thoroughly ill tempered afterward. He was hit
on the head by a rock thrown from a Zuni post. In all, he destroyed
a dozen pueblos, breaking a promise he had made to the viceroy of

New Spain that any conquest would be "Christian and apostolic, and not a butchery."

His low point may have been on the plains of Kansas, at the far eastern edge of the rumor-chase. When he found grass huts and animal-skin lean-tos instead of the gilded city of Quivera, Coronado garroted his guide, the latest in a string of artful liars. Quivera, the conquistadors had been told, was a city where the emperor took his afternoon nap under a tree bedecked with bells of gold, lulled to sleep by wind against the ornaments. That story sustained them on the march to Kansas, but the way home had no similar motivating myth. Retreating back to the Rio Grande, Coronado said of the Great Plains and its bison herds, "It is nothing but cows and sky."

Nearing the top of Acoma, Coronado's men must have felt like a party that climbs Mount Everest only to find someone lounging on the summit with a bag of chips and a portable TV. They were shown kivas, the ceremonial cellars, and the elaborate village, windows facing the southern sun, cisterns filled with drinking water, pathways on the hard stone, hundreds of people going about their business atop the rock of Acoma. Women climbed up the ladders, water-filled pots balanced atop their heads, without spilling a drop. The villagers said their perch was impenetrable: nobody would ever take the fortress Acoma. And Coronado's men wondered, clambering back down the rock, who would want it?

The 500 or so homes atop Acoma are still heated by wood, with mounded clay ovens outside that look like big beehives. The old timbered ladders, baked white by the sun, still rise to the top terraces, and there are deep footpaths along the tabletop of the rock. It is not a museum, but a living town, somewhat iced in time. The wind dominates all other sounds.

The Acoma people always had a cacique, the top religious head of the pueblo. His job was to watch the sun, keeping careful track of its movement so that the people would not miss the solstices. This did not impress the Spanish, who had their own fetishists but seemed well assured that the sun would rise every day, regardless of whether they paid any attention to it or not. Also, in this land where the dry air was full of illusion, Pedro de Castañeda had written, "What they worship most is water."

Signs of the ancient religion abound atop the pueblo, but the tallest, most dominant structure has nothing to do with sun worship or water shortages. As you move through the village, hearing half-stories of wars and miracles at Acoma, of the silver-crowned cane that was a personal gift from Abraham Lincoln for loyalty to the Union, of priests being thrown from the cliff, and defeat and redemption of the residents, you wonder about the church bell hanging above the Sky City, in San Esteban de Rey Mission. It seems so out of place. Coronado, the deflated conquistador, fled the rock, claiming no use for Acoma. The Spanish had come to New Mexico, one conquistador wrote, "to give light to those who were in darkness and to get rich as all men desire to do." The Acomans did not seem worth the effort of conversion, and they certainly had little that would fill the crown's coffers. Coronado went back to Mexico City in disgrace, later to be tried for mismanagement and cruelty to the Indians. But the Spanish were not done with Acoma.

Old age was to the sixteenth century what drawn-out male adolescence is to the late twentieth century. You married as a teen, mourned the death of many of your children during the first few years of their lives, and counted yourself lucky if you lived past your thirty-fifth birthday—five years beyond life expectancy for European males. Don Juan de Oñate was nearly fifty years old, a fossil in armor and silk, when he finally pushed north out of Mexico City on a colonizing journey to the Kingdom of New Mexico in 1598. It was the same year that Cervantes started writing *Don Quixote*, so windmill-chasing was not yet ingrained into Spanish life as a national metaphor.

After years of delays and debate, Oñate had persuaded the Crown that it was worth taking another look at the cold, high mesas of the north. More than half a century had passed since Coronado's disaster. The soul-saving argument carried much sway, of course. But there were other incentives to prod the two-mile-long column that moved through the dust of El Camino Real—the 2,000-mile trail from Mexico City that for centuries was the longest road in North America. The Spanish, like other Europeans, were still in ardent pursuit of a waterway across North America, the fabled shortcut to Asia. The ill-fated march of Coronado had not chilled the urge for chasing rumors; the Northwest Passage, known to the Spanish as the Strait of Anian, would be a wondrous trophy. Maps of the time also showed a distant and vast island named California, somewhere off the coast of present-day Nevada.

Gold lust had not dissipated. The Spanish Crown was bankrupt, having frittered away its huge profits from New World mines on endless meddling in European wars. Maybe, some of Oñate's men told themselves, Coronado had missed something. A snowballing rumor had it that there were silver bars just lying around the ground of the Rio Grande pueblos. As a sweetener, Oñate offered prospective settlers prime New Mexican real estate, for the taking, and a low-level noble title. Essentially, it was the first American dream, conquistador version. Every man who lived in New Mexico for five years would receive a patent of hidalgo, the lowest rank of Spanish nobility.

As for the people already living there, that issue was in flux. There were an estimated 20 million natives in all of Mexico and Central America around the mid-sixteenth century. At one point, King Charles V suspended new expeditions into the Americas until the question of whether these people had souls or not was settled. A widespread view held that some races and groups were by nature set aside to be slaves to people of a higher order. This certainly was not a uniquely European concept. North American Indians, from the Haidas of the rain forests in southeast Alaska to the Apaches of the deserts of Mexico, raided and traded in human beings. The Spanish had their dark-skinned slaves, which they preferred to call servants, of Moorish and North African descent. Pope Julius II issued an encyclical in 1512 declaring that the native people of North America were more than muscle and fiber; in fact, he declared they had souls. The bad news was, this meant that they were also burdened with Original Sin, thus putting them in urgent need of baptism, which would wipe the stain from their souls. So for many natives, the inaugural ritual of Christianity as practiced by sixteenth-century Spain came only after deciding it was better than the hell-fire of eternal damnation or a torching from juniper twigs. Spain had forged a violent Catholicism. Its leaders, both spiritual and political, were tramping around the world forcing people to become Roman Catholics or die at the grill. This is still known, in some history books, as the golden age of Spain.

With a clean conscience, the Spanish Crown issued a *cedula* in 1583, authorizing the conquest, er, pacification, of New Mexico, for the purpose of saving the spiritually bereft. The stage was set for Acoma's tangle with the last of the conquistadors.

It took Oñate six months to move 1,500 miles up the trail to New Mexico, the old Plus Ultra banners fraying in the desert wind. He had the kind of family background where the word "destiny" likely followed the word "mama." He married a woman who was a descendant of both Montezuma and Cortés. His father, Cristóbal, had landed in those first Spanish boats to arrive in Mexico and had marched to the Aztec capital with

> Those old Spanish conquerors had a monstrous greed for gold and a wonderful lust for saving souls. Treasures they must have, if not on earth, why, then, in heaven; and when they failed to find heathen temples bedecked with silver, they propitiated Heaven by seizing the heathen themselves. There is yet extant a copy of a record made by a heathen artist to express his conception of the demands of the conquerors. In one part of the picture we have a lake, and nearby stands a priest pouring water on the head of a native. On the other side, a poor Indian has a cord about his throat. Lines run from these two groups to a central figure, a man with beard and full Spanish panoply. The interpretation of the picture writing is this: Be baptized as this saved heathen or be hanged as that damned heathen.
>
> —John Wesley Powell (1874)

Cortés. Oñate had done nothing of real substance in his entire life. He was desperate for the New Mexico *entrada*, and he brought along two of his adult nephews to share in the family triumph.

When he arrived, a few months shy of the last year of the sixteenth century, it marked the end of about 500 years of relatively uninterrupted Pueblo life—a point that Oñate tried to make immediately. This time, the Spanish were not just visiting. They brought an army, cattle, building tools, and several walking levels of Roman Catholic Church hierarchy. Moving up the Rio Grande, Oñate set up a colony just north of modern Santa Fe, in a place he called San Juan de Caballeros. He then called together Indians from throughout the valley for what was known as the standard conquistador speech. The Pueblo people should consider their land occupied. There was much to learn from the Europeans. Most important, they could earn themselves a passage to heaven. But they had to submit. They had to give up the sun god talk and corn worship and kachina dances. They had to replace their sustaining myth—the southern exodus, shouting into sandstone walls waiting for an echo—with a new story, one of a predestined salvation at the hand of the One True Church. No one would be harmed, no women raped, no villages burned, if the people would take an oath of loyalty to the King of Spain.

Many of the Rio Grande villages, seeing an ally in their long fight with Apache and Ute raiders, took the pledge. One by one, the Indians came to kneel, kiss the hand of a priest, and then swear fealty to King Phillip II. Acoma held back. They sent spies to watch it, who then returned a hundred miles to the rock, reporting all they had seen. One bit of intelligence they brought back from the ceremony was that the Spanish fired off these massive metal weapons, the cannons and harquebuses, but they didn't seem to do much harm.

In the fall, Oñate became restless, and set out to find an ocean that was supposed to be just west of the big New Mexico mountains, between the mainland and the Isola de California. He went through Zuni and Hopi country, and they seemed agreeable enough, despite what happened to Coronado. Then he came upon

Acoma. It was, one of his men wrote, "the best situated Indian stronghold in all Christendom." Though, of course, it was not Christian. Acoma was ancient, by New World terms; it had the settled rhythms, detailed oral history, the rigid religion, the too-familiar local powers, the cluttered byways, and the petty politics of a prosperous city that had been around for several hundred years. Consider the parallel to Avignon, in southern France. Avignon, another sky city, built atop a rock, was where popes lived for much of the fourteenth century. It had the same pretensions as Acoma, with, of course, much more of an army to back its conceits.

The people of Acoma believed in premarital sexual experimentation, war, and property rights, to a degree. They were generally monogamous, with family clans regulating marriage. Their main weapon was the big rock itself. Looking down at the high plains 400 feet below, and across to Mount Taylor, then away west to the purple and blue horizon at day's end, they believed themselves invulnerable. Nobody in their known world lived higher up than the Acomans.

Oñate pranced around the base of the rock, looking for a strategic advantage, wondering what such a conquest would mean back in Seville. The Acomans fretted. They had spent the summer beefing up their defenses. It was only a matter of time, they felt, after watching what happened in the Rio Grande Valley, before the conquistadors would attack. At first, Oñate tried the old superstitious Indian trick, which had worked well elsewhere. He knew horses were something of an exotic presence in the north. A few of Coronado's mounts had gotten loose, but the Pueblos were still foot-bound. Oñate had his soldiers move their horses around, facing each other. He was trying to make it appear that horses could talk.

High above the chattering steeds, the Acomans considered their defensive strategy. They were going to roll boulders down from the perch, crushing the soldiers and their talking horses. But at the last minute, they decided to hold the stones. A delegation went down to see the Spanish, bearing gifts. Oñate and several men crawled up to the top. Once on the summit, the *adelantado*, or governor, of all the Kingdom of Nuevo Mexico, fired his big, unwieldy rifle. The harquebus made a great kaboom, the sound bouncing off the walls of Enchanted Mesa, Acoma's twin to the northeast. But again, nobody suffered a consequence, so the firearm was deemed harmless. Oñate gave The Speech, demanding that the Acomans subscribe to the Act of Obedience and Homage. At the end of the day, he clambered down the rock and left.

Two months later, in early December, Oñate's nephew arrived at Acoma with thirty men on horseback. Captain Juan de Zaldivar wanted to trade for flour. This time, the Acomans seemed surly, telling Zaldivar it would be a few days' wait while they ground the flour. When Zaldivar took his men to the top to pick up the bags, they were attacked. Acoma could wait no more; these men in beards and armor, with their pledges and threats, their talking horses and booming metal sticks, must go. Stones and arrows were fired in one direction, steel balls and swords the other. An Acoma warrior crushed the skull of Zaldivar. Soldiers were tossed from the cliff; others jumped. In all, eleven Spaniards died in the first battle of Acoma.

When news of the fight arrived back down at the Rio Grande, Oñate went into a rage. Acoma would pay, and the punishment would send a message to all of New Mexico. By Spanish protocol, he needed church and state justification to declare war, which the friars granted him. Three days after Christmas, he dispatched nearly a hundred soldiers for a war "by blood and fire." His surviving nephew, Vincente de Zaldivar, would lead the attack.

When young Zaldivar arrived at the base of Acoma, he called on the Indians to surrender. Their response was a storm of stones, arrows, and ice chunks. Thereupon he issued a formal declaration of war. Trumpets blared, weapons fired, and the Spanish charged forth at the base of the impenetrable mesa. The large frontal attack drew the Acomans to the edge. At the same time, a small detachment led by Zaldivar sneaked around the rear, climbed up the backside, and mounted a surprise attack. For three days, they fought for the rock, a battle later celebrated in a Spanish narrative poem. Clubs pulverized skulls, and balls ripped apart chests. By the end of the first day, Zaldivar's men had managed to haul one of their cannons up by rope to the summit. From then on, it was no contest, as the boom was no hollow sound. By the third day, the natives were in desperate retreat. The Spanish burned their homes, throwing wounded Indians over the side.

Others committed suicide or killed their brothers and sisters, sons and daughters, in order to spare them death at the hands of the conquistadors.

In the smoke of the smoldering Sky City, the Spanish pronounced it a miracle. They had lost only one soldier. Acoma was nearly wiped out. The Place That Always Was lay in ruins. Nearly 600 Indians had died. But the worst was yet to come.

The hands of the remaining men and the Acoma women and children were tied and they were marched down the rock and east to the Rio Grande. It was freezing, in the dead of winter, the hard winds blowing from the north with snow squalls. At the village site on the river, the defeated Acomans met the victorious Oñate. They would now stand trial for the crime of breaking the Act of Obedience and Homage, though most of them had never taken such an oath. They were given a defense counsel who pleaded a sixteenth-century version of insanity: the Indians were uncivilized, he said, and therefore incapable of knowing what they had done. The outcome was never in doubt, and after a three-day trial, a guilty verdict was pronounced. Then Oñate issued his sentence.

Men over the age of twenty-five were to have one foot cut off and spend twenty years in personal servitude.

Males from age twelve to twenty-five were condemned to twenty years as slaves, as were women of the same age. This amounted to war booty for the soldiers who had found no silver bars in New Mexico. As Oñate said, "I order that all the Indian men and women who have been sentenced to personal servitude shall be distributed among my captains and soldiers in the manner which I will prescribe and who may hold and keep them as slaves for the said term of twenty years or more."

Two Hopis—then called Moquis—who had been captured on the rock were each sentenced to amputation of the right hand. They were ordered to return to their tribes with their bloody stumps as graphic warning.

Children under the age of twelve were given to the friars for Christian schooling. Sixty of them were later sent to convents in Mexico City.

And that was it. The book was closed. There would be no appeal, Oñate said, "this being a definite and final sentence I so decree and order."

Over a period of days, in front of crowds of Indians, men had their feet hacked off or their hands amputated. Slaves were given over to the soldiers. And the Kingdom of New Mexico, breached in blood and blessed by bishops a full generation before an Englishman tied up on the Massachusetts coast, was ready to enter its second year. Four hundred years later, the West has the lowest rate of church participation of any region in the country.

You hear the bells ringing at the old mission tower atop Acoma this morning, the sound drifting out of the rock-and-dirt tower and falling away in the winter air. Nobody bothers to look up from what they are doing in the pueblo. The bell was a gift from the King of Spain. Beyond that, there is barely a remnant scrap from the empire that won the battle at Sky City. As it was before 1540, the pueblo is still governed by a cacique, and Acomans still look to the snows of Mount Taylor for divine inspiration, and to the neighbor of Enchanted Mesa for spiritual sustenance. They talk about the sun and corn and water, as always, as parts of a world in which everything fits. And they talk about these things in English, but also in Keresan—the same language that was used while searching for the Place That Always Was. You hear very little Spanish spoken atop Acoma.

Even if Oñate had not made a second *entrada*, the river of Western history already had jumped channels, never to return to the old course. The Spanish brought horses, and the effect on North America was not unlike what happened after Henry Ford started mass-producing the Model T. From the Rio Grande, the tough desert mustangs, a Moorish breed, spread north. They ran wild, living on prairie grass and desert sage. With horses, the Plains Indians went from being part-time hunters to big nomadic tribes, chasing bison across far-away river drainages. The ripple spread to their social structure. It was men's work to hunt, women's to tan the hide. More women meant more hides. Monogamy faded; polygamy became tolerated, as did increased raiding and slaving to build up a harem of forced-work hide-tanners.

The Apaches, effective raiders on foot, became feared desert pirates on horseback, forcing Pueblo Indians to look south for allies. The Utes, Shoshone, and Arapaho roamed over an enormous area of the Great Basin with their hoofed mounts. Horses were glorified in rock art and ritual. By the early 1700s, horses had crossed the Continental Divide deep into the Pacific Northwest and were used by Yakamas and Nez Perce, who would later be known for their own hybrid, the Appaloosa. The Blackfeet moved out of the central Plains and started to set up camps across the raw country of northern Montana. All of this flowed from the few horses that had gotten loose from the Plus Ultra marches up the Rio Grande.

It took nearly 400 years for the population of Acoma to reach what it had been when the Spanish first took a count; about 1,000 people were recorded just before World War II, the same as in 1540. Barely a year after Acoma men had had their feet cut off and been ordered into bondage, the Sky City resumed many of its old rituals. Some Acomans had never left. But, more remarkably, the condemned ones, the men with a single foot and a severed stump, had also made it back. That part of the city that had been destroyed was rebuilt, this time of adobe brick—a technique learned from the friars.

Acoma lives up to its name. As for Oñate, he left his mark—a disputatious note in the desert. The only physical evidence remaining from the first governor's reign is the hieroglyphic scratching of a rock north of Acoma, called El Morro. It is still visible.

"Passed by here the Adelantado Don Juan de Oñate from the discovery of the South Sea on the sixteenth of April 1605," he wrote, in Spanish. He said he discovered the Gulf of California, having dipped his toe in the brackish waters. But the Spanish had already been there. In the end, desperate to achieve something other than a court-martial and ridicule, he was chasing another rumor—that men lived underwater at the far edge of the desert.

The "poor, isolated, cold and unlovely Kingdom of New Mexico," as Oñate's biographer Marc Simmons put it, went through drought, food shortages, and finally a mutiny. You can't eat a patent of hidalgo, the low-ranking noblemen-to-be concluded. After several years of grubbing and bitterness, the settlers fled south. Oñate sent Zaldivar after them, with orders to cut off their heads. But they made it safely back to New Spain, where they told of the tyrant Oñate, an *adelantado* out of control. He had, they said, thrown an Indian out of a second-story window in Santa Fe, among his recent fits of rage. Much later, back in Mexico City, Oñate was found guilty of numerous crimes, among them cruelty to the Indians at Acoma. He spent the remaining decade of his life trying to save his reputation. A man of nearly eighty, the last conquistador was reduced to a piteous figure in Madrid, begging the royals to grant him a pardon, or at least listen to his story one more time. Gradually, with great regret, the Cities of Gold were erased from the map of Nuevo Mexico. In their place, scrawled over a great area, the Spanish labeled most of what they had seen in the American Southwest as simply *despoblado*, an unpeopled howling wilderness.

Over time, the forced weave of two cultures took hold. There was enough of the Old World that the New World liked. Horses would stay, as would some farming techniques, and orchards. To this day, an Acoma peach is a summer treat, distantly descended from a Spanish fruit. New Mexico has most of the strand of the modern West, with a heavy Spanish and Pueblo texture. Its cities are full of urban exiles looking to the glow of nearby mountains to put an extra dimension in their lives. People run up and down mesas, trying to squeeze meaning from the land. New Agers come and go, sampling the rarified air but never letting it get into their bones.

Acoma goes on; it has no other way. A handful of people attend Mass at the mission built in 1629, while men in long, black hair track the motion of the sun. The secret to old age in the West? Find your place, dig in, and defend it, just as Gary Snyder said. The Spanish thought this land, these views, this air, was foreign. Today, Europeans make up the bulk of visitors who marvel at the red rock, the wondrous light, the fact that in the American West, where trailer parks have historical designations, something shaped by human hands is still standing from a thousand years ago. In Avignon today, at the Palace of Popes, the walls are covered with graffiti; like French rock 'n' roll, it is a bad combination. Nothing of any real religious significance emanates from inside the stone fortress in Provence. Acoma never had the power of Avignon, but it still controls its small universe. It is not a reservation, a ruin, a ghost town, a toxic Superfund site, or a faux-Indian theme park. It is a city in the sky, looking out to the world as before, the Place That Always Was.

Timothy Egan, a third-generation Westerner, is the author of The Good Rain, Breaking Blue, *and* Lasso the Wind: Away to the New West, *from which this story was excerpted. The Pacific Northwest correspondent for* The New York Times, *he lives in Seattle with his wife, Joni Balter, and their children.*

✳

Rising 2,000 feet above the Montezuma Valley at Cortez, Colorado, the Mesa Verde has a commanding presence. Named by early Spanish explorers, the "green table" takes its name from the Douglas fir, piñon pine, and juniper trees that cloak its upper elevations. Uplifted through the geologic past, Mesa Verde reaches elevations of 8,200 feet and slopes gently southward.

The Mesa is actually a wonderful combination of canyons and cliffs, a beautiful dendritic pattern of finger-like mesas when seen from the air. The entire Montezuma Valley was the home of a culture which spread throughout the Southwest. Archaeologists know these people as the Anasazi, but a more accurate name for them is Ancestral Puebloans. After leaving the Four Corners area (the point of contact of Colorado, New Mexico, Arizona, and Utah) sometime around A.D. 1300, these people moved south and east and eventually became the modern Pueblo tribes along the Rio Grande River.

Mesa Verde National Park was established in 1906 to protect one of the most concentrated and best-preserved areas of archeological sites in the nation. Over 4,500 sites have been identified, including 600 cliff dwellings. The park is probably best known for the cliff dwellings Cliff Palace, Balcony House, and Long House. The archaeological sites in the park represent Ancestral Pueblo settlements dating from A.D. 550 to A.D. 1300.

These sites are all listed on the National Register of Historic Places and, in 1978, Mesa Verde was the first national park to be designated a World Cultural Heritage Site by the United Nations Educational, Scientific and Cultural Organization (UNESCO). The park maintains a collection of over 2 million artifacts, representing one of the largest archaeological collections in the National Park System.

—William R. Morris, "Mesa Verde"

PART FOUR

IN THE SHADOWS

CRAIG CHILDS

Haunted Canyon

The danger here is sudden and awesome.

SEPTEMBER. A THUNDERSTORM CELL ARCHED ITS BACK NEATLY around the curve of the North Rim of the Grand Canyon. A radio call came down in the afternoon. Heavy rain. From the interior of the canyon, 5,700 feet below, skies were partly cloudy with occasional light rain. Sprinkles, really.

Bryan Wisher sat in the bunkhouse set just east of Bright Angel Creek in a cluster of small Park Service Buildings. The only buildings on the floor of the Grand Canyon, they seem huddled for dear life below the huge, black, scowling faces of Vishnu schist. Screens instead of windows wrap the outside walls, the way they would on a bungalow in the tropics. For eleven years, Wisher has been a ranger in this park, now stationed at Phantom Ranch at the bottom of the great chasm, where all things eventually flow to the Colorado River. People come here by trail. Wisher rescues some of them. Sprung muscles, dehydration, ridiculous falls from loose-rocked edges, old men who make it only halfway by sunset. It is a longer, steeper walk than most people think. He knows weather, and has grown familiar with the quick alterations the canyon causes. He looked outside. Rain is as common to the North Rim as sweltering heat is to the floor. There were no more messages on the radio. He returned to his business.

Four o'clock. The sound of power and motion entered the canyon, like continents grinding together. The bunkhouse shook.

Wisher hit the screen door and sprinted toward Bright Angel Creek. A waist-high wall of muddy water, tree parts, and boulders was rolling over the placid crystalline water below, traveling about six miles an hour—just slow enough that Wisher could jump into the lead and run alongside, looking over his shoulder. The flood grabbed every rock it could, lifting even the biggest ones from their settings and putting everything in motion.

He squinted into the froth and debris, hoping not to see a water bottle or a backpack or the flash of someone's face gone slack in death. He also had to be careful, and not let himself become seduced by the flood. He had sensed it before, an almost hypnotic effect that can wash over a person when in the presence of such might. Only certain events have this kind of focused rage: the breaking of ice on northern rivers, an avalanche, a flash flood. All from water. To be there at the exact moment is indisputable, exquisite.

The canyons farther upstream are markedly narrower, making the water that surges through them violent. Wisher had pulled people from this kind of water before. Once, during a midnight

---

The Colorado is never a clear stream, but for the past three or four days is has been raining much of the time, and the floods poured over the walls have brought down great quantities of mud, making it exceedingly turbid now. The little affluent which we have discovered here is a clear, beautiful creek, or river, as it would be termed in this western country, where streams are not abundant. We have named one stream away above, in honor of the great chief of the Bad Angels, and as this is in beautiful contrast to that, we conclude to name it Bright Angel.

—John Wesley Powell (1874)

flood, he locked arms with others in a human chain to breach the water, rescuing five people out of Bright Angel Creek.

This time, there were no signs that people had been captured by the water. He stopped running and the flood passed him, kicking and shouting on its way to the Colorado River. Even if he had seen the people, a husband and wife who had been hiking earlier, he wasn't sure he could have done anything. The water was picking up speed, and he probably would have had to stand helplessly as they washed away.

The canyon of Bright Angel Creek drops twenty-four miles to the river, passing two dozen major side canyons on the way: Roaring Springs Canyon, Manzanita Creek, The Transept, Wall Creek, Phantom Creek, and many unnamed canyons. These lesser canyons are further dissected to form even more canyons, which are then again split so the whole place looks like a kindergartner got at it with scissors. Combine this confusing mazelike terrain with desert cloudbursts, and you have an unpredictable, often dangerous situation. One canyon floods, but not the other right next door. Here and not there.

This particular flood began at about 7,800 feet and cascaded toward the desert 4,000 feet below. When it entered Haunted Canyon, it ripped the world apart. New channels were excavated by the force, old ones slopped over with mud. One fresh cut in the sediment—later measured at fifteen feet wide by six feet deep—wound through a stately grove of cottonwood trees. Some trees bridged from side to side, felled by the flood. Others were missing entirely. Meaty, arm-wrestling roots of old cottonwoods were exposed, along with the fishnet roots of everything else. Imprinted into a treeless quarry of roots was the shape of a boulder estimated to be five feet tall and four feet across. The boulder was nowhere to be found. Against the still-standing trees were aprons of debris—some hurled nine feet up the trunks—made of riparian grasses, horsetails, reeds, slabs of dismembered cottonwoods measuring three feet around, roots, branches, stones, pieces of cactus, and sodlike earth woven together with roots. Thick branches were frayed into papery strings. The trees hosting the debris aprons were peeled of bark, as if they had been relentlessly chewed by animals. And everything was draped with blackened horsetail rhizomes and bits of tree bark curled like chocolate confections.

The flood emerged from Haunted Canyon into Phantom Canyon, then angled southeast, moving through thickets of coyote willow. Most were laid flat, their topmost, lance-shaped leaves sewn into the debris on the ground. In the main channel, twenty-foot-tall willows were pressed plumb to the creek bed, some fitting nearly around rocks as if they were soft and pliable.

Eventually the waters reached a place where a canyon dumps into a hole. After a flood, no debris ever shows here. The canyon is narrow and clean, and the force of water surging through is great. The floods comb everything out, always. Three people had been down there, near the mouth of the canyon, when it was scoured clean this time, when the wall of water came down. They had been camping below Phantom Ranch and had come in the afternoon to explore the waterfalls of Phantom Creek. Signs of scattered rain did not offend them. They had no idea how long this canyon was, how many tributaries and daughters of tributaries hung above them. Still, it was the kind of deep, narrow canyon that should have smelled of apprehension. Most of the sky was blindfolded. Black walls crowded at the already dull light.

A terrace of waterfalls masked the sound of the approaching flood. There was no time, no warning. If there had been four seconds, maybe, they could have scuttled up the ledges. They could have found some break, but it came quickly, like a car accident. The flood buried the waterfalls above them. They had one second, maybe two. They dove behind a grayish, leaning boulder, the crease where the eight-foot boulder meets the wall no more than nine inches wide. The water struck the rock with a back-handed, chin-deep slap. The wife and husband, both forty, were pulled down and cartwheeled into the muddy, frothing water choked with trees and rocks. The woman's brother, in his mid-thirties, managed to point his feet downstream, flailed his arms, and stayed on top of the flood. Likely it was luck. It's impossible to explain, or understand, how someone lives and someone else dies in a flood. In the haystack pulses of the floodwater, there is no sense.

The brother hit the east shore at Bright Angel Creek and pulled himself out. If he'd gone any farther he would have been stripped bare, his clothes ripped from his body by the water. Farther still, and he would have been dead.

Badly abraded and drenched, he stumbled to the ranger station where he found Bryan Wisher. The man's words came out monotone and hollow, as if rattling around in an empty cardboard box. He sobbed. He tried to tell the story. The flood had let him go. He was always the better swimmer.

In the safety of human company, he tried to put it all in order, but the event was inexplicable. He started sobbing again.

Wisher had no time for wasted words. He is not a callous man, but he had to know where the people were seen last. As the man babbled and cried, Wisher broke in: "Where did you last see your sister and brother-in-law?"

"At the boulder."

Wisher could not find the couple. Helicopters and dogs could not find them. They were gone, spilled into the river miles beyond.

This incident was the last of the summer flood season. A month earlier, fourteen illegal immigrants had been caught in a flash flood as they crawled through culverts beneath the Arizona border town of Douglas. They were nine city blocks into a four-foot-wide storm drain when the fist of water hit. Six made it out alive and were found crammed beneath a jammed manhole cover. They were lucky.

Three days later, an Amtrak train derailed in a flash flood in western Arizona. Just before sunrise, before the dining car opened with its fresh flowers and linen, the train traveling ninety miles per hour struck a flooding arroyo. The three engines separated while cars toppled and snapped from each other. The manifest listed 307 passengers and 18 crew members—roughly half were injured, many critically, but luckily no one died.

The following afternoon, a flash flood destroyed the village of

Supai in Havasu Canyon of the Grand Canyon. A helicopter flew ahead of the flood, swerving through the narrow canyon to warn hikers who immediately scrambled up the cliffs. When the flood reached the Colorado River, it pounded into river outfitters' boats docked inside the canyon. Two fully loaded twenty-two-foot snout boats, three eighteen-foot canyon rafts, and other large boats were hurled end over end. Deck canoes, kayaks, and trees blew out like confetti. Every rope, metal D-ring, and chock holding boats to rocks snapped. When a Park Service crew was sent to survey the damage, one ranger found a polypropylene rope and life vest still clipped to a rock. Reaching down to cut them loose, he found that the force of the flood had essentially melted them into each other. Luckily, no one was killed.

Two days after the Havasu flood, twelve people were struck by a flash flood in a popular northern Arizona slot called Antelope Canyon. Only one of them, the hiking guide, survived. He was thrown onto a ledge, mud packed beneath his eyelids, stripped naked by the force of the flood. He was delirious when found and asked over and over why he lived and the others had not. A rescuer, experienced at the task of finding bodies, later reported that she was left particularly uneasy by the implications—the anger, as it were— of this flood. Each body was stripped. Jewelry and tightly laced boots were torn free breaking bones in the process. Two bodies were never found.

Bryan Wisher eventually gave up his search for the husband and wife. They were declared dead. Seven days later, well out of search range, a raft outfitter sighted the woman's body near Tapeats Creek along the Colorado River. The guides tied the body to a bush to keep it from drifting. She had floated forty-eight miles from the tilted gray boulder where she'd taken shelter with her husband and brother, down Phantom Canyon, into Bright Angel Creek, and finally some distance down the Colorado River. It was farther than any drowning victim had traveled in the Grand Canyon. The way it was discussed among Park Service people and those who under-stood the circumstances, it was a sort of postmortem victory that she out-traveled those who drowned in the river itself. There was admiration for how she was propelled through Crystal Rapids and past Elves Chasm, all the way to the clear, converging waters of Tapeats Creek. It was as if she had done it herself. By those well-versed in this territory, she was offered a fleeting sainthood.

Twenty-one days later, another group of rafters found her husband's body in an eddy a short distance down river from Bright Angel Creek. His body, like his wife's, was naked. Bones were broken. All that remained was flesh.

The mechanics of a flood can be understood and its causes defined: thunderstorms, paths of least resistance, stream flow, currents. But many times, reason cannot be found even after the waters recede. One canyon floods while all others around it remain dry and still. A two-year-old survives while strong, healthy adults wash away. Seven bodies are found clogged together, almost arm in arm, while another from the same group of friends is deposited 100 yards up a side canyon.

Then, there are those times when a certain divination seems to lie beneath it all. The deadly Antelope Canyon flood originated from a place the Navajo call Many Ghosts Hill. This most recent flood formed in Haunted Canyon, killing the husband and wife when it hit Phantom Canyon. The brother lived and emerged from the water at Bright Angel Creek. Patterns show in the most unlikely places.

Wisher was the man sent down the Colorado River to recover the woman's well-traveled body. When he later described the scene, his voice was fluid, almost pleasant, but occasionally sliding into whispers. While explaining the disturbing shape of her limbs and face, he spoke no differently than when talking about being chased by the flood down the canyon. But if you listened closely, carefully, his voice showed traces of emotion. It was obvious the sight of the woman, his first recovery of a female corpse, haunted him.

When asked what these people could have done to save themselves, he almost answered, but did not. It was a question he had been asked before, a search for a simply worded answer tying everything about death and flash floods into an unsoiled package. From his station at the bottom of the Grand Canyon, he did not have any colorful quotes to offer anyone. All he could do was look west. West, where Phantom Creek ran deceivingly clean, and newly ordered boulders stood like statues.

Craig Childs is a former river guide, natural history field instructor, and writer who lives near Crawford, Colorado. This story was excerpted from his latest book, The Secret Knowledge of Water: Discovering the Essence of the American Desert. *He also contributed "Seeking Father Kino's* Tinajas" *to Part Two.*

JAMES CONAWAY

The Kingdom of Deseret

*There are some unusual people out
there in the wide open spaces.*

I WANTED TO FIND A POT HUNTER. THE ARCHAEOLOGICAL
Resources Protection Act had made them publicity-shy and poten-
tially dangerous. The arrest on the Strip for pot-hunting had been
made by the deputy in Colorado City, Arizona, a polygamous LDS
[Latter Day Saints] settlement hard up against the Utah border,
isolated and schismatic. Pot-hunting was popular around there, but
then so it was throughout Deseret, a Mormon word for honeybee,
and an old LDS designation for the church's part of the Southwest.
The patriarch of Colorado City reputedly had twelve wives and
more than seventy children, and a power struggle was in progress to
determine his successor. Outsiders were not welcome.

I had passed Colorado City the day before, on the way back from
the Buckskins. It lay a mile or so off the two-lane highway, at the
end of a rutted dirt road that would discourage the odd tourist from
seeking a cold Coke and directions to the North Rim. Rough-
hewn houses put up by their inhabitants remained in what appeared
to be a long-lived state of incompletion, and were surrounded by
public lands. Boys in crossed suspenders and bowl cuts, girls in long
dresses with white smocks over the top, their hair in single braids,
stood among the garden plots and watched my approach as I pulled

in after the drive from St. George. I felt oddly exposed as I got out of the van.

The deputy sat with his elbows propped on a bare desk, a bright Mohave County patch on one arm, He was friendly enough, though guarded. Catching pot thieves on public land was not high on his list, he said, since he was one of only two deputies in a vast jurisdiction cut off from the rest of Arizona by the Grand Canyon. People had been collecting pots there for years; he was more concerned with car theft.

I told him I wanted to meet a pot hunter, expecting him to laugh. He said, "You ought to talk to Vernal."

Vernal was a woodcutter working on the Kaibab; when he got home the deputy's brother would drive me over to meet him. Meanwhile, I crossed the road to the communal cafeteria, where a school board meeting was in progress. The men wore shiny black suits and black ties, the women, black dresses and white smocks, fashions from another age. The proceedings seemed subdued for a town supposedly in the middle of social upheaval.

The sign on the coffee machine read, "The management appreciates people who clean up after themselves. Do it here and be a wife-saver." There wasn't much to eat: some well-cooked green beans, and oatmeal. The old woman at the cash register watched me with what I thought was distrust, then gave me a slice of fresh-baked bread with my decaf.

> ───※───
>
> The Arizona strip, an area of remote and wild country beginning at Marble Canyon and the Vermilion Cliffs outside the town of Page, runs past the Northern Rim of the Grand Canyon and continues on beyond Diamond Creek and other points north and west. This is one of my favorite places in Arizona. Isolated ranches and townships give the impression of being at the very edge of the West, at the last roundup of all the wildness and freedom in the world.
>
> —Sean O'Reilly, "Notes from the Southwest"

Later I strolled up to the co-op store. Big sacks of flour, hardware, and a few sundries changed hands, but I never saw any money. The salesgirls tittered at the presence of a stranger. I went back into the sunlight. A hammer rang in the late afternoon, a preindustrial sound. Children in their old-fashioned clothes ran in circles outside the adobe schoolhouse, clapping their hands. And singing.

The deputy's brother was also a deputy, and a Mormon. He had a glass eye and the jaunty assurance of someone just graduated from law enforcement school. We drove around looking for Vernal, and I asked him about dissension in Colorado City. "Some of these people think they've been hard done by," he said, sitting low in the seat of his black sedan, a local boy made good. "This is all community property. If they decide to leave, they give up the improvements, which means the house."

The houses were incomplete, he said, because you didn't have to pay county tax on unfinished dwellings. "We've had a surge of problems lately—people apostatized for smoking and drinking, and child molestation. Two cases of that in the last three years. You'd think a man with four wives would be busy enough."

There were 2,000 souls in Colorado City, governed by a patriarch whose authority came from God. He headed the Council Priestship. His own grandfather had been a patriarch. I asked how many children the patriarch had fathered. "I couldn't really say—he had over 400 offspring. I don't think there's anybody around here I'm not related to."

We passed two teenagers in long dresses; their hair was parted down the center, the lacquered curls pressed to their foreheads. They ran along the red dirt road behind us, bound for graduation ceremonies at the school, it being June already. Laura Ingalls Wilder would have appreciated that scene, but not the fact that they were married and pregnant.

"We try to look modest," the deputy said, "and be modest. All we ask is that people try to live right, and work together." Everyone had pitched in to build the school. "I tromped them adobes all one summer."

The town had been raided back in the fifties by the state police, and the mothers and children taken to Phoenix. There, an attempt to "adopt them out" had been unsuccessful, and most ended up back in Colorado City in the same polygamous relationships. There was still a lot of bitterness toward the state authorities over that, he said, and more faith than ever in the institution of polygamy. As far as Colorado City was concerned, the Mormons in Salt Lake were apostate. "When they accepted the concept of monogamy, they lost the priesthood."

He had four children. I asked if he wanted another wife.

"You betcha!"

"What do you do to get one?"

"We don't believe in dating. Dancing is about as far as we go in that direction. The elders will decide when I'm ready, and who the celestial bride will be." There were enough females to provide celestial brides for Colorado City males because "more of the boys run off. There's Vernal now."

Vernal had a lantern jaw and three days of blond beard. His battered Bronco was full of tools of his trade: Swedish power saws, calk boots, gas cans, a splitting ax, chaps, and ammo cans full of spare chains. He had cut 80,000 board feet on the Kaibab that week, making close to a thousand dollars. His face, hands, and clothes were covered with dirt.

The deputy told him what I wanted; to my surprise Vernal said, "Want to see what I've got?"

He lived in a trailer on the edge of town. It had once been two-tone, but the colors had merged into a muddy approximation of the surroundings; the battered screen door hung limply. Vernal produced a key, although the thin metal barrier would have opened with a kick. He turned on the light, and out of the shadows leaped shapes of such beauty and sheer archaic richness that I caught my breath. Bowls, slender-necked ollas, ceramic canteens, arrowheads— Shoshone and Paiute points, some white, some of obsidian— Anasazi drills, *manos* for grinding maize, awls, dart shafts, flat turquoise beads, ax heads, stone knives, were all arranged on a plywood shelf next to an uncurtained window.

Vernal picked up a small pot with a spigot and matching handles, painted orange and black. I asked where he found it. "Somewhere," he said. He had been collecting since he was a child, inspired by the sight of the school principal's collection. Some of the things Vernal had found himself, others he obtained in trade. He figured the collection was worth upward of a hundred thousand dollars but wasn't sure. He dug for the pots—R and R after the rigors of tree-felling—and brought them back to his own little Smithsonian set amidst rabbitbrush and sage, where he mended the broken ones with epoxy, working deep into the night.

"Why?"

He slammed a muscular palm against the wall, rattling pots. "I love to hunt 'em," he said. "The shovel goes in, sometimes you feel something on the first stroke. You have to dig away real careful. They're wet, incredibly easy to break. You take 'em out and set 'em in the sun for a while…." The words trailed off.

He led me into the bedroom, where picture books about Indians lay on the floor. He reached under the mattress and pulled out Harold E. Driver's academic *Indians of North America*, then tossed it aside. "That don't do nothing for me." He opened the narrow closet, and a large olla rolled out. On hands and knees, he raked past lithic scraps, shards, pieces of bowl, and a Ruger rifle with a fifty-round circular clip before he found what he was searching for—a loose-leaf binder in which he had copied the name of every Indian tribe in America by hand. He was trying to match them up with the names of the chiefs, a home-grown anthropologist.

"I feel sorry for the Indian," he said. "The white man treated him bad, gave him smallpox and that."

His own ancestors were no exception. His great-grandfather had run Lees Ferry on the Colorado after Lee. That stretch of the Strip near Short Creek had been in constant contention between Indians and Mormons, and a hotbed of polygamy from the time Utah entered the Union. Vernal belonged to a long tradition of church independence. He was twenty-eight and so far unmarried. I asked if the elders had a bride in mind for him, and he said, "Oh, you know about us. Well, I'm too busy to get married."

He had only recently heard about the existence of the Anasazi;

he wanted to know more but was unsure how to proceed. Meanwhile the artifacts piled up. The same urge that drove kids all over the country to collect arrowheads had in Vernal's case gotten out of hand. He never dug in burial sites, he said, and disapproved of mechanized pot-hunting. The notion of the slit-eyed artifact dealer doing some dope on the side could not have been further from this reality: another American hunter-gatherer picking up scraps of previous cultures and trying to make sense of them.

He avoided public lands now because of the fines and jail sentences involved, but spoke wistfully of choice BLM sand just waiting for the spade. Artifact collecting had become a recognized outrage in academia, but many of those same outraged archaeologists had been inspired first by picking up something man-fashioned. Now they had job security in mind. How could anyone not pick up artifacts as Vernal had, when backhoes building roads had dumped colored pottery in front of him all his life, and exotic things protruded from the earth in every canyon beyond the narrow confines of his fundamentalism?

He had yet to sell anything. A dealer had come by once to look at the collection, but Vernal had sent him away empty-handed. "I can't stand the idea of getting ripped off."

On the way out he picked up a little corrugated bowl with a broken rim—an Anasazi porridge warmer. "Here," he said, handing it to me.

"I don't have money for pots."

"Take it anyway."

"Why would you give something so precious to a stranger?"

"Because you want it."

The breeze from the cliffs smelled sweetly of juniper; night moved on the sandstone hoodoos like a lover.

"If you come back through," Vernal said, "stop in. I'll either be cutting trees or digging pots."

I had come to the Arizona Strip in pursuit of the Anasazi on public lands; I found myself thinking about Mormons. Both cultures had flourished in difficult country; both were highly individualistic and imbued with an overriding notion of divinity. The Anasazi had dropped off the edge of the Colorado Plateau, a fate unlikely to overcome the members of the Church of Jesus Christ of Latter-Day Saints. Assimilation was more likely. Future archaeologists digging among Mormon genealogical records might well wonder what happened to these once exclusive, sometimes fierce, followers of a self-proclaimed prophet.

Mormon towns were built like medieval villages, centers of close-knit social and religious life from which radiated paths to useful employment. St. George, Utah, was a triumph of revealed religion over environment. Brigham Young kept a winter residence in St. George. Today the main drag is lined with symbols of American consumption—Chevron, Sizzler, Best Western, Montgomery Ward—and loud with the traffic of pickups and customized sedans. It was June when I stopped there, and half of St. George's blond Lotharios had discarded their shirts in celebration of summer. Broad side streets were set about with spacious lawns—Mormons have always been great waterers—and were full of kids on bikes.

An iron fence and well-watered trees surrounded the temple. I saw St. George burghers in business suits straighten their ties in the mirrored glare of their car windows before entering the temple. Some had removed Stetsons to reveal the rancher's white head and walked oddly in city shoes. They became something other than cowboys on the other side of the ironwork, but I wasn't sure what.

Mormonism grew out of the revivalist fervor of the early nineteenth century in the eastern United States. Its founder, Joseph Smith, Jr., a visionary New York farmboy, supposedly found gold plates bearing the text of Mormon scriptures after digging where an angel named Moroni directed him, and led the faithful west ahead of their persecutors. He was martyred by lynchers in Carthage, Illinois, in 1844, and Brigham Young took over. The murdering stopped at the Rockies. Young told his followers, when they came to the Salt Lake Valley, "This is the place."

The Mormons were hated in the West as well. No doubt horny outfitters, trappers, cowboys, and cavalrymen resented a man having several wives when there weren't enough women to go around, and making a go of it in barbarous country by the force of communal life. The United States acquired what the Mormons were to call Deseret in 1848, after the war with Mexico; Utah was granted statehood, in 1896, on the condition that the church give up polygamy.

The Mormons might have been cultish, but they counteracted some of the excesses that passed for individualism in the West. The word *Deseret* was coined in the *Book of Mormon*; the honeybee became the symbol of the Mormons. But bees seemed slovenly compared to Mormons and their accomplishments: the expeditions among the Indians by Jacob Hamblin, who assisted John Wesley Powell in making the first descent of the Colorado River; and the greening of canyon country that even the natives considered uninhabitable. The temple at St. George was built before the one in Salt Lake City, to bolster flagging colonists who had already made so many sacrifices. Newly married Mormons would travel hundreds of miles over the Honeymoon Trail to get "sealed" for eternity in the temple.

The Hurricane Canal, which early settlers had dug by hand, was small potatoes compared to the TransColorado passage through the Hole in the Rock, when Mormons' wagons climbed onto the plateau over a road supported by logs driven into the cliff face by Mormon men dangling at the ends of ropes.

Nowadays Deseret unofficially includes Utah, Nevada, northern Arizona, northwest New Mexico, western Colorado, southwest Wyoming, most of Idaho, and the fringes of Oregon and California. The empire reveals itself in odd ways: the absolute order of cultivated farms and ranches, the tidiness of city streets, the hint of suspicion in otherwise guileless expressions.

The owner of the shop where I took my van to be tuned up had come to St. George by way of Los Angeles after marrying a Mormon and converting. His wife had since gone off with another man, he said, and he had fallen away from the church. He wanted to talk about that. "They chip away at you," he told me, while his mechanic poured dust out of my air filter. "They came around here and tried to set my prices." Customers wanted to pay him with little plastic vials full of gold dust. "I tell them, 'I don't assay, I fix cars. I want money!'"

He shook his head. "They say taxes don't exist because the Prophet never gave his permission. My wife's like that. She says the IRS don't exist because the president of the church in Salt Lake didn't give permission. She won't pay her light bill for the same reason—the power companies don't exist. You know what does exist, don't you? Alimony exists."

The manager of public lands on the Strip was Bill Lamb, a bishop in the Church of Jesus Christ of Latter-Day Saints. He had grown up in Cedar City, Utah, and had moved ten times in his twenty-two years with the Bureau of Land Management, including a stint in Washington essential to his career, before coming to St. George. Bishop Lamb looked like a professional golfer: neatly combed black hair, good smile, striped sport shirt. He sat on the couch facing his desk and invited me to do the same. I asked if there were many Mormons in the BLM, and he said yes. Most Westerners were interested in land use, and since so many Westerners were LDS there were a lot of Mormons in the BLM. Utah State University had developed one of the first schools in range management, and over the years it had contributed many to the bureau.

I asked if Mormons were generally in favor of development in the West. He pressed his fingertips together, a man divided between secular and ecclesiastical duties. "You have to look at the history of the church," he said, "and Joseph Smith. The main idea was to *progress*. You don't sit idle, you continue to develop—your mind, and whatever else you can."

The resources were here to be developed and used, but prudently. The millennium would not be the end of the world. "The millennium simply means a thousand years—the amount of time that Jesus Christ will reign as king after the Second Coming. Then there will be the final judgment to determine who will go to the kingdom of glory. During that thousand years we will need the resources."

"I thought the Second Coming meant destruction."

"There will be some, to purify the earth. There'll be a partial judgment at that time, and some people, like murderers, won't be resurrected. There'll be a big change, no doubt about it."

The murderers would go to the telestial kingdom, the lowest, but most people would remain in the terrestrial kingdom—the here and now.

"I think during the millennium you'll see a lot of people going to the celestial kingdom, too, but they'll continue to develop. They'll retain their physical being. Satan will be bound, and there'll be a lot of righteousness throughout the world. A lot of work will be done for the people who have already passed. It's an American kingdom, all spelled out by Joseph Smith. Christ will be very unhappy with anyone who has abused the resources."

The conversation turned to Indians. I had heard Mormons refer to them as Lamanites, descendants of Old Testament characters. I asked if Mormons viewed the Lamanite story symbolically, as some Christians viewed the Garden of Eden.

He shook his head. "We believe in the historical truth of the Garden of Eden, and the Lamanites. We know the Lamanites came over here by boat from the Holy Land, like the Nephites. That was before the fall of Jerusalem. I'm not sure exactly where they landed—somewhere in Central America."

They were all descendants of the sons of Levi and Sarah, he said. Christ appeared before them in Central America. There occurred 200 years of righteousness during which time the Aztecs developed their calendar and other advancements were made. The Lamanites grew corrupt and began to disagree violently with their cousins, the Nephites. They migrated northward, the first people to enter what became the United States, fighting all the way.

"About 400 A.D.," Lamb said, "there was a big battle in the New York area. Millions were killed, most of them Nephites. The Lamanites wandered off in bands. They developed their own dialects, becoming what we call Indians today. Originally the languages brought to the United States were Arabic and Hebrew, but they were lost."

It seemed to me that the Mormons had a problem in the implications of carbon dating. I said, "Some anthropologists think the Indians came from Asia by way of the Bering Strait."

"Oh, I can't say the land bridge didn't bring over some Asians. They could have migrated there and *come back* again."

There was no righteousness left on the continent at the time, Lamb said. The Lamanites had fallen from grace, but that didn't mean they couldn't "progress" like everyone else. "The Indians should be proud—they have a great heritage. They come from the house of Israel, part of the chosen people."

He smiled, trying to help me understand. Here was an administrator of public lands, in charge of fifty BLM employees, twenty-three vehicles, and a $2 million annual budget. "They're Jews, really," he added.

He stepped to the bookcase and came back with a little blue volume, supposedly written by Moroni, son of Mormon. Gold leaf showed an angel standing on a globe, blowing a trumpet.

"The Book of Mormon is just an abridgement of what happened in the previous 900 years. There are thousands of volumes on gold plates still buried somewhere in the mountains of New York." He handed it to me. "It's all in there. Read it, and try not to fall into the same traps."

James Conaway was born in Memphis, Tennessee. He is a novelist and the author of several works of nonfiction. His articles have appeared in numerous publications, among them The New York Times Magazine, Harper's, *and the* Atlantic. *He has been a Wallace Stegner Creative Writing Fellow at Stanford University and a recipient of an Alicia Patterson Journalism Fellowship. This story was excerpted from* The Kingdom in the Country.

TOM MILLER

✦ ✦ ✦

Saguaro

Be careful what you shoot at in the desert.

CRUELTY OFTEN COMES WITHOUT WARNING AND TAKES MANY
guises. I've told the story of David Grundman's untimely death to
hundreds of people over the years, and not one of them has ex-
pressed sorrow. His killer gets all the sympathy. To fully appreciate
the showdown that early February afternoon in 1982, let's go back
125 years earlier. James Buchanan succeeds Franklin Pierce as president, Louis Pasteur proves that living organisms cause fermentation,
and the U.S. Supreme Court hands down the Dred Scott decision.
In the western part of the New Mexico Territory, gold is discovered
along the Gila River. Anglo trappers from back east have already
made an appearance along some rivers. Mexicans, whose *patria* had
lost two-thirds of its territory to the United States the previous
decade, are manipulated out of their land and their labor. And just
south of what's now called the Hieroglyphic Mountains, in the
northern reaches of the Sonoran Desert, a saguaro cactus seedling,
one of some 40 million from the same plant, takes root.

Saguaros have been on earth an estimated 10,000 years, and although they have come to symbolize the rugged and boundless
West, they live only within the Sonoran Desert. In the United States
this means in Arizona, with precious few interlopers east of the

Peloncillo Mountains in New Mexico or across the Colorado River in California. We have a national park out here devoted to the saguaro, and caricatures from Playboy bunnies to Snoopy's brother, Spike, have leaned against them for national exposure.

To say that our seedling that fell in 1857 took root is too hopeful. First, saguaro flowers have to fertilize each other, a process that occurs when a bat or a white-wing dove or other bird carries the nectar from one plant to another. This can happen only during a five-week period in late spring and early summer when the flower opens its white petals at night, exposing its pollen, only to close up the next afternoon in time for *Oprah*. Several weeks later the flower gives way to a lusty, juicy fruit with red pulp that some birds find irresistibly delicious. Its sweet taste has been likened to a cross between a watermelon and a fig. The saguaro fruit that falls to the ground gets eaten by any number of creatures, from insects to small critters on up the chain. No matter who eats the fruit, though, bird or land-walker, its seeds are defecated throughout the desert.

Let's name our seedling Ha:san (pronounced *hah-shiñ*), the word for saguaro within the Tohono O'odham Nation, which exalts the cactus in its traditions, ceremonies, and lore. For Ha:san to actually germinate requires a wide range of natural conditions to fall into place in a given sequence during a finite period of time. These include, over the precious first couple of years, good rainfall, the absence of freezing temperatures, a larger plant nearby to protect the seedling from too much direct sun, and the good fortune to stay out of the way of a jackrabbit or rodent or any animal that, merely by bumping into Ha:san, would kill it. I asked George Montgomery, chief horticulturist at the Arizona-Sonora Desert Museum, how big the saguaro would be if all these conditions held for two years. He took my pen and paper and made a speck no bigger than the period at the end of this sentence.

We're up to 1859 now. *A Tale of Two Cities* comes out, Oregon becomes a state, and John Brown is hanged for leading the raid on the federal arsenal at Harpers Ferry. More germane to our drama, however, Charles Darwin's *On the Origin of Species by Natural Selection* is published. After its second birthday, little Ha:san can relax slightly.

True, its life would be over if a cow stepped on it, but now the night temperature can dip below freezing and Ha:san will still be alive the next morning. For a number of years it manages to avoid cow hooves, hungry rabbits, excessive sun, and prolonged frost.

The year Ha:san celebrates its tenth birthday, Walt Whitman publishes *Leaves of Grass*. In Europe, Karl Marx brings out *Das Kapital*. Although the Civil War has come and gone, misguided troops loyal to the Confederacy skirmish with a U.S. Cavalry scouting party at Picacho Pass, eighty miles south of Ha:san's desert land. Of zero significance to Ha:san, the U.S. Congress has now divided the New Mexico Territory in two; Ha:san's half is called Arizona. At age ten, Ha:san stands one-and-a-half inches tall. Four years later the first known photograph of a saguaro is taken, not too far west of Ha:san's dwelling place.

By age thirty, in 1887, Ha:san has grown to a sturdy two feet tall. Prescott is the territory's capital, an honor soon shifted to Phoenix. Arizona's five-year Pleasant Valley War begins, a violent conflict over sheep and cattle and turf and family dominance. Ha:san has no enemies; though still a young cactus, it has survived its most vulnerable years. In March of Ha:san's forty-forth year, Ha:san and its species get friendly news: The saguaro blossom is named Arizona's territorial flower. Finally, at age fifty-five in 1912, the year that Arizona gains statehood, Ha:san claims another level of maturity for itself: A crown of Arizona's flower grows on its top for the first time, providing nectar for its airborne visitors. Soon seedlings from Ha:san's own fruit will reach the desert floor. Ha:san stands eight feet tall now, closer to the popular image of a saguaro. None of its 39,999,999 sibling seedlings made it this far.

Ha:san has an easy life. Statehood schmatehood, no one bothers the growing saguaro cactus and it bothers no one. A narrow east-west road a few miles south connects Wickenberg to the west to some small towns much farther east, but Ha:san remains secure in the desert with bald eagles and great blue herons flying about and rattlers and Western diamondbacks slithering below. Other cactus such as ocotillo and prickly pear and trees such as ironwood and paloverde live nearby. Mule deer and wild burros trot by on occasion, and coyotes and rabbits are regular passersby. Ha:san weighs 800 pounds by now, 90 percent of which is water sucked up from the ground. It is landlord to the Gila woodpecker, which bores out a hole in its skin big enough for a nest; when the woodpecker moves on, elf owls, curve-billed thrashers, and cactus wrens move in.

Ha:san's biggest breakthrough takes place about the same time. It starts to grow arms. The arms take on some of the same characteristics as the trunk—slow growing, with flowers eventually blossoming at the ends and with woodpeckers and other birds as permanent guests.

In 1933 at age seventy-six, Ha:san is at the peak of its form. Mature, one arm growing nicely and another on the way, plenty of water to drink in the rainy season and retain through the dry season, its outer pleats evenly spaced, birds at home among its needles. It is the first year of the New Deal and the last year the Washington Senators win the American League pennant. Almost a quarter of a century later—in Ha:san's centennial year—Jack Kerouac's *On the Road* is published, the Brooklyn Dodgers move to Los Angeles, and David Michael Grundman is born in New York State.

We know far more about Ha:san's formative years than we do about Grundman's. Let's give him the benefit of a doubt and assume he graduated from high school. At age twenty-one, Grundman lived in Johnson City, a New York town near the Pennsylvania border three-and-a-half hours northwest of Manhattan. In the middle of the winter he lured a sixteen-year-old boy to a friend's apartment, intent on stealing the lad's $1,200—money with which the kid hoped to buy three pounds of marijuana. Grundman pulled a gun on the boy but botched the job, and he was arrested for armed robbery. A day before he was to go on trial, he agreed to a plea bargain: He would plead guilty to second-degree robbery, which carried a maximum sentence of four years, rather than stand trial and risk a more severe sentence. On January 29, 1981, after eighteen months in Attica, David Michael Grundman was released on parole.

He stood six-one, with brown hair and blue eyes, and weighed 200 pounds. By the end of the year, he and a buddy named Jim Suchocki—who had been arrested for possessing a nice quantity of marijuana a few years earlier—had moved to the Southwest. Grundman's mother lived in a quiet working-class neighborhood in northwest Phoenix, and the two moved in with her. They were fifty-three miles southwest of Ha:san.

About this time I lived in a small adobe adjoining the Tucson Botanical Gardens. It was a tranquil and captivating place, surrounded by thick desert growth that absorbed noisy traffic and blocked nosy neighbors. Late one midsummer afternoon I discovered a Papago woman a few yards from my house brandishing a long saguaro rib. (This was before the tribe changed its name from Papago to Tohono O'odham.) I recall her name as Henrietta. Saguaro ribs—sturdy, lightweight, woody poles that grow within the cactus's trunk—are used to lift, or sometimes knock, the fruit off the top of tall saguaros. The ribs, which litter the desert floor as part of decaying saguaro carcasses, are also used in home and fence construction. To simplify gathering the fruit, the far end of one rib is often fashioned into a two-pronged fork; to extend their length, two ribs are frequently strapped together. I stood and watched admiringly as the woman delicately lifted one fruit after another off the tops of saguaros and handed them to her young daughter, who carefully placed each in a plastic bucket. Finally Henrietta noticed me and smiled as I complimented her on her ability to lift the fruit from the plant.

Proprietorship was no concern; I was a mere Anglo renter, and this harvesting of the saguaro fruit was an ancient tradition in her tribe. The saguaro even played a role in their creation stories. A teacher I know grew up on the Tohono O'odham reservation with Papago as his first language. "I used to take my bow and arrow as a kid," he told me, "and shoot at the saguaro. My grandfather said, 'Don't do that. All things are alive. That plant is very special to the O'odham. It bears fruit that we use for food. When Mother Earth decides not to give any more life to the saguaro, we use its ribs for many things.'"

In a manner both gallant and sociable, Henrietta asked if I would like a jar of saguaro jelly once she boiled the pulp down into syrup. (Most syrup is fermented for wine, to be used in ceremonial gatherings on the reservation.) That was our bond; we parted all smiles. For weeks I told anyone who would listen this little episode about the friendly encounter with the saguaro-gatherer in my yard. When Henrietta had not returned by late fall, however, I realized I would never taste saguaro jelly from the cactus beside my house.

On February 4, 1982, David Grundman didn't go to work at the Sun Kountry Kitchen. Instead, he and Jim Suchocki headed out into the desert an hour northeast of Phoenix with lots of beer, a 16-gauge shotgun, a box of rifle slugs, and their dog. It was a weekday with temperatures in the comfortable mid-60s. They drove toward Wickenberg through swap-meet country, over the railroad tracks leading to Los Angeles, and past Del Webb's Sun City. The only town they passed was Surprise. At Route 74, the Carefree Road, they turned east 12.7 miles and then north on a dirt road into Bureau of Land Management desert land. After bouncing along the road a couple of miles, they parked the car and walked east a bit, settling in near an arroyo full of wolfberry shrubs and squat mesquite trees. Instead of the usual incessant weekend noise of all-terrain vehicles tearing up the land, all the two could hear was desert. They had the Sonoran Desert to themselves, or at least that swatch of it. On north-facing slopes grew jojoba; on south, saguaro. Some were younger, shorter, and lighter than Ha:san; others were older, taller, and heavier.

After a few beers, David Grundman started shooting. At saguaros. They made easy, immobile targets, almost humanlike with their arms in the air. He began with smaller saguaros and worked up to bigger ones, each time shooting the cactus enough so that the *Carnegiea gigantea* fell over dead.

"The first one was easy," he told Jim after killing two saguaros, "and the larger one was partly dead already." In the silent desert, the final fall of each cactus must have sounded thunderous. Javelina, common there at that time of the year, stayed away from the drunken marksman. Grundman must have killed a half-dozen saguaros, leaving each one lying on the ground as he moved to the next.

Finally David Grundman encountered Ha:san. A couple of rounds didn't do it. Ha:san, 125 years old, remained erect.

Grundman moved slightly to another angle and pumped a few more slugs into the splendid 3,000-pound saguaro, but it refused to fall. He tried again from farther over. In all, he moved about a third of the way around Ha:san. Frustrated at this particular cactus's resistance to his gunshots and determined to best it, Grundman picked up a saguaro rib from the ground and started poking at Ha:san's lowest arm, which had grown almost five feet in its 70 years. Grundman's poking finally dislodged the arm, which rested about four feet above him and weighed close to 500 pounds.

Well, the joke was on David Grundman, and so was Ha:san. The arm crashed down on him, and the twenty-five-foot trunk of the mighty cactus, suddenly unstable, started wobbling. It could have fallen anywhere in a 360-degree radius, but it too fell square on David Grundman. His last word was, "Jim!"

I've never given much thought to retribution or karma, yet surely both of those were at work in the Sonoran Desert on February 4, 1982. David Michael Grundman lay face-up, dead beneath a ton and a half and 125 years of cactus, saguaro needles piercing his face and torso. Natural selection had played its hand.

Jim Suchocki, full of beer and bravado, went into momentary shock, then ran over and rolled the cactus off his dead buddy just as a car passed by on the lonely road nearby. Suchocki flagged it down and asked the driver to get someone quick from Lake Pleasant, the Maricopa County park slightly to the east. Grundman was an accidental-gunshot victim, he said. By the time park manager Doug Collup arrived, Jim had gathered up all the beer bottles and rifle slugs and put them in the car with the dog. Collup had called for a helicopter, but when he saw Grundman, he changed that to a hearse. Ha:san's arm had hit David between the neck and shoulder, and the trunk had landed directly on top of him. The side of his face was mashed in and yellow. You could still smell beer around his mouth.

"The cactus probably broke his neck on impact," Collup said when we spoke at his home years after the fact. Collup had returned to the site to photograph it the day after the accident, and he found Grundman's teeth prints still visible in the big cactus.

"See that?" Collup held up one of his photos. "The cactus is reddish from the blood. Some of the needles are bruised and some are missing. The cactus popped his gums like they were little water balloons." The county medical examiner's description for Grundman's cause of death: "external compression of chest."

The falling-cactus story makes for great telling and retelling. Within a few years it had graduated to urban-myth status; people weren't sure if it was true or not, but it had all the elements of a noir morality tale. It has surfaced a few times in print, but only Michael Stevens of the Austin Lounge Lizards and a friend have artfully immortalized Ha:san and its calamitous end by composing a ballad. "Saguaro" appears on the Lounge Lizards' album *Creatures from the Black Saloon*. It turns the affair into a Western in which Grundman "a noxious little twerp" sees himself as Wyatt Earp to the saguaro's Clanton gang. At the end, though, the roles are reversed: "One mighty arm of justice came hurtling toward the ground."

Guided by the initial sheriff's reports and Collup's memory, I set out one day to locate the scene of the crime. I started at the house where Grundman had lived in northwest Phoenix, trying to emulate his last journey, but nothing along the way encouraged a warped and wasted mind. A billboard said, "KEEP DRIVING IF YOU LOVE AVOCADOS." As I neared my goal, I ran into construction for a new golf course and had to park the car and go by foot. After hiking north up and down small hills for a mile or two, I found a bone-dry arroyo with a lightly sloping, south-facing stretch on the other side. It was the sort of desolate spot where *Bloodbath at Massacre Creek* might have been filmed had anyone ever filmed a movie called *Bloodbath at Massacre Creek*. During late-summer monsoons, arroyos like this one can fill up quicker than your Maytag. Some Bud Light cans lay nearby; tangled in the scrub was the bullet-riddled side of a Remington game load box.

Dead saguaros disintegrate within a few years, and I wasn't exactly expecting to find Ha:san's corpse or even its ribs. But I did look at the surrounding saguaros in a new light. There was no logic behind it, but I stepped lightly when I got near them, and I never ventured close enough that one of them could fall on me if it wanted to.

They were part of Ha:san's extended family, and I simply wanted to pay my respects.

Tom Miller is the author of Jack Ruby's Kitchen Sink: Offbeat Travels through America's Southwest, *from which this piece was excerpted, as well as six previous books including* Trading with the Enemy: A Yankee Travels through Castro's Cuba, On the Border, *and* The Panama Hat Trail. *He has been covering culture and conflict in Latin America and the American Southwest for more than three decades, and has written for publications ranging from* The Berkeley Barb *to* Smithsonian, Life, *and* The New York Times. *Miller has appeared on National Public Radio, produced the Rhino Records album, "The Best of La Bamba," and given talks to students in the United States, Canada, Mexico, and Cuba. He is editor of* Travelers' Tales Cuba.

Living as an Alien

*Riding the underground to El Norte may break the
law, but for many it is the key to a new life.*

JUST TWO BLOCKS NORTH OF THE BUSTLING BORDER OF MEXICO,
the Golden Arches of McDonald's stand tall, a tantalizing symbol
of the coveted riches to be won in the land of opportunity.

This balmy Tuesday morning, the restaurant teems with people,
mostly Mexicans. Among the diners are those whose thoughts
reach far beyond this border city; illegal immigrants, chasing a
dream not theirs for the taking.

To begin the chase, though, they first must elude *la migra*,
the U.S. Border Patrol, sometimes zealous guard of a porous
international border. This day, *la migra* floods the streets with uni-
formed agents.

Inside the jam-packed McDonald's and out, people who have
slipped through the ten-foot-high chain-link fence that attempts to
separate the two nations hastily cook deals with coyotes, who, for a
price, will smuggle them inside the United States.

Outdoor pay phones buzz as coyotes verify that relatives and
friends of penniless immigrants indeed will pay cash on delivery.
Once the deal is cut, the race against *la migra* is on.

It's about 11:30 A.M. when we approach our first coyote, a weary,
suspicious young man inconspicuously holding a two-way radio, in

the lively parking lot. Two amigos, standing behind him, look us over silently.

"Why doesn't the gringo just take them?" the coyote asks in Spanish, glancing at my aunt's husband. "He can speak English to *la migra* at the checkpoint and they will let him through."

The ice behind his eyes chills me. This is not a man I would trust my life with. My aunt explains that her husband fears the Border Patrol. The coyote offers to take us to Phoenix for $200 each.

But only after *la migra* takes down its checkpoint on Interstate 19, about ten miles north of Nogales.

Suddenly, the *coyote* steps back, turns and speaks in hushed tones into his radio. He looks up to see Border Patrol agents nab four illegals across the street. Spooked, the *coyote* and his buddies vanish into the sea of faces.

Hearts racing, we enter the restaurant and pretend we're there to eat. My nerve is ebbing; even if I dodge the Border Patrol, what of the smugglers? Plenty of coyotes rob, rape, and abandon women.

My aunt and uncle are buying cold drinks when one of the weary coyote's associates comes up to our table, a dollar bill in hand. He needs quarters to make a phone call. He leaves when I say we have no change.

It was a test: someone fresh from Durango is unlikely to carry quarters. But we never see that coyote or his friends again.

My aunt spots another smuggler, a shabby man with red, bleary eyes and dirty hands. His price to drive us to Phoenix is $300 apiece. He doesn't have a place to stash illegals temporarily, as do many coyotes, so he suggests we wait at McDonald's until the checkpoint comes down. That could be hours.

I'm not going anywhere with this *maleante*, who stinks and clings to us like cheap polyester. His eyes hint of guile, betrayal.

My aunt hails a chubby young man walking past our table, who promptly offers to find a smuggler. Within minutes, we are joined casually by a personable man in his early twenties. A fast talker, Marcelino is wearing expensive ostrich-skin boots. He wants to know where my cousin and I are going, how we crossed the border, where we're coming from. The other coyotes hadn't been so inquisitive.

We say we're from Durango, on our way to Phoenix to look for work. We found a hole in the fence, up in the hills. He seems satisfied.

Like the others, Marcelino says the trip will cost us a little more than usual, $300 each, because *la migra* is out in force this day. We bargain down to $250, to be paid upon delivery to Phoenix, and he agrees to our request to stay together.

Marcelino exudes confidence and seems to know his craft. I nod to my aunt, who quickly seals the deal.

We'll have to wait at a local hotel until the coast is clear, maybe early afternoon or as late as 7 P.M. Everything hinges on *la migra*.

Marcelino points to a group of illegals posing as diners and says they, too, have hired him.

Told to act like a couple, my cousin and I drape our arms around each other and follow the coyote to a late-model, air-conditioned Chevrolet van, where a middle-aged woman with scraggly hair waits. She scarcely glances at us.

As we climb in, Marcelino promises my aunt that he will deliver us safely later that day.

It's too late to turn back, this is no Sunday drive in the desert. I'm with lawbreakers, and if they go down, I go with them. Worse yet, the coyotes could be pirates, even killers.

On the way to the hotel, Marcelino tells us his classy blue van is a rental. He doesn't want to lose his own car if *la migra* catches him. The Border Patrol tends to focus on older vans, he says, so a new one is good cover.

The van stops at a motel on Grand Avenue. Scraggly Hair watches the traffic. We wait until Marcelino signals, then dash for the first-floor room. The door opens from inside. It's 12:30 P.M.

Nine men and a teenage girl are crammed into the spare room, which is big enough for three people at most. We make it twelve. A prematurely gray man in his thirties sits in the only chair; everyone else rests on the floor or the two unmade beds. *Santa Fe* blares from a color TV atop the dresser.

Keeping vigil at the door is a courteous man in his early twenties, who is wearing leather *huaraches*, a sandal common in Sinaloa, Mexico. He's probably an illegal immigrant himself.

Although he's low man on the coyote totem pole, this certainly beats picking lettuce or washing dishes.

The Sinaloan suggests we take a nap because the wait might be long. I pray it isn't, darkness would only heighten my fear.

We sit on the bed and stare at the tense faces. The girl, who looks about sixteen, cozies up to a frazzled young man who hasn't seen twenty. They are traveling with a quiet youth of about seventeen who looks like a scolded child on the verge of tears.

Everyone is in their late teens or early twenties. The oldest is the graying man in the chair. The others sprawl on the floor, failing to relax. Only occasional muttering and the TV break the silence. People file in and out of the tiny, reeking bathroom, which glistens with urine. Holding my breath, I swear to drink nothing more.

The watchman starts pacing, chain-smoking, clicking the remote control. He's been here since early morning.

A soft knock and in comes Marcelino, who has replaced his $500 boots with white Nikes. The pall offends him. He orders the Sinaloan to stub his cigarette. *La migra* is still watching I-19, he reports.

He leaves. Returning a short time later with bread, bologna, mayonnaise, jalapeños, paper cups and a gallon of chocolate milk. It's 1:30 P.M.

The food goes quickly. This is the first meal of the day for most of the immigrants. I'm too nervous to eat.

Another knock and in come a gaunt man and a stubby woman, her arms bangled with gold. Too friendly with Marcelino to be illegals, they must be associates. They glance about without looking; they've seen too many like us before.

The woman, Juanita, slumps on my bed, lamenting that she must work on her birthday. A dozen of her *pollitos*—chicks, or clients—wait in another room.

The coyotes talk among themselves, as if we are invisible. They plot the safest route to Phoenix, and how to divvy up the twenty-four illegals in the two rooms.

Juanita phones a Phoenix number and speaks to someone caring for her little girl. She asks about diapers and rashes, then makes a request: "Go to my dresser and light a votive candle and please, please say a prayer for us so we can arrive there safely."

Juanita and her gaunt friend leave with Marcelino.

Soon, a weary Marcelino comes back, showers quickly and leaves again. When he returns about 2:30 P.M., it's to say that we might be leaving soon, when *la migra* is distracted during a shift change.

Marcelino advises his cargo that if *la migra* stops us on the highway, do not give away the true identity of our driver, who could be jailed instead of sent back across the border.

"You all have to stick together and say that he is one of you, not a coyote. You tell *la migra* that the coyote is following you in another car," he says.

He leaves minutes later, telling us to be ready to dash out when he returns. My heart surges; I hit the bathroom a final time.

When Marcelino comes back, we are hustled out to his van and another six-seater rental van, this one red with Florida license plates. Juanita and part of her group take off in a passenger car. Nine of us file into the red van. It's 2:45 P.M.

"Get inside, sit down, hurry up!" orders the driver, who's wearing a frown, a cowboy hat and white tennis shoes. He talks down to me, and I resent it. Defeating the impulse to fight back, I turn as submissive as the men around me. I have no choice; my life is in his hands.

I'm discouraged to have ended up with this man who treats me like filth. I'm almost glad to see the scraggly haired woman who was with Marcelino climb into the van. At least she's a familiar face.

I sit behind the coyotes, between my cousin and the gray-haired man. Beneath my feet, Filiberto lies on his back. I have to put my feet on the seat back so I don't step on him. Another man crouches in the small space between the two front seats. The last four men are in the back.

We follow Marcelino's van up Arizona 82 toward Patagonia, away from the I-19 checkpoint. Passing motorists see only five of the eleven people jammed into our van.

None of the illegal immigrants moves or speaks. And no one glances back as the van speeds away from Mexico, which can't hold onto them.

The woman with the scraggly hair, Concha, who is in her early fifties, is fretting over a spiritual matter. "Where is my prayer to San Pedro? I need to say my prayer before we get on the road!" she squeals, tearing through the glove compartment.

At the beginning of each smuggling run, Concha prays that the Roman Catholic saint will protect her from the Border Patrol. In twenty years as a coyote, she says, St. Peter never has failed her.

Giving up her search, Concha recites a few passages from memory. "Holy Father, I beg for your guidance during this trip. Please allow me and my chicks to get to Phoenix safely."

If you're interested in knowing more about border issues, here are three terrific books: *Coyotes: A Journey through the Secret World of America's Illegal Aliens,* by Ted Conover; *Cutting for Sign: One Man's Journey along the U.S.-Mexican Border,* by William Langewiesche; and *By the Lake of Sleeping Children: The Secret Life of the Mexican Border,* by Luis Alberto Urrea.

—SO'R and JO'R

Several miles into our trip, the driver, Ray, and Concha begin to laugh about the Border Patrol crackdown in Nogales. The smugglers say word of the heavily guarded checkpoint spread like wildfire among the coyotes, who spent the morning waiting for it to ease. Only one smuggler was concerned enough to quit for the day, Concha says.

To my right sits gray-haired Manuel, a native of the northern state of Chihuahua. His stubbly face is somber, as if he had just lost a loved one. *La migra* is a big worry to him.

Manuel and five male friends had traveled seventeen hours by bus from their hometown to Nogales, Sonora. Last night, they sneaked into Arizona through a hole in the fence but were robbed at knifepoint by *pandilleros*, gang members, and chased back into Mexico by the Border Patrol.

Broke, the six Chihuahuans roamed the Mexican city all night. After sunup, they slipped into Arizona again, this time guided by an experienced coyote, who stashed them at the motel. Many illegals are intercepted at the border and deported at least once before crossing successfully.

For Manuel, beating the border is easy compared with leaving home and family. But there were few choices. His job baling hay ended weeks ago, and there was no other work. Even at minimum wage in Arizona, he'll make in an hour what he makes in a day in Chihuahua.

Manuel worked here illegally once before, five years ago. He and three of the men behind us are headed for Maricopa, where Manuel's brother-in-law will pay the coyote and find them field work. The other two Chihuahuans want work in Phoenix.

Fatigue submerges tension, and I close my eyes—until the coyotes mention that we're passing the Border Patrol station in Sonoita. The news jolts the illegals. The eyes of the man crouched between Ray and Concha open wide as hubcaps, and Manuel looks down, as if refusing to face an unpleasant truth.

But no swarm of agents pursues our van.

My relief soon turns to dread, however. Marcelino, who had been leading Ray, is nowhere in sight.

From here, we could take Arizona 83, a shorter route to Interstate 10 and Phoenix, but Ray continues straight on 82, which ends in a few miles. He and Concha consider asking directions at a nearby supermarket, but are leery with *la migra* so close. Knowing this area well, I bite my lip to keep quiet. Filiberto, squirming beneath my feet, is a veteran undocumented worker from Navojoa, Sonora, who also is familiar with southern Arizona's back roads.

My cousin and I read highway signs aloud, furtively prompting Filiberto to direct the clueless coyotes. Concha curses imaginatively, blaming Marcelino for their confusion.

Filiberto says little, perhaps fearful of offending our guides. My cousin can hardly restrain himself. "If I ever got into the smuggling business, I would make it a point to always carry a map with me," he says with a sneer before my jab shuts him up.

Where Arizona 82 ends and 80 begins, arrows point Tombstone, right, and Benson, left. Ray picks Tombstone—back to the border.

Instead of screaming at this pair of imbeciles, I nonchalantly read the sign aloud, hoping Filiberto will take charge. He bolts upright and tells the coyotes that Phoenix is the other way. Ray, bemused, makes a U-turn. Relief washes over Filiberto's face. My cousin rolls his eyes, but no one dares utter a word.

Ray, a legal U.S. resident in his late thirties, says he recently was caught transporting eleven illegal immigrants, which is a felony. But he didn't spend a minute in jail, he adds with a grin.

In tiny St. David, Concha warns the men in back to stay down. I spot a Chevy Blazer in the white and green of the Border Patrol, heading toward us on the narrow two-lane. My heart hammers. Our van is moving so slowly that the agent couldn't help but see how we're crammed into it.

However, *la migra* zooms past without a glance.

"*Pinche migra*, they're running around like hound dogs," Concha spits.

A Chevron station is ahead, and Ray mentions that we need gas. As he signals the turn, my cousin shouts that a Border Patrol car is parked next to the pumps, fifty feet away. There's no way we can get past the agent, who's standing by his car.

"*¡Síguele! ¡Síguele!*" Concha shouts to keep going. Ray accelerates so abruptly that I can't imagine the agent wouldn't be suspicious.

Ray drives a quarter-mile and pulls into a grocery store to ask directions. Concha goes in while the rest of us wait nervously. My hands are clammy, my head primed to explode. The immigrants look as if they've seen a ghost. Manuel peers out the window for signs of the pursuing agent.

But the agent must be too tired, too bored to try. It's 4 P.M.

Carefree Concha reappears about ten minutes later with several bottles of water and directions to Phoenix. We continue north spotting yet another Border Patrol agent, this one on the shoulder talking with someone.

We finally reach I-10 at Benson. For miles, Concha and Ray joke about the close call at the Chevron station.

Near Tucson, Ray takes the Ajo Way exit. I ask whether we're going to drop people off there. Concha replies they are trying to get on I-19 to go to Phoenix. I-19, however, ends in Tucson. My cousin and I are astonished.

"I'm pretty sure that the last time I was smuggled, the coyotes took 10 from Tucson to Phoenix," he tells Ray, who pays no heed.

Ray pulls into a gas station, parks at a full-service pump and walks inside. Within seconds, a pump jockey comes up to the driver's open window and asks Concha, in English, "Fill it up?"

She nods.

His eyes widen when he spots the man crouched up front. He does a double take when he sees the hidden men, but starts pumping gas quietly.

Concha takes the wheel and Ray moves to the passenger's seat, swigging from a bottle of Budweiser. Fortunately, the coyotes spot a freeway sign up ahead, and Concha gets back on I-10. It's after 5 P.M.

Finding the interstate puts Ray in a good mood. He pops in a Chalino Sánchez cassette, and for most of the rest of the trip, the late Mexican *norteño* singer croons of unrequited love and men of valor.

As dusk falls and the lights of metropolitan Phoenix begin to dance on the horizon, we take the Maricopa Road exit off I-10. I'm beginning to think we're going to make it.

A few miles later, Concha tells the men in hiding that they can sit up. Immobile for nearly five hours, their collective relief is tangible.

Concha says all of us are going to a drop house, where coyotes stash illegals before they are delivered to friends and relatives. We stop at a Circle K to use a pay phone. Concha is worried about Marcelino. Ray makes the call and reports that he hasn't arrived.

"I thought they would be home by now. I just hope *la migra* didn't catch them," Concha says.

It is dark by the time we get to a plain, fenced-in house next to a run-down market near Buckeye.

No matter. What's important is that I'm finally here, on familiar soil, unharmed. I'm impatient for the freedom I've always taken for granted. But the wait is not yet over.

"I think the Guatemalans are still here," Concha observes.

Two men and a teenage boy come out to greet the coyotes. They want to hear about the trip, but Concha is more interested in Marcelino's whereabouts. We're still outside when Marcelino arrives with seven of his illegal workers. He must have stopped somewhere first and dropped off the rest to another drop house.

Business was good today. Marcelino and his associates made a killing off the two-dozen travelers.

It's 7:45 P.M. Our cramped, maddening journey took five hours.

The coyotes gather in the kitchen to talk, the rest of us in the living room. The dirty linoleum floor is full of holes. A worn crib, pushed into a corner, is piled with clothes and folded blankets. Three skinny boys and a girl huddle on the old couch. The oldest boy looks fifteen, and the youngest, ten. They must be the Guatemalans.

I look at their frightened faces and wonder what pushed them from their distant homeland, trying to imagine living in such uncertainty at their tender age.

Ed Abbey and I shared a common antipathy toward cameras. Once, quite by coincidence, we ran into each other at a small border crossing three hours from home. It was early on a weekday morning, about twenty past coffee, and we were each surprised to see the other. "For the first time in my life," he said after a characteristically long silence, "I wish I'd had a camera with me. I just passed a pickup parked by the side of the road. This Mexican fellow was driving his pig somewhere and the pig was up in the cab with him. It seemed like a very well behaved pig. The guy got out to take a leak, leaving the pig sitting upright looking out the windshield. Where are those damned photographers when you need them?"

—Tom Miller,
"Camera Sty"

In another corner is a religious shrine with Concha's sacred relics. Six votive candles burn next to a large framed image of Jesus and a smaller print of San Isidro, another of Concha's serving saints. She has a lot to be thankful for today.

But she's not praying. She's in the kitchen discussing the trip with her associates, making plans for the next one. The smugglers help themselves to cold drinks but offer none to us.

I call my aunt, who speaks to a coyote I've never seen before. We're to meet at a nearby restaurant in half an hour. Manuel and the others take turns calling friends and relatives

Before we leave, Ray gives us his and Concha's phone numbers in case we ever need their services again. We get into an old, dark van, where three anxious men, barely twenty, are waiting. These natives of the central Mexican state of Hidalgo are on their way to Sky Harbor International Airport in Phoenix to fly to North Carolina.

Like Manuel and his group of Chihuahuans, the trio were robbed in Nogales and chased back into Mexico. In the confusion they dropped a duffel bag, and now they've been told they must leave the rest of their meager belongings with the coyotes.

"If you take that bag with you to the airport," Marcelino warns, "*la migra* is going to catch you." The Chihuahuans reluctantly comply.

Without a word, we drive about ten miles to Goodyear. There they are again: the Golden Arches of McDonald's, ultimate symbol of opportunity and escape. Escape from the world's most desolate corners to the world's richest, most powerful nation. Difficult to resist.

My aunt and uncle wait in the parking lot. They pay the coyote $500, and he leaves after shaking hands with everybody. It's 8:30 P.M.

Exhausted, hungry, relieved, I am appalled at how easy it was to hire a coyote amid the flood of Border Patrol agents. I'm equally appalled at how little effort it took, even with two boneheaded guides and a beefed-up checkpoint, to get through the busy Nogales-Tucson stretch.

Reaching Phoenix required only a little money and a little patience. Will it be so easy to create a false life here?

Lourdes Medrano Leslie now writes for the Star Tribune *in Minneapolis,*

Minnesota. She frequently travels to the Southwest, where she grew up, to stock up on the desert warmth that helps her through Minnesota's mean winters. Exploring the U.S.-Canada border remains on her list of future travels.

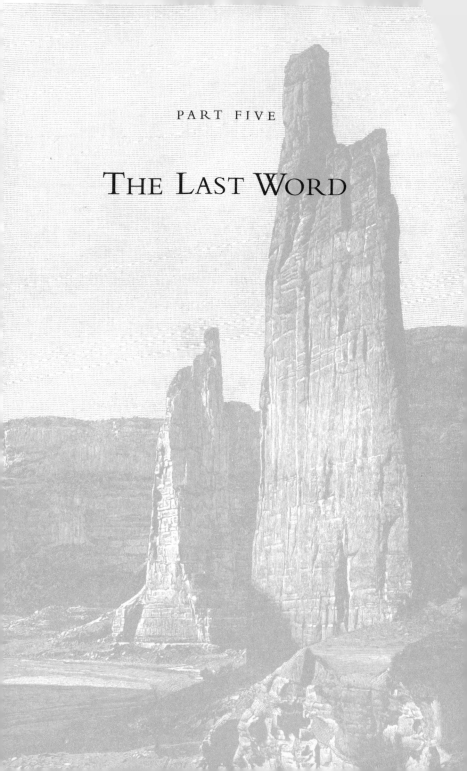

PART FIVE

THE LAST WORD

LEO W. BANKS

Searching for the Good Spirit

The mysteries of the Southwest are legion.

THIS BLASTED WIND IS ALL I HAVE. IT FILLS MY HEAD. IT CLOUDS MY mind. It threads my clothes. It blows sand into my mouth and brings on black clouds, the smell of rain, and voices that stand out even above the howling.

I hear children's voices, way off, in some place behind the beyond, but still clear, as though coming from lips pressed to my ear.

My partner, Edward McCain, walked off looking for the only thing photographers seek. Light. How strange to look at the world the way he does. To hunt light. To be consumed by it. To be in conversation one moment, and the light shifts, and something turns over in his brain, and he's off, chasing one ethereal, always moving, always changing commodity. Light.

My own master is no less bizarre. A spirit.

I'm approaching a canyon on the western end of the Navajo reservation. This land, particularly Begashibito Canyon, is said to be inhabited by a benevolent force called the Good Spirit.

It's a preposterous legend. Not a tale that could be told in my world without a nudge and a wink. Long beyond understanding.

But not up here, where the wind makes the rocks bow, a world of rust mesas, shimmering horizons that only get farther away as

285

you move toward them, and moonlike ground so parched it could
make a lizard weep.

I've been chasing the Good Spirit for almost two years. Several
times I've come to this other world, searching. Now I feel as if I'm
closing in. The children's voices pull me forward.

We're on foot, McCain and I. We had turned left off U.S. Route
160 some thirty-eight miles outside Tuba City, onto State Route 98
over Shonto Wash, then onto dusty reservation roads. We drove
about thirty-five miles from the boarded-up Cow Springs Trading
Post on U.S. 160 before we started walking.

They call it a canyon, but it's so shallow it hardly seems to merit
the description. The English name for this place is Cow Springs
Canyon. *Begashibito*, pronounce ba-GOSH-ibito in Navajo, means
"place where the cows water."

The voices lead me down a split in the side of the wash that cuts
the canyon, and I bounce on my rear end to the bottom. The wash
banks are high, maybe twenty-five feet. They channel the voices and
carry them to me, clear as the noon sun.

Still, I'm not sure they're real. It might just be the wind talking.

McCain heads in the opposite direction, hauling his gear over
fine sand, like he's running in a dream. That's what photographers
do, run in their dreams hoping to catch fleeting light.

I go a long way. I don't know how far, a mile, maybe, when a
blast of thunder shakes the ground, and it occurs to me, for the first
time, that I'm in danger.

I'm walking in a wash as though on a Sunday stroll, and there's a
storm building. Flash flood. The single most obvious peril of the
desert didn't occur to me until this instant, and even now that it has
penetrated my consciousness, I feel no fear.

I keep walking toward the voices and out loud I say to myself
something I don't believe: "It's the Good Spirit."

My research brought me to one brick wall after another. Talking
to a Navajo about spirits is a bit like being at the boss's dinner party
and mentioning the corpse propped at the head of the table.

Let me tell a story.

I'd stopped at the Old Red Lake Trading Post in Tonalea. A typical afternoon on the Big Rez. Pickup trucks whirled in, one after another, with bumper stickers that proclaimed: Rodeo!

Young men stepped out, shook off the dust, and strutted past, in uniform: slant-heel cowboy boots, turquoise rings, black Stetsons with rope hatbands and feathers dangling from the back brim. And that odd way Navajo men have of saying hello by pursing their lips. Those are the gregarious ones.

After an hour of leaning against the wall and watching the show, I went inside. The clerk was a young fellow, and beside him, at the movie-rental counter, stood three boys. They were imitating some variety of mayhem from the latest martial arts movie.

I wanted to ask about the Good Spirit. I had my presentation planned. My cover was a gum purchase. I dropped the gum on the counter. "Say, have you ever heard of a Good Spirit that inhabits the Cow Springs area?"

I swear, you would've thought I'd lit the fuse on a stick of dynamite and held it in his face. I'd noticed the corpse at the table. I pressed on, soothingly. "I read something about the Good Spirit of Begashibito Canyon. Gets people out of jams and such."

The clerk was so nervous, he couldn't stop laughing. His shoulders shook. I took the hint and got out of there.

The truth is, stories are told of the Good Spirit. At least they're told in print. A half-century-old magazine tells of a man riding through a sandstorm along what he thought was a trail into Begashibito Canyon.

But he got lost, and the storm grew violent. He felt his horse shake in fear beneath him. Squinting, he caught sight of something moving through the swirling air ahead of him. He had no idea what it was. Desperate, with no choice but to ride or die, he urged his horse forward.

The horse, suddenly finding its legs, followed whatever it was to safety. It was the Good Spirit, the man claimed later.

Three Navajo boys wandered from their mother's sheep camp and got lost. Night fell. A search party was organized. When dawn broke, the children were seen walking serenely toward the camp. Asked how they found their way home, the oldest boy looked surprised. "Why, the man in the long coat came to us when the big star arose. We followed him."

An old woman, also on horseback, was in the canyon when a rainstorm blew in, and with it came a tremendous roar. Soaking wet, she listened to identify the sound.

Just then she saw the figure of a man walking out of the bed of the canyon wash. His head was bare, and he wore a gray robe tied with a rope at his waist and grass sandals.

"I'd no sooner cleared the wash," the old woman said, "when a great wall of water swept past, overflowing to the depth of several feet the place I had just left. I would have been slain by the Water Monster."

The clouds hang low now, black beasts hovering above me. The wind blows relentlessly, almost painful as it hammers away.

As I struggle against it, I'm thinking about those published legends. Preposterous, inexplicable. But I realize again, as I always do on this great and unknowable reservation, that this isn't a land of answers, only questions.

When McCain and I were wheeling along State 98, we drove over a pair of work gloves. Nothing around them, no other traffic, just two gloves.

They were on fire. Smoke rose off them, fanned by the wind. Neither of us said a word as we passed over them. A few hundred feet down the road, I couldn't stand it any longer.

"Did you see that back there?" I asked.

"I sure did."

"What the heck was it?"

"Gloves? I don't know."

McCain turned around to get a look, but by then I was swinging into a U-turn. They were exactly what they appeared to be, burning black work gloves. Only by the time we got there, one of the gloves was gone. The other was still burning.

Preposterous. Inexplicable. Like the white saddled horse we saw tied to a range fence with no rider in sight. And no place for a rider on flat landscape without buildings or concealment to the farthest limits of our vision.

Here we were chasing a spirit, and we came upon burning gloves and a riderless horse. We did what people from our world do. We joked about it, had ourselves a good laugh.

The wash zigzags across the Earth, its walls revealing deep gashes from previous floods. The sand on the wash bottom shows red, and that makes the pile of animal bones stand out. They're bleached white, scattered at my feet.

I step over them. Lightning splits the sky. It seems to bring the voices closer than ever. McCain catches up, and we crawl out of the wash and climb a hill and lie on our bellies to have a look.

Until this instant, peering over flat red tundra, I wasn't sure the voices were real. Now I see them, three children, looking tiny in the distance playing and giggling in the wash. Nearby stretches a cornfield, with two women working it.

The scene appears idyllic. Like a painting. Peaceful to watch.

McCain and I kick around the idea of approaching and asking about the Good Spirit. But that would be foolhardy, two strangers appearing out of a wash to inquire about an apparition.

Reluctantly, feeling we again have failed to find what we were looking for, we drive on steep dirt hills out of Begashibito Canyon to Shonto Plateau and Indian 16. The long-expected downpour starts the moment we reach pavement.

"Wow," I say to the racket of the rain beating on the car.

"Yeah," says McCain, "if we hadn't gotten out of there when we did…"

He looks over at me, and his voice trails off. Nothing more is said. But I can see the realization in his eyes. I recognize it because I have the same thought:

Those children in the wash were protected, and they knew it. So were we, only the dictates of our world concealed it from us until just now. In following their gleeful voices, maybe we found the Good Spirit, too.

We stop joking about the burning gloves and the riderless horse and the rest of it. We don't understand what any of it means, if there is anything to understand.

But we no longer laugh. We drive on quietly in the rain.

Leo W. Banks has been writing about the Southwest for various newspapers and magazines for twenty-five years. He also has written several books of Western history. For a brief time a decade ago, he taught school on the Navajo reservation in Shiprock, New Mexico. He lives in Tucson, Arizona.

Recommended Reading

Abbey, Edward. *Desert Solitaire: A Season in the Wilderness*. New York: Ballantine, 1990.

Annerino, John. *Adventuring in Arizona: The Sierra Club Travel Guide to the Grand Canyon State*. San Francisco: Sierra Club Books, 1991.

Annerino, John. *Running Wild: Through the Grand Canyon on the Ancient Path*. Tucson: Harbinger House, 1992.

Babbitt, Bruce., ed. *Grand Canyon: An Anthology*. Flagstaff, Ariz.: Northland Press, 1978.

Bowers, Janice Emily. *Fear Falls Away and Other Essays from Hard and Rocky Places*. Tucson: The University of Arizona Press, 1997.

Brown, Kenneth A. *Four Corners: History, Land, and People of the Desert Southwest*. New York: HarperCollins Publishers, 1995.

Calvin, Ross. *Sky Determines*. Silver City, N. Mex.: High-Lonesome Books, 1993.

Childs, Craig. *Grand Canyon: Time Below the Rim*. Phoenix: Arizona Highways, 1999.

Conaway, James. *The Kingdom in the Country*. New York: Avon Books, 1987.

Darlington, David. *The Mojave: A Portrait of the Definitive American Desert*. New York: Henry Holt and Company, 1996.

Egan, Timothy. *Lasso the Wind: Away to the New West*. New York: Vintage Books, 1998.

Ellis, Rueben, ed. *Stories and Stone: Writing the Anasazi Homeland*. Boulder, Colo.: Pruett Books, 1997.

Fletcher, Colin. *The Man Who Walked Through Time*. New York: Alfred A. Knopf, 1967.

Foster, Joseph. *D. H. Lawrence in Taos*. Albuquerque: University of New Mexico Press, 1972.

Ghighlieri, Michael P. *Canyon*. Tucson: The University of Arizona Press, 1992.

Goldwater, Barry M. *Delightful Journey: Down the Green and Colorado Rivers*. Tempe: Arizona Historical Foundation, 1970.

Gosnell, Mariana. *Zero Three Bravo: Solo Across America in a Small Plane*. New York: Touchstone, 1993.

Hall, Edward T. *West of the Thirties: Discoveries among the Navajo and Hopi*. New York: Doubleday, 1994.

Kingsolver, Barbara. *High Tide in Tucson: Essays from Now or Never*. New York: HarperPerennial, 1996.

Lane, Belden C. *The Solace of Fierce Landscapes: Exploring Desert and Mountain*. New York: Oxford University Press, 1998.

Lopez, Barry H. *Crossing Open Ground*. New York: Vintage Books, 1988.

McCairen, Patricia C. *Canyon Solitude: A Woman's Solo River Journey Through Grand Canyon*. Seattle: Adventura, 1998.

McGrath, Melanie. *Motel Nirvana: Dreaming of the New Age in the American Desert*. New York: Picador's Books, 1995.

McNamee, Gregory. *Blue Mountains Far Away: Journeys into the American Wilderness*. New York: Lyons Press, 2000.

Miller, Tom. *Arizona: The Land and the People*. Tucson: The University of Arizona Press, 1986.

Pfister, Patrick. *Pilgrimage: Tales from the Open Road*. Chicago: Academy Chicago Publishers, 1995.

Preston, Douglas. *Talking to the Ground: One Family's Journey on Horseback Across the Sacred Land of the Navajo*. New York: Simon & Schuster, 1995.

Pyne, Stephen J. *Fire on the Rim: A Firefighter's Season at the Grand Canyon*. Seattle: University of Washington Press, 1989.

Pyne, Stephen J. *How the Canyon Became Grand: A Short History*. New York: Viking Penguin, 1998.

Reisner, Marc. *Cadillac Desert: The American West and Its Disappearing Water*. New York: Penguin Books, 1987.

Shoumatoff, Alex. *Legends of the American Desert.* New York: Borzoi, 1997.

Shukman, Henry. *Savage Pilgrims: On the Road to Santa Fe.* New York: Kodansha America, 1997.

Snyder, Gary. *A Place in Space: Ethics, Aesthetics, and Watersheds: New and Selected Prose.* Washington, D.C.: Counterpoint, 1995.

Stegner, Page. *Grand Canyon: The Great Abyss.* New York: Tehabi Books, 1995.

Stevens, Larry, ed. *Colorado River in Grand Canyon: A Comprehensive Guide to Its Natural and Human History* (5th ed.). Flagstaff, Ariz.: Red Lake Books, 1998.

Teal, Louise. *Breaking into the Current: Boatwomen of the Grand Canyon.* Tucson: The University of Arizona Press, 1994.

Welch, Vince, Cort Conley, and Brad Dimock, eds. *The Doing of the Thing: The Brief Brillant Whitewater Career of Buzz Holmstrom.* Flagstaff, Ariz.: Fretwater Press, 1998.

Williams, Terry Tempest. *An Unspoken Hunger: Stories From the Field.* New York: Vintage Books, 1994.

Williams, Terry Tempest. *Pieces of White Shell: A Journey to Navajoland.* Albuquerque: The University of New Mexico Press, 1997.

Work, James C. *Following Where the River Begins: A Personal Essay on an Encounter with the Colorado River.* Provo, Utah: Charles Redd Center for Western Studies, Brigham Young University, 1991.

Zwinger, Ann Haymond. *Downcanyon: A Naturalist Explores the Colorado River Through the Grand Canyon.* Tucson: The University of Arizona Press, 1995.

Index

Index of Contributors

Acknowledgments

We would like to thank our families and friends for their usual forbearance while we are putting a book together. Thanks also to Lisa Bach, Susan Brady, Deborah Greco, Raj Khadka, Jennifer Leo, Kathy Meengs, Natanya Pearlman, Tara Austen Weaver, Patty Holden, Tim O'Reilly, Michele Wetherbee, and Judy Johnson. Further thanks to Anna Jenness-Wells and Mary Pratt, research editors at *Arizona Highways,* for their help in locating hard-to-find stories.

"Land of the People" by Douglas Preston excerpted from *Talking to the Ground: One Family's Journey on Horseback Across the Sacred Land of the Navajo* by Douglas Preston. Copyright © 1995 by Douglas Preston. Reprinted by permission of Simon & Schuster Inc. and Thomas C. Wallace.

"Making Peace" by Barbara Kingsolver excerpted from *High Tide in Tucson: Essays from Now or Never* by Barbara Kingsolver. Copyright © 1995 by Barbara Kingsolver. Reprinted by permission of HarperCollins Publishers, Inc. and Farber and Farber Ltd., London, UK.

"The Recruiter" by Patrick Pfister excerpted from *Pilgrimage: Tales from the Open Road* by Patrick Pfister. Copyright © 1995 by Patrick Pfister. Reprinted by permission of Academy Chicago Publishers.

"The Navajo Way" by Alex Shoumatoff reprinted from the November 1998 issue of *Men's Journal.* Copyright © 1998 by Men's Journal Company, L.P. All rights reserved. Reprinted by permission.

"John Ford's Monument Valley" by Jeb J. Rosebrook and Jeb Stuart Rosebrook reprinted from the July 1999 issue of *Arizona Highways.* Copyright © 1999 by Jeb J. Rosebrook and Jeb Stuart Rosebrook. Reprinted by permission of the authors.

"News from Nowhere" by Zeese Papanikolas excerpted from *Trickster in the Land of Dreams* by Zeese Papanikolas. Copyright © 1995 by the University of Nebraska Press. Reprinted by permission of the University of Nebraska Press.

"The House of Time" by Colin Fletcher excerpted from *The Man who Walked Through Time* by Colin Fletcher. Copyright © 1967 by Colin Fletcher. Reprinted by permission of Alfred A. Knopf, a division of Random House Inc., and Brandt & Brandt Literary Agents, Inc.

"Water" by Edward Abbey excerpted from *Desert Solitaire: A Season in the*

River Begins: A Personal Essay on an Encounter with the Colorado River by James C. Work. Copyright © 1991 by James C. Work. Reprinted by permission of the author.

"In the Superstitions" by William Hafford reprinted from the January 1992 issue of *Arizona Highways*. Copyright © 1992 by William Hafford.

"The Place That Always Was" by Timothy Egan excerpted from *Lasso the Wind: Away to the New West* by Timothy Egan. Copyright © 1998 by Timothy P. Egan. Reprinted by permission of Alfred A. Knopf, a division of Random House, Inc., and the Carol Mann Literary Agency.

"Haunted Canyon" by Craig Childs excerpted from *Secret Knowledge of Water: Discovering the Essence of the American Desert* by Craig Childs. Copyright © 2000 by Craig Childs. Reprinted by permission of Sasquatch Books and the author.

"The Kingdom of Deseret" by James Conaway excerpted from *The Kingdom in the Country* by James Conaway. Copyright © 1987 by James Conaway. Reprinted by permission of Houghton Mifflin Co. and Knox Burger Associates. All rights reserved.

"Saguaro" by Tom Miller excerpted from *Jack Ruby's Kitchen Sink: Offbeat Travels Through America's Southwest.* Copyright © 2000 by Tom Miller. Reprinted by permission of National Geographic Adventure Press.

"Living as an Alien" originally titled "Living as an Illegal" by Lourdes Leslie reprinted from the April 30, 1995 issue of *The Arizona Republic*. Copyright © 1995 by The Arizona Republic. Reprinted by permission of The Arizona Republic.

"Searching for the Good Spirit" originally titled "Searching for the Good Spirit of Begashibito Canyon" by Leo W. Banks reprinted from the March 1999 issue of *Arizona Highways*. Copyright © 1999 by Leo W. Banks. Reprinted by permission of the author.

Additional Credits (Arranged alphabetically by title)

Selections by Stephen Trimble excerpted from *Arizona: The Land and the People* edited by Tom Miller copyright © 1986 by The Arizona Board of Regents. Reprinted by permission of the author

Selection from *Arizona: The Land and the People* edited by Tom Miller copyright © 1986 by The Arizona Board of Regents. Reprinted by permission of the author.

Selection from "Camera Sty" by Tom Miller published with permission from the author. Copyright © 2001 by Tom Miller.

Selection from "Clear Vision of Elvis' Final Days" by Edvins Beitiks reprinted from the February 1, 1999 issue of the *San Francisco Examiner*. Copyright © 1999 by the *San Francisco Examiner*.

Selection from "Comes True, Being Hoped For" by Cynthia S. Larson reprinted from *PARABOLA, The Magazine of Myth and Tradition*, Vol. 25, No. 1, (Spring 2000). Copyright © 2000. Reprinted by permission.

Selection from "Driving Across the Southwest" by Brenda Davis published with

About the Editors

Sean O'Reilly is a former seminarian, stockbroker, and prison instructor who lives in Arizona with his wife Brenda and their five small boys. He's had a life-long interest in philosophy and theology, and is at work on a book called *How to Manage Your Dick: A Guide for the Soul*, which makes the proposition that classic Greek, Roman, and Christian moral philosophies, allied with post-quantum physics, form the building blocks of a new ethics and psychology. Widely traveled, Sean most recently completed an 18,000-mile van journey around the United States, sharing the treasures of the open road with his family. He is editor-at-large and director of international sales for Travelers' Tales.

James O'Reilly, president and co-publisher of Travelers' Tales, wrote mystery serials before becoming a travel writer in the early 1980s. He's visited more than forty countries, along the way meditating with monks in Tibet, participating in West African voodoo rituals, and hanging out the laundry with nuns in Florence. He travels extensively with his wife Wenda and their three daughters. They live in Palo Alto, California when they're not in Leavenworth, Washington.

TRAVELERS' TALES

THE SOUL OF TRAVEL

Footsteps Series

KITE STRINGS OF THE SOUTHERN CROSS

A Woman's Travel Odyssey
By Laurie Gough
ISBN 1-885-211-54-6
$14.95

"Gough's poetic and sensual string of tales richly evokes the unexpected rewards—and perils—of the traveler's life. A striking, moving debut." —*Salon.com*

— ★ ★ ★ —
ForeWord Silver Medal Winner
—*Travel Book of the Year*

THE SWORD OF HEAVEN

A Five Continent Odyssey to Save the World
By Mikkel Aaland
ISBN 1-885-211-44-9
$24.00 (cloth)

"Few books capture the soul of the road like *The Sword of Heaven*, a sharp-edged, beautifully rendered memoir that will inspire anyone."
—Phil Cousineau, author of *The Art of Pilgrimage*

STORM

A Motorcycle Journey of Love, Endurance, and Transformation
By Allen Noren
ISBN 1-885-211-45-7
$24.00 (cloth)

"Beautiful, tumultuous, deeply engaging, and very satisfying."
—Ted Simon, author of *Jupiter's Travels*

TAKE ME WITH YOU

A Round-the-World Journey to Invite a Stranger Home
By Brad Newsham
ISBN 1-885-211-51-1
$24.00 (cloth)

"Newsham is an ideal guide. His journey, at heart, is into humanity."
—Pico Iyer, author of *Video Night in Kathmandu*

THE WAY OF THE WANDERER

Discover Your Hidden Selves Through Travel
By David Yeadon
ISBN 1-885-211-60-0
$14.95

Experience transformation through travel with this delightful, illustrated collection by award-winning author David Yeadon.

Travelers' Tales Classics

THE ROYAL ROAD TO ROMANCE
By Richard Halliburton
ISBN 1-885-211-53-8
$14.95

"Laughing at hardships, dreaming of beauty, ardent for adventure, Halliburton has managed to sing into the pages of this glorious book his own exultant spirit of youth and freedom."
— *Chicago Post*

UNBEATEN TRACKS IN JAPAN
By Isabella L. Bird
ISBN 1-885-211-57-0
$14.95

Isabella Bird gained a reputation as one of the most adventurous women travelers of the 19th century with her unconventional journeys to Tibet, Canada, Korea, Turkey, Hawaii, and Japan. A fascinating read for anyone interested in women's travel, spirituality, and Asian culture.

Europe

GREECE
True Stories of Life on the Road
Edited by Larry Habegger, Sean O'Reilly & Brian Alexander
ISBN 1-885-211-52-X
$17.95

"This is the stuff memories can be duplicated from."
— *Foreign Service Journal*

IRELAND
True Stories of Life on the Emerald Isle
Edited by James O'Reilly, Larry Habegger & Sean O'Reilly
ISBN 1-885-211-46-5
$17.95

Discover the wonder of Ireland with Frank McCourt, Thomas Flanagan, Nuala O'Faolain, Rosemary Mahoney, Colm Tóibín, and many more.

FRANCE
True Stories of Life on the Road
Edited by James O'Reilly, Larry Habegger & Sean O'Reilly
ISBN 1-885-211-02-3
$17.95

The French passion for life bursts forth from every page of this invaluable guide, featuring stories by Peter Mayle, M.F.K. Fisher, Ina Caro, Jan Morris, Jon Krakauer and many more.

PARIS
True Stories of Life on the Road
Edited by James O'Reilly, Larry Habegger & Sean O'Reilly
ISBN 1-885-211-10-4
$17.95

"If Paris is the main dish, here is a rich and fascinating assortment of hors d'oeuvres."
—Peter Mayle, author of *A Year in Provence*

ITALY
True Stories of Life on the Road
Edited by Anne Calcagno
Introduction by Jan Morris
ISBN 1-885-211-16-3
$17.95

ForeWord Silver Medal Winner —
Travel Book of the Year

SPAIN
True Stories of Life on the Road
Edited by Lucy McCauley
ISBN 1-885-211-07-4
$17.95

"A superb, eclectic collection that recks wonderfully of gazpacho and paella, and resonates with sounds of heel-clicking and flamenco singing."
—Barnaby Conrad, author of *Matador*

Asia/Pacific

AUSTRALIA
**True Stories of
Life Down Under**
Edited by Larry Habegger
ISBN 1-885-211-40-6
$17.95
Explore Australia with
authors Paul Theroux,
Robyn Davidson, Bruce
Chatwin, Pico Iyer, Tim
Cahill, and many more.

JAPAN
**True Stories of
Life on the Road**
*Edited by Donald W.
George & Amy
Greimann Carlson*
ISBN 1-885-211-04-X
$17.95
"Readers of this entertain-
ing anthology will be better
equipped to plot a rewarding course through
the marvelously bewildering, bewitching
cultural landscape of Japan." — *Time* (Asia)

INDIA
**True Stories of
Life on the Road**
*Edited by James O'Reilly
& Larry Habegger*
ISBN 1-885-211-01-5
$17.95
"The Travelers' Tales series
should become required
reading for anyone visiting
a foreign country."   — *St. Petersburg Times*

NEPAL
**True Stories of
Life on the Road**
*Edited by Rajendra
S. Khadka*
ISBN 1-885-211-14-7
$17.95
"If there's one thing tradi-
tional guidebooks lack, it's
the really juicy travel infor-
mation, the personal stories about back
alleys and brief encounters. This series fills
this gap." — *Diversion*

THAILAND
**True Stories of
Life on the Road**
*Edited by James O'Reilly
& Larry Habegger*
ISBN 1-885-211-05-8
$17.95

— ★ ★ ★ —

*Winner of the Lowell
Thomas Award for Best
Travel Book—Society of
American Travel Writers*

HONG KONG
**True Stories of
Life on the Road**
*Edited by James O'Reilly,
Larry Habegger &
Sean O'Reilly*
ISBN 1-885-211-03-1
$17.95
"Travelers' Tales Hong Kong
will delight the senses and
heighten the sensibilities, whether you are
an armchair traveler or an old China hand."
— *Profiles*

The Americas

AMERICA
**True Stories of
Life on the Road**
Edited by Fred Setterberg
ISBN 1-885-211-28-7
$19.95
"Look no further.
This book is America."
—David Yeadon, author
of *Lost Worlds*

HAWAI'I
**True Stories of
the Island Spirit**
*Edited by Rick &
Marcie Carroll*
ISBN 1-885-211-35-X
$17.95
"Travelers' Tales aims to
convey the excitement of
voyaging through exotic
territory with a vivacity that guidebooks can
only hint at."—*Millenium Whole Earth Catalog*

GRAND CANYON
**True Stories of Life
Below the Rim**
*Edited by Sean O'Reilly,
James O'Reilly &
Larry Habegger*
ISBN 1-885-211-34-1
$17.95
"Travelers' Tales should be
required reading for anyone
who wants to truly step off the tourist track."
—*St. Petersburg Times*

SAN FRANCISCO
**True Stories of
Life on the Road**
*Edited by James O'Reilly,
Larry Habegger &
Sean O'Reilly*
ISBN 1-885-211-08-2
$17.95
"Like spying on
the natives."
—*San Francisco Chronicle*

AMERICAN SOUTHWEST
True Stories
Edited by Sean O'Reilly and James O'Reilly
ISBN 1-885-211-58-9
$17.95
Put on your boots, saddle up, and explore
the American Southwest with Terry Tempest
Williams, Edward Abbey, Barbara Kingsolver,
Alex Shoumatoff, and more.

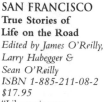

BRAZIL
**True Stories of
Life on the Road**
*Edited by Annette Haddad
& Scott Doggett
Introduction by Alex
Shoumatoff*
ISBN 1-885-211-11-2
$17.95

—★*★*★—
**Benjamin Franklin
Silver Award Winner**

MEXICO
True Stories
*Edited by James O'Reilly
& Larry Habegger*
ISBN 1-885-211-59-7
$17.95

—★*★*★—
*One of the Year's Best
Travel Books on Mexico*
**—The New York
Times**

Women's Travel

A WOMAN'S PASSION FOR TRAVEL
More True Stories from A Woman's World
Edited by Marybeth Bond & Pamela Michael
ISBN 1-885-211-36-8
$17.95

"A diverse and gripping series of stories!"—Arlene Blum, author of *Annapurna: A Woman's Place*

A WOMAN'S WORLD
True Stories of Life on the Road
Edited by Marybeth Bond
Introduction by
Dervla Murphy
ISBN 1-885-211-06-6
$17.95

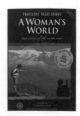

— ★ ★ ★ —

Winner of the Lowell Thomas Award for Best Travel Book — Society of American Travel Writers

WOMEN IN THE WILD
True Stories of Adventure and Connection
Edited by Lucy McCauley
ISBN 1-885-211-21-X
$17.95

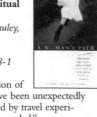

"A spiritual, moving, and totally female book to take you around the world and back." —*Mademoiselle*

A MOTHER'S WORLD
Journeys of the Heart
Edited by Marybeth Bond & Pamela Michael
ISBN 1-885-211-26-0
$14.95

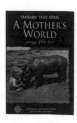

"These stories remind us that motherhood is one of the great unifying forces in the world" —*San Francisco Examiner*

Spiritual Travel

A WOMAN'S PATH
Women's Best Spiritual Travel Writing
Edited by Lucy McCauley, Amy G. Carlson & Jennifer Leo
ISBN 1-885-211-48-1
$16.95

"A sensitive exploration of women's lives that have been unexpectedly and spiritually touched by travel experiences…highly recommended."
—*Library Journal*

THE ULTIMATE JOURNEY
Inspiring Stories of Living and Dying
James O'Reilly, Sean O'Reilly & Richard Sterling
ISBN 1-885-211-38-4
$17.95

"A glorious collection of writings about the ultimate adventure. A book to keep by one's bedside—and close to one's heart." —Philip Zaleski, editor, *The Best Spiritual Writing series*

THE ROAD WITHIN:
True Stories of Transformation and the Soul
Edited by Sean O'Reilly, James O'Reilly & Tim O'Reilly
ISBN 1-885-211-19-8
$17.95

— ★ ★ ★ —

Best Spiritual Book — Independent Publisher's Book Award

PILGRIMAGE
Adventures of the spirit
Edited by Sean O'Reilly & James O'Reilly
Introduction by
Phil Cousineau
ISBN 1-885-211-56-2
$16.95

A diverse array of spirit-renewing journeys—trips to world-famous sites as well as places sacred, related by pilgrims of all kinds.

Adventure

TESTOSTERONE PLANET
True Stories from a Man's World
Edited by Sean O'Reilly, Larry Habegger & James O'Reilly
ISBN 1-885-211-43-0
$17.95

Thrills and laughter with some of today's best writers: Sebastian Junger, Tim Cahill, Bill Bryson, Jon Krakauer, and Frank McCourt.

DANGER!
True Stories of Trouble and Survival
Edited by James O'Reilly, Larry Habegger & Sean O'Reilly
ISBN 1-885-211-32-5
$17.95

"Exciting...for those who enjoy living on the edge or prefer to read the survival stories of others, this is a good pick." — *Library Journal*

Travel Humor

NOT SO FUNNY WHEN IT HAPPENED
The Best of Travel Humor and Misadventure
Edited by Tim Cahill
ISBN 1-885-211-55-4
$12.95

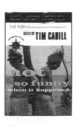

Laugh with Bill Bryson, Dave Barry, Anne Lamott, Adair Lara, Doug Lansky, and many more.

THERE'S NO TOILET PAPER...ON THE ROAD LESS TRAVELED
The Best of Travel Humor and Misadventure
Edited by Doug Lansky
ISBN 1-885-211-27-9
$12.95

— ★ ★ ★ —
**Humor Book of the Year
—Independent
Publisher's Book Award**

Food

THE ADVENTURE OF FOOD
True Stories of Eating Everything
Edited by Richard Sterling
ISBN 1-885-211-37-6
$17.95

"These stories are bound to whet appetites for more than food."
—*Publishers Weekly*

FOOD
A Taste of the Road
*Edited by Richard Sterling
Introduction by Margo True*
ISBN 1-885-211-09-0
$17.95

Sumptious stories by M.F.K. Fisher, David Yeadon, P.J. O'Rourke, Colin Thubron, and many more.

— ★ ★ ★ —
**Silver Medal Winner of the
Lowell Thomas Award for
Best Travel Book—Society
of American Travel Writers**

Special Interest

THE GIFT OF RIVERS
True Stories of Life on the Water
Edited by Pamela Michael
Introduction by Robert Hass
ISBN 1-885-211-42-2
$14.95

"*The Gift of Rivers* is a soulful fact- and image-filled compendium of wonderful stories that illuminate, educate, inspire and delight. One cannot read this compelling anthology without coming away in awe of the strong hold rivers exert on human imagination and history."
—David Brower, Chairman of Earth Island Institute

THE GIFT OF TRAVEL
The Best of Travelers' Tales
Edited by Larry Habegger, James O'Reilly & Sean O'Reilly
ISBN 1-885-211-25-2
$14.95

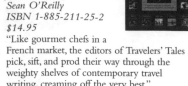

"Like gourmet chefs in a French market, the editors of Travelers' Tales pick, sift, and prod their way through the weighty shelves of contemporary travel writing, creaming off the very best."
—William Dalrymple, author of *City of Djinns*

FAMILY TRAVEL
The Farther You Go, the Closer You Get
Edited by Laura Manske
ISBN 1-885-211-33-3
$17.95

"This is family travel at its finest." —*Working Mother*

LOVE & ROMANCE
True Stories of Passion on the Road
Edited by Judith Babcock Wylie
ISBN 1-885-211-18-X
$17.95

"A wonderful book to read by a crackling fire."
—*Romantic Traveling*

THE GIFT OF BIRDS
True Encounters with Avian Spirits
Edited by Larry Habegger & Amy G. Carlson
ISBN 1-885-211-41-4
$17.95

"These are all wonderful, entertaining stories offering a *birds-eye view!* of our avian friends."
—*Booklist*

A DOG'S WORLD
True Stories of Man's Best Friend on the Road
Edited by Christine Hunsicker
ISBN 1-885-211-23-6
$12.95

This extraordinary collection includes stories by John Steinbeck, Helen Thayer, James Herriot, Pico Iyer, and many others. A must for any dog and travel lover.

Submit Your Own Travel Tale

Do you have a tale of your own that you would like to submit to Travelers' Tales? For submission guidelines and a list of titles in the works, send a SASE to:

Travelers' Tales Submission Guidelines
330 Townsend Street, Suite 208, San Francisco, CA 94107

You may also send email to *guidelines@travelerstales.com* or visit our Web site at *www.travelerstales.com*

Travel Advice

SHITTING PRETTY
How to Stay Clean and Healthy While Traveling
By Dr. Jane Wilson-Howarth
ISBN 1-885-211-47-3
$12.95

A light-hearted book about a serious subject for millions of travelers— staying healthy on the road—written by international health expert, Dr. Jane Wilson-Howarth.

THE FEARLESS SHOPPER
How to Get the Best Deals on the Planet
By Kathy Borrus
ISBN 1-885-211-39-2
$14.95

"Anyone who reads *The Fearless Shopper* will come away a smarter, more responsible shopper and a more curious, culturally attuned traveler."

—Jo Mancuso, *The Shopologist*

THE PENNY PINCHER'S PASSPORT TO LUXURY TRAVEL
The Art of Cultivating Preferred Customer Status
By Joel L. Widzer
ISBN 1-885-211-31-7
$12.95

World travel expert Joel Widzer shares his proven techniques on how to travel First Class at discount prices, even if you're not a frequent flyer.

SAFETY AND SECURITY FOR WOMEN WHO TRAVEL
By Sheila Swan & Peter Laufer
ISBN 1-885-211-29-5
$12.95

A must for every woman traveler!

THE FEARLESS DINER
Travel Tips and Wisdom for Eating around the World
By Richard Sterling
ISBN 1-885-211-22-8
$7.95

Combines practical advice on foodstuffs, habits, & etiquette, with hilarious accounts of others' eating adventures.

GUTSY WOMEN
More Travel Tips and Wisdom for the Road
By Marybeth Bond
ISBN 1-885-211-61-9
$12.95

Second Edition—Packed with funny, instructive, and inspiring advice for women heading out to see the world.

GUTSY MAMAS:
Travel Tips and Wisdom for Mothers on the Road
By Marybeth Bond
ISBN 1-885-211-20-1
$7.95

A delightful guide for mothers traveling with their children—or without them!